CRICUT

10 Books in 1:

The Complete Beginner's Guide to Design Space and Profitable Project Ideas, Mastering All Machines, Tools, and Materials. All You Need to Know Including Advanced Tips and Tricks

TABLE OF CONTENTS

HERE ARE THE BONUSES!

FOR READERS OF THIS BOOK ONLY

Scan this QR code with your smartphone or go to https://campsite.bio/jennifermichaels for accessing a collection of video tutorials, official manuals, best communities to meet other makers, thousands of project ideas, and millions of free SVG files and images.

Introduction

Cricut machines are a versatile help in doing any project you can think of and using various materials and tools. They can cut cardboard, balsa, vinyl, flex, burlap, and fabric. Yes! You read that right, fabric! And not just cotton! These devices are great for people who enjoy making their gifts and for those looking for a side hustle to get creative while also being able to sell the products they make. Many Etsy online shops on the internet these days usually include some articles for sale that are made using a Cricut machine.

Also, scrapbooking was not a simple procedure back when I was still in my baby years. The whole process was so repetitive and careful that one little misstep was sufficient to cause you to go insane because you needed to start from the very beginning once more. Be that as it may, things have gotten a lot simpler and progressively helpful with the innovative approach. Presently, we have the Cricut machine, which makes it infinitely easier.

The Cricut machine also has large collections of designed images in its library that will make your work super simple. As a beginner, you need to get access to one or more images, place the desired material to be cut onto the sticky mat, and get the Cricut machine to cut it for you.

Cricut Design Space is the software where all the magnificent designs are made before they are sent to be cut. It is one of the most critical aspects in the creation of crafts in the Cricut setup. As a crafter, without proper knowledge of Design Space, you're not only going to cut out poor products, but you will also make little or no in-road in your quest to find success.

Most Cricut machines will work over Bluetooth or Wi-Fi, which means you can design with your iPad, iPhone, or computer. This makes designing your passions easier than ever, with complete versatility that will help you to be able to do whatever you want. There are a variety of creative options available to you.

If you don't have too much experience with these types of devices, don't worry. We've got you covered. You will find the guidelines presented in this book are both easy to understand and simple to implement. You won't have to contend with complicated technical instructions written by some electronics nerd. You will find the information contained in this book in simple and understandable English. This is what makes using Cricut machines so easy. Plus, you will find that it's much more fun when you don't have to deal with elaborate explanations.

But the most important thing is to have fun and enjoy yourself. That is what crafting is all about, doing what you love. Don't beat yourself up if, at first, your design does not come out perfect; some of the best artwork is made by mistake. For those of you who are new to the craft, the most important thing is to learn to get comfortable with the Cricut. Learn what works and what does not work. The best way to learn is to work with the system.

You will soon be well on your way to creating great items to spruce up your home, making customized gifts and handmade greeting cards.

PART 1:

CRICUT CONCEPT AND ORIGIN

CHAPTER 1:

What Is Cricut?

A Cricut is an electronic cutting machine that helps you cut and produce elegant and gorgeous creations with resources you didn't even realize existed. You can also emboss, draw, and develop folding lines to create 3D creations, picture frames, boxes, etc., based on the prototype you have.

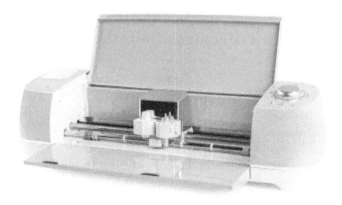

The Cricut is a perfect machine for individuals who enjoy crafting and those who like to cut various stuff and all kinds of materials.

A Cricut is an extraordinary cutting machine, otherwise known as a die-cutting device or an art plotter. These systems used to be relatively pricey and bulky, but now they're inexpensive and compact like a computer printer.

They are basically, in more respects than one, like a computer printer. You submit a pattern like a printer, except instead of inserting ink on a sheet of paper, the computer swings a blade around to slice through the material you have selected.

They automatically do this and will cut through all kinds of material: Cloth, paper, and sheets of adhesive, some of them also cut through metal!

Instead of cutting, several of the Cricut models allow you to use a marker; therefore, you can use the device to draw pictures or compose text. It performs amazingly to create invites for parties and weddings that appear handwritten, however, without really cramping your hands. Some also have a tool for scoring to create frames, stamps, ornaments, and all kinds of papercraft.

Designs are kept digitally and simple to pick and modify patterns from any interface, such as computers, iPad, or smartphones. The Cricut Picture Collection has approximately 50,000 photos and fonts, or you can even upload your custom templates.

History of Cricut Machines from the First to the Last Generation

We sum up Cricut's past by looking at Cricut devices' styles, including the original to the newest and latest, the Cricut Maker! You will cringe or chuckle at the older Cricut units, or maybe both!

The old Cricuts were clunky, had plenty of buttons, and used cartridges. They had minimal cutting areas and were frustrating to operate.

We should be happy to get devices like the Maker and Explore Air 2 now; however, it is a lot of fun to peek back at the past.

Cricut targeted the initial devices at card designers and scrapbookers. At least among home craftspeople, electronic cutting devices were somewhat novel and offered an inexpensive way for doing it all by yourself from home.

Today, anything from producing iron-on transfers and vinyl decals to cloth and sewing designs and even cutting wood or other heat transfer forms is done using Cricut machines.

Here is a list of the older Cricut machines in general order, from first to last:

Cricut Original

While not as aesthetically appealing, the Cricut personal began the revolutionizing method of cutting and pasting.

You used Cricut cartridges on this system, and you didn't require a computer for it to operate.

It was a very compact unit, with a relatively limited area for cutting. It could not render exceedingly complicated cuts, nor could it complete projects greater than 5.5 by 11 inches.

The cutting mat's width was just 6 inches wide; therefore, it was just a simple handicraft cutting unit.

Cricut Create

The next machine placed out by Cricut, the Cricut Create, was also simply known as Provo Craft back in the day.

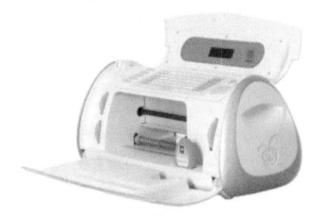

The Create device was the same scale as the first Cricut device, although Cricut made a few improvements.

Compared to the first unit, it has a significantly new look and had the newest colors.

It also enhanced the monitor panel.

Technology and hardware features were both enhanced, and an 8-way rotating blade was also introduced with it.

Cricut Expression

Next came the Cricut Expression, bringing some more substantive improvements.

Most importantly, it was the initial Cricut with a cutting capability of 12 by 24 inches, and the smaller cuts were best. A wider variety of materials could be sliced by Expression 1, including thicker materials such as vellum and poster board.

It was still possible to operate this gadget directly without a device, but the computer use program was undoubtedly improving. Cricut Craft Room was the predecessor to Cricut Design Space, and this program was in full usage for the Expression.

Cricut Expression 2

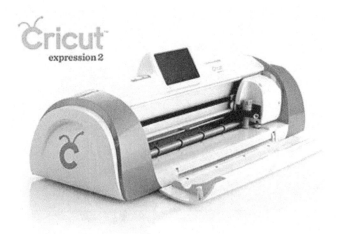

The Cricut Expression 2 was considered a very successful product at the time of its creation. There were many incredible features and enhancements to this machine, such as:

- 200+ designs pre-loaded (images, fonts, sayings, etc.).
- Better concepts for manipulation-resizing, rotating, turning, mirroring.
- Using Cricut Craft Area for more photos.

Cricut was progressively becoming more popular and better known among crafters by the time Expression 2 came out.

Cricut Imagine

Do Cricut machines print? It is one of the essential questions that Cricut newbies have.

The Cricut Imagine is exceptional since it is the only one that can print as well as cut. It was a cutter printer by Cricut! In addition to the Imagine, to print and cut, you just should get a contour cutting machine—we don't know about any other devices that do this.

Cricut partnered with HP to create a specially formulated black and 3-color ink to fit with the Imagine.

Unfortunately, at the moment, the machine was not the most successful for consumers, and it was discontinued very soon. At the same time, Cricut tried designing devices that were more aligned with the original.

Cricut Mini

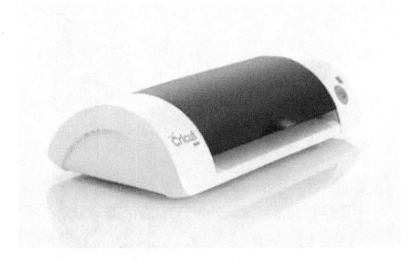

The Cricut Mini cutting device, not mistaken with the Cricut EasyPress, was just another little personal cutter.

It was the first unit to be used, along with a computer that had a narrower cutting range of 8.5 inches. While it was not as large a success as the Expression series, Cricut marketed this machine as a quieter and more manageable machine to carry.

Cricut Cake

This Cricut Cake device was a part of the Martha Stewart Collection.

Remarkably, cake crafters used this equipment to decorate desserts, cakes, and cupcakes!

It would cut fondant, sheets of frosting, gum paste, and more. We believe this is another device that did not really click. How often would people like to waste hundreds of dollars on icing machines? It was a cool concept, nevertheless.

Cricut Explore One

The Cricut Explore One is the first device to carry on the current Cricut cutting machines' theme—pretty much like all the newer machines until the Maker.

With Explore One, you can discover your own online fonts and graphics or select from tens of thousands of image formats in the Cricut Image File. This machine was much simpler to use and worked well with home computers.

It had holding compartments for additional knives, pens, etc., and was used with a Bluetooth adaptor wirelessly.

Cricut Explore Air

A trendy machine—the Explore Air was the initial Cricut to have a double tool holder.

The items that could be cut up with the Explore Air were also improved, with more than 60 separate recommendations. It was designed with Bluetooth, and it had a Smart Set Knob for the most typical settings.

Although there's always a place to mount a Cricut Cartridge—the template files are connected to your account, and you can practically put away the cartridge after doing that.

Cricut Explore Air 2

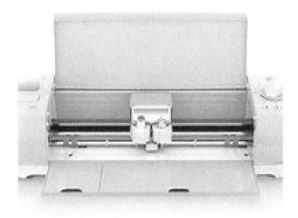

Despite being considerably cheaper, the Explore Air 2 is nevertheless a popular machine.

This machine has much of the same features and functions as Explore Air, and the only improvement is that it is twice as fast. The Explore Air 2 is also accessible in more colors than every other machine, 22 at the moment of printing!

Cricut Craft Area and the Cricut Picture Library have become the Cricut Design Space, which has also recently experienced a significant shift in the sense that it is no longer based on a browser.

Cricut Maker

The Cricut Maker is the most incredible machine ever.

It is the machine with the best specifications and the best capability. It's a massive jump from the Explore Air 2, so if it's in your budget, it is the only device you need to consider today.

The latest Cricut blades (in specific QuickSwap tools) are only compliant with the Maker, which certainly opens up the kinds of projects you can create.

Cricut Joy

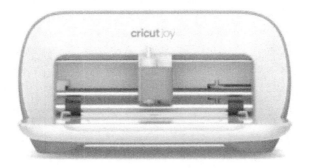

Cricut Joy is the newest and smallest Cricut device in the Cricut family.

It is around one-fourth of the scale of the Explore Air 2 and the Maker with a cutting range of almost 4 inches. The significant difference is that it will cut larger areas of up to 20 feet than all other devices!

This gadget is useful as a lightweight cutter for producing stickers, tags, vinyl decals, and quick heat transfers. It's convenient to pack and transport and adds to every art space for fun.

Now you know all of the various styles of Cricut devices.

The Cricut machine is a fantastic creation. It helps you cut paper, cloth, and vinyl sheets to whatever pattern you would like. These actual production designs may be achieved via software tools like the Cricut Layout Studio or via Capsules using pre-engineered structures assembled into them. Therefore, if you're an enthusiastic scrapbooker, this system is a must-have.

What Can I Make with Cricut?

There are several one-of-a-kind problems for you to use a Cricut. While you know what type of task you want to perform, and at the same time considering what kind of decoration and supplies you need to use the machine, please take a look at the rest of the other projects and parts that Cricut has just started. Demand (and what are basically "decent possessions" that you can spend when you need them) scrapbooking and card making.

There are loads of scrapbooking thoughts and scrapbook designs that you can discover for your Cricut!

Or, once you don't want the opportunity to make cards yourself, there are some pointers and special effects for making cards quickly.

Weddings and Gatherings

Cricut machines are great for making custom stylistic themes for weddings and gatherings!

Occasions

Use your Cricut to make an occasional stylistic layout for any event!

Home Stylistic Theme

You can make loads of various undertakings to improve your home!

Everything from cushions and divider craftsmanship to big business thoughts!

Clothing and Extras

One of my preferred designs to make with my Cricut is shirts, onesies, and tote sacks. You can put warmness switch vinyl on exceptionally much any material surface. However, you can likewise use a Cricut to make adornments, headbands, and then some!

Vinyl Decals and Stickers

Our concern is cutting vinyl decals and stickers, and you can do this with the Cricut Maker. It can cut through any vinyl in no time easily—you should simply make your format in Cricut Design Space, teach the PC to begin cutting; at that point, weed, and change the arrangement to your picked surface.

Texture Cuts

One of the Maker's essential selling elements is the truth that it comes outfitted with the new product Turn Cutting edge. On account of uncommon coasting and moving movement—by and large with the gigantic 4 kg. of power at the back of the Cricut Maker—this ability that the work area can lessen unmistakably any texture.

The truth is out. Denim? Check. Overwhelming canvas? Check. Silk? Check. Chiffon? Check. We've continually constrained using a particular texture sooner as the registering gadget cutting machines essentially weren't compelling to deal with more massive textures. We cherish the truth that a Maker is an across-the-board machine.

It comes furnished with a texture-cutting mat so that you can cut bunches of textures aside from the utilization of any support. Astonishing!

Sewing Examples

Another key prepared of the Maker is the gigantic Sewing Test Library that you'll get passage to when you've purchased the machine.

It comprises earnestly many examples—some from Effortlessness and Riley Blake Designs—and capacity you can genuinely pick the model you like. The Maker will remove it for you.

No additional removing designs physically yourself (and not any more human blunder ruins!)

Additionally, secured is a launder-able texture pen that will call attention to the spot the example parts intend to stable together.

Balsa Wood Cuts

On account of the incredible 4 kg. of weight and the Blade Sharp Edge (sold independently), the Cricut Maker can slice using substances up to 2.4 mm. thick. That limit-thick texture that had before been beyond reach with the Cricut and outline machines is currently open to us. We can hardly wait to start cutting wood with it!

Thick Cowhide Cuts

In a similar vein as factor #4, thick cowhide can be cut with the Maker!

Natively Constructed Cards

Paper crafters aren't forgotten about with the Maker either. Paper and card cuts will be less complicated and snappier than at any other time because of the machine's vitality and exactness. Your Scratchpad playing cards just went up a level.

Jigsaw Riddles

We understand that the Cricut Maker can cut through significantly thicker substances with the Blade Edge than any time in recent memory. The central perspective we give it a shot? Making our special jigsaw confound. We'll save you, refreshed!

Christmas Tree Adornments

The Revolving Cutting edge that vows to cut through any texture is the ideal gadget for designing occasion improvements. Scour the Sewing Design Library for Christmassy designs (we've purchased our eye on the "Gingerbread Man Adornment"!) cut out the example utilizing felt or whatever texture you want, and after that, sew it all in all independently.

Blankets

Cricut has collaborated with Riley Blake Designs to give various sewing designs in the Sewing Design Library. This capacity that you can utilize the Maker to remove your sewing correctly divides before sewing, them aggregately independently.

Felt Dolls and Delicate Toys

One of the Effortlessness designs we have our eye on in the Sewing Design Library is the "Felt Doll and Garments" example. We understand a couple of little women and young men who'd love a natively constructed dish to add to their collections. Just pick the bar, cut, and sew. Simple peasy!

Shirt Moves

You need to arrange the switch in Design Space, load the glow switch vinyl to the manufacturer (or flash it drastically on the HTV if you may feel timid); it recommends that the PC start cutting and ironing your switch shirt. Or, on the other hand, you should use the fresh-out-of-the-box new Cricut EasyPress to switch the vinyl—it's everything, the solace of an iron meets the adequacy of a warmness press!

Texture Appliques

Additionally, available to get individually is the Fortified Texture Sharp Edge in lodging, which will allow you to cut additional unpredictable material designs, similar to applique.

In contrast to the sharp rotating edge, the Fortified Texture Edge requires reinforced sponsorship on the material to diminish adequately.

Calligraphy Signs

The Cricut Maker's significant selling element is its versatile apparatus framework. It is the element that will verify that you keep up your Maker until the end of time. In reality, it's a gadget machine that exclusively suits every one of the instruments and sharp edges of the Explore family. However, it will fit as a fiddle with every future device and cutting edges made using Cricut. The vitality of the Cricut Maker limit that you can cut thicker substances sooner than that is appropriately perfect for intricate gems designs.

And keeping in mind that you aren't in any way, shape, or form to cut gold, silver, or jewel on there, at whatever point soon, an excellent pair of cowhide rings are just inside reach.

Wedding Invitations and Spare the Dates

As a whole, we know about how "little" costs like welcomes can add to the super price of a wedding.

As makers, we also know how to counter-balance a portion of those costs using making matters like ourselves.

The Cricut Maker is perfect for designing staggering welcomes—presently, not exclusively, would you remove confusing paper patterns, anyway that calligraphy pen will come in reachable once more.

Wedding Menus, Spot Cards, and Support Labels

You're nearly no longer compelled to create before the wedding function—you can likewise utilize your Maker to adorn for the gigantic day itself. The sky is just the confinement directly here; however, in all reality, make menus, region playing a card game, and lean toward labels. Attempt and ensure you use a practically identical arrangement for all your stationery to protect the subject upfront.

Shading Book

Do you know these "careful shading" books that are extremely popular at present? And after that, the Maker's total direction is to make your own unique, unquestionably extraordinary, shading book utilizing the fine-point pen device.

Liners

Another part we can hardly wait to make with our new Maker is liners.

The world you claim, as far as substances go—whatever from cowhide to sew, to steel sheets, and everything in the middle.

There are likewise some fabulous liner designs in the Sewing Library to investigate as well.

Texture Key-Rings

Something different that got our attention in the Sewing Test Library was, at one time, a couple of simple designs for fabric key-rings.

Once more, the Maker makes it advantageous—totally cut the example, and after that, sew it together.

Headbands and Hair Adornments

Presently, Cricut has propelled a registering gadget that is cutting through thick calfskin; we are fearless thought for mind-boggling, steampunk-motivated hair designs and even headbands.

Who realized the Maker ought to be so convenient for significant pattern articulations?

Cut-Out Christmas Tree

We know, we know, every individual needs a real Christmas tree eventually of the get-away season. In any case, just on the off chance that you don't have space for a transcending tree in your residence room or, God prohibits, you're hypersensitive to pine, you may need support to make your tree. As the Cricut Maker successfully cuts thick substances like wood, we guess an interlocking wood tree is an incredible task to check with this year. No laser is required when the Maker is available to you no matter what!

How Does It Work?

When you see the finished product from a Cricut machine, you will definitely be blown away. The neatness and appealing look of a typical project done with the Cricut machine will take your breath away. However, only a few people understand the process involved in the creation of such amazing designs.

Curious to know how the Cricut machine is able to cut out materials effectively? There are 2 major steps involved when using the Cricut machine:

Have a Design

If you have a PC, you can access the Cricut Design Space to access the library of designs. If you have a Mac, you can access the same platform to select a huge variety of patterns. In case you don't have any of these 2 but possess an iPhone or iPad, you can use the Design Space for iOS.

If what you have is an Android, you are covered as well. This is because you can take advantage of the Design Space for Android. These are online platforms where you can select any design that best suits your taste.

You can also customize a ready-made design to suit your needs. For example, you can resize it or modify the shape. You can also add a text or image as you wish till you have the design just as you want it.

Prepare the Machine

Having selected the design you intend to cut out with the machine, you are ready for the next step. The machine needs to be prepared by turning it on. Once you switch on the machine, you actually don't need to do anything.

You don't have to press any button unless you are using the machine for the first time. In that case, the machine will give you instructions on what to do. It is that simple.

What Cricut Machines Are Out There Right Now?

We will try to break this down quickly for you! Right now, there are 3 different types of Cricut machines on the market:

- **Family Cricut Explore:** These are perhaps the most popular machines that initially had 3 options to choose from. All 3 devices will cut the same items, but every one of them has unique features.
  - o Cricut Explore 1 and Explore Air are the very first models of Explore Air 2. The first had just one tool holder, while the second had 2 gear holders and Bluetooth. Note: You could purchase them used, as Cricut no longer offers them on the website.

- o Cricut Explore Air 2 has the same functionality as Explore Air (draws, score, cuts, prints, then cuts), except that it's 2 times quicker.
- **Cricut Maker:** The Maker is better than the Cricut Explore Air 2 since it enables the strength to be sliced by 10X. You can score, deboss, cut, and do a lot more with the Maker!
- **Cricut Joy:** The latest device launched by Cricut. It's pretty small, and an extensive range of materials can be cut and drawn upon. The Cricut Joy allows the vinyl cut and laser-cutting vinyl without a cutting mat.

CHAPTER 2:

What to Know Before Buying

Here we will explore the machines available and help you decide the option that is the best value for money for you. We will cover each of the currently available versions, what they can do, and the characteristics ideally suited to what types of crafts are outlined here.

Different Cricut Machines in the Market Today

Cricut Explore One

This is the simplest machine they sell in terms of what's typically available from Cricut. This machine promises the ability to cut 100 of the most common materials presently available for use with your Cricut machine and is also extremely user-friendly.

The Cricut Explore One is regarded by Cricut craft plotters as the no-frills beginner model and runs at a slower speed than the other available versions. The Cricut Explore One has just one component clamp within, so cutting or scoring can't be performed simultaneously, as compared to the others found in the current model line. Nevertheless, they can be performed in quick succession, one right after the other.

While this is a fantastic tool for a wide variety of crafts on 100 different materials and will get you on the right track to create beautiful crafts that are often cut from others, the cost is not as high as you would think. If you're going to use your art plotter mainly for those special occasions, then this is a fantastic tool to have on hand.

Cricut Explore Air

With all of the features of the Cricut Explore One and more capabilities, the Cricut Explore Air model comes loaded with Bluetooth functionality, has an integrated-in storage container to hold your tools in one place while you're working, so they won't roll away or get lost in the shuffle.

This model does have 2 on-board accessory clamps, which allow for marking, cutting, or scoring simultaneously. These clamps are labeled with an A and a B, so each time you load them up, you can be confident that your tools are going in the right positions.

This model is designed to handle the same 100 materials as the Cricut Explore One and runs at the same pace, so the price difference represents individual variations and similarities! A fantastic deal and a powerhouse of a machine.

Cricut Explore Air 2

The Cricut Explore Air 2 is the current top-selling craft plotter from Cricut and is probably the best value they can give for the price. This model cuts materials at twice the previous ones' speed and has Bluetooth support and 2 adapter clamps on board. The storage cup at the top of the unit features a smaller shallower cut to hold your replacement blades while they aren't in use. If you want to swap to a different project between several different tips, they're all readily accessible. All cups have a smooth silicone rim, so you won't have to worry about your blades getting rusty or scratched.

It is the perfect tool for the job for someone who finds themselves using their Cricut with some frequency. You will be able to do your crafts twice as quickly, and each time, even at that pace, you will get a favorable outcome!

Cricut Maker

The Cricut Maker is known as the flagship model of Cricut. It's the one that can do almost anything under the sun on almost any material you can bring into your machine's mat guides. The price point is the only drawback of this powerhouse model, and unless you want to make crafts to sell, this model proves to be quite expensive. Either way, you can be confident that whatever you do with this machine will always be of the highest quality. This baby is going to pay for itself in a short time if you sell your crafts.

This machine is full of exciting features for the enthusiastic crafters who want to turn up at the party with the most exquisite creations that are ahead of their colleagues. This model really has everything.

There is no other Cricut machine with the speed of the Cricut Maker. The cuts that can be made using the precise blades that fit this machine are smoother than anything from a straight knife or other craft cutters you could ever expect. You can easily remove the tip from the housing using blade housings, add the next one, clip it back into place, and start to roll your designs. Moreover, the machine will identify the loaded material, so you won't have to specify the type of material at the start of the project. One common problem in the other models is that the project is halfway completed before the crafter discovers that the dial has been set wrongly.

Like some other models, the machine is fully Bluetooth compatible and 10 times more powerful than any other, with a specialized rotary cutter attachment that allows it to glide effortlessly through fabrics with accuracy.

Cricut Mini

These models were compatible with a Cricut device called the Gypsy, not the same as the Cricut Design Space currently in use today. Each machine has triumphed in innovating the processes of handcraft cutting.

Cricut's main goal was to amend the complexity of operating with its machinery while creating its newest line of models. Some crafter groups exchange hacks and mathematical leads to plan their machines as precisely as they want them to, and this machine makes it easier than ever to operate.

The new selection of models available allows you to be as imaginative as possible in the design process so that no operations are unmanageable and take away from your creative flow.

When you own one of these machines, it needs upgrading, but you don't need to upgrade if you've done your crafting well with the one you have on hand. Cricut has always created superior quality products, and Cricut Design Space still supports cartridges containing various thematic design elements.

Cricut Cartridge Adapter is a USB adapter that enables the import of your cartridges into Cricut design space so that all your elements are accessible in an organized place.

Design Space

Like many machines placed on the shelves, this device also comes with a unique software filled with different settings and features to toggle with. All these components ensure that you end up with a beautiful, customized, and accurate product when you are using this instrument. Cricut's very own software is called "Cricut Design Space," and all of Cricut's devices come with this software, whether it is Cricut Mini or Cricut Explore Air. Every Cricut owner must have this software installed on their device. The Cricut must be directly connected to the device via cable or by Bluetooth. Either way, the device needs to be close to the machine. The software is free and has a good user interface that makes it clear and easy to work with, even if you don't have any prior experience working with a similar device. Its user-friendly feature encourages creativity in an individual. The program is based on the Cloud, so even if your device is destroyed or has become inaccessible for any reason, the different design files can be safely recovered. It can be opened onto almost every device and be available at any moment. A laptop, tablet, or mobile can be used as well, and starting a project on one device and switching in between to another is possible. It can even be accessed offline.

After the program has been installed, you need to create the designs from the beginning or use any one of thousands of templates already stored in its library. Design Space has a large, diverse collection to motivate a new crafter to start constructing and inventing. One can play around with varieties of fonts and images and new inspiring ideas. For optimum usage, a Cricut Explorer connected to a computer will be amazing. This way, all of the features are available, and the machine works without lag.

Cheat Sheets

The cheat sheets refer to the 12 functions of design space that can be used from the "Layers" panel. These features are amazing when it comes to customizing your pictures. Therefore, in this panel, you will be able to see some interesting features such as slice, weld, connection, disconnection, flatten, unflatten, visible/hide, outline, group, ungroup, duplicate, and delete. So, let's go through each function and find out what you can do:

- **Slice:** This feature is for 2 superimposed layers and can be divided into separate parts.
- **Weld:** Helps more layers join in a single form, eliminating any cutting lines that overlap.
- **Attach:** You can use this feature to keep your cuts in position so that your pictures on the cutting show exactly like on the design screen. Besides, with this option, you should be able to inform the machine which image layer you wish to place the marker or text on.
- **Take off:** It is exactly the opposite of the above function, as it can remove any bonded layer, allowing a separate cutting or removing of all other layers.
- **Flatten:** This feature can convert any of the images to a printable form by merging all selected layers in a single layer.
- **Unflatten:** Dividing the printable layers of an image into individual printable layers.
- **Outline:** If you want to cut roads in a layer or to hide/contours, this is the option you need to use; however, if the image has several layers, these will be grouped first.
- **Ungroup:** This is the reverse of the group function as the function divides sets of images or text layers to be sized and moved individually on the screen design. For example, if you

click "Ungroup" on a single layer of text, you will be able to resize and move each letter of the text independently. This option does not influence how the images are presented in the cutting.

- **Double:** If you want to create multiple versions of the same image, this is the option to use.
- **Remove:** Just select an item on the screen design, and it will be removed.
- **Score:** You can also set the layer to score, but scoring a pencil is needed.
- **Print:** With this option, you can transform your layer into one-printable, so it can be printed and only then cut with the Cricut machine. The Flatten function mentioned above can be very useful because it can transform your multiple layers image on one to print a layer.

Remember that the Cricut Essentials iOS app does not come with the Layers panel or the Edit menu, so you only need to tap in this case.

PART 2:

<u>CRICUT MACHINES</u>

UPGRADE 2022 – NEW MACHINES

<u>CRICUT MAKER 3 & CRICUT EXPLORE 3</u>

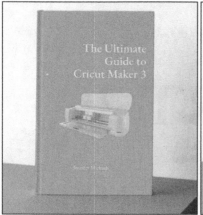 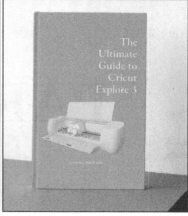

Scan this QR code with your smartphone or go to https://campsite.bio/jennifermichaels **for accessing a the ultimate guide to Cricut Maker 3 & Explore 3** and collection of video tutorials, official manuals, best communities to meet other makers, thousands of project ideas, and millions of free SVG files and images.

CHAPTER 3:

Explore Air 2

What You Need to Know

If you are a lover of craft or want to engage in crafting from home, you need to get an advanced cutting machine suited for your needs.

The Cricut Explore Air 2, in this instance, is probably the best electronic cutting machine you can buy and can be used with a variety of materials.

Cricut is the industry leader in the craft machine industry, and the Explore Air 2 leads in the home craft cutting market. The Explore Air 2 is the latest in the Cricut machine series, and it is 2 times faster in performance than the previous models.

The Explore Air 2 cutting machine can be miniature in looks, but it is efficient. It can carry out different projects like cutting, writing, draw, or edges on various materials. The Explore Air 2 is very suitable for beginners and for those who work on smaller tasks. It is also ideal for artisans who design craft products or access some excellent ready-made designs.

What Is a Cricut Explore Air 2 Machine?

The Cricut Explore Air 2 is a beautiful and well-built machine tool that can cleanly cut and draw at the same time on all common materials used for craft. The Explore Air 2 has the newest technology for vinyl cutters, and it is the fastest cutter you can find. It is reputed as the smartest cutting machine in the market. Unlike the traditional tools, the Explore Air 2 is designed to work perfectly with intelligent devices. The machine is compatible with mobile phones, personal computers, and tablets.

Altogether, this gives you the flexibility to access designs and print them for your projects on the go. This makes the machine so easy to use, unlike other smart devices.

Key Features of Cricut Explore Air 2

The Explore Air 2 possesses some excellent features that make it easier for anyone to produce beautiful and professional-looking crafts. One thing you cannot find on the machine is a touch screen. Instead, every function is controlled by the dial and the software program on your phone or computer.

Cutting Width

Even though the Explore Air 2 is not suitable for heavy commercial use due to its small size, the compact size machine still offers an excellent cutting width to get the basic craft project done.

The machine measures 14 inches long and 12 inches wide. That is not the most significant width available to do a more massive cut, but it is the best you will get amongst the desktop home cutting machines. Also, note that the cutting width will further reduce in size depending on the type of material you want to cut.

Cricut Design Space Software

The Explore Air 2 can be used with the free Design Space software that is cloud-based. This action requires internet connectivity to log on to the software, and you can have access to an entire library of images and designs for your project. You can access the software seamlessly through your phone, tablet, or personal computer.

A major setback for the Explore Air 2 design space software is that you will need reliable internet access to design and to cut with your material. A new version only allows offline mode access but is only available for the iOS app.

Performance (2X Fast Mode)

The Explore Air 2 has a 2X fast mode, which enables you to cut common lightweight materials like vinyl, paper, and cardstock twice as fast as the regular speed setting. You can save a considerable amount of time by simply switching to fast mode to speed up your cutting when you want the project done quickly, although some thick materials may slow down the machine's speed.

Smart Set Dial

The machine comes with a Smart Set Dial to smoothly help you choose the type of material you are cutting, and the Cricut will automatically adjust the depth and speed appropriately. This saves you so much time or helps you to set up your work in real-time by removing any frustration you might encounter in guessing the amount of material needed for your project.

Pre-Installed Patterns

The Cricut Explore Air 2 comes with pre-installed ready-to-use designs that you can use to work on different applications for your project. With more than hundreds of pre-loaded printable patterns on the machine, you are given many choices to select a unique profile based on your preferences. You can also upload new printable images for your next cutting project, in addition to more than half a million printable images that come with the machine.

Durable Cutting Blades

The Cricut Explore Air 2 uses a robust German carbide blade, specifically designed to perform all sophisticated cuts on light and medium-weight materials efficiently.

Parts of the Cricut Explore Air 2

Tool Cup

The tool cup provides a practical storage space where you can keep tools handy. You can keep scissors, pencils, pens, rulers, etc. in the tool cup without fear of having a cluttered workspace. The tool cup helps you keep your workspace organized.

Open Button

The "Open" button is the button to push to unfold the Cricut Explore Air 2. Users can close the Cricut Explore Air 2 to keep it safe and dust-free. The "Open" button is the "open sesame" that opens it up and gets it ready for use.

Clamp

The clamp holds the blade housing in place and ensures it delivers maximum precision while cutting.

Tray

The tray is the flat surface where the cutting mat and material are placed. The tool holder and blades work on materials placed on the tray.

Mat Guides

The mat guides are found on the sides of the tray. They keep the cutting mat firmly in place and prevent it from moving as the material upon it is being cut. This helps achieve very precise and intricate cuts.

Storage Compartments

There are 2 storage compartments. Both compartments are found under the tray. The first compartment is used for storing blades and blade housing safely. The second compartment is used for the storage of other accessories like markers, pens, and housing adapters.

USB Port

This is where the USB cord is connected.

Power Port

This is where the power cord goes in.

Power Button

This button wakes up the Cricut Explore Air 2. It is also the button to push when you wish to shut down the machine.

Smart Set Dial

The "Smart Set Dial" sets the machine to the type of material being cut. There are different materials pre-set; what you just need to do is to turn the dial to the preset material you wish to operate on. For instance, if you are working on vinyl, you will simply turn the dial to "Vinyl."

Load/Unload Mat, Go, Pause

These are 3 buttons found near the Smart Set Dial. They are used to control movements of the cutting mat.

The "Load/Unload Mat" button loads the cutting mat with materials to be operated on by the tools. When the button is pushed and the material is already loaded, it rolls out the cutting mat so that the material can be removed.

The "Go" button starts an operation. After you have loaded material to a machine, you push the "Go" button to start operations.

The "Pause" button puts any ongoing operation on hold.

Rollers

The rollers work to push the material being operated under the tool holders to be worked on. The cutting mat is placed on the rollers, and they roll back and forth to push the cutting mat back and forth. This is the tool holder that can reach all parts of the material being worked on, to give a very precise cut.

How to Open the Machine

When you want to open the machine for use, you should click on where the red arrow is pointing at. You can raise the cover where the arrows are pointing below, to hide some of the accessories you will be using for making your designs.

Pros and Cons

There are +3,000 easy-to-use projects predesigned in the library, and the Cricut Explore Air 2 can use this large image library, therefore, you do not need to be a professional to make use of the Cricut Explore Air 2 machine to create beautiful and super amazing crafts that you have always desired to produce.

The Bluetooth-enabled device gives you the freedom to send designs directly from another Bluetooth-enabled device, including your phone, thereby eliminating the need for an adapter. The speed at which this machine performs the cutting and writing operation is its main selling point. It has both normal and fast modes of operation.

Another pro for this exciting crafter's companion includes the fact that it comes in nice and very beautiful colors, easy storage compartments, and powerful cutting blades for different materials, including wood and leather.

Like every manufactured device, Cricut Explore Air 2 has its cons. One drawback of the Cricut Explore Air 2 machine compared to the other cutters out there is that it is only compatible with the web-based Design Space software. This means that you need internet connectivity before you can work with this software to design those super amazing projects.

The software is very powerful and can be used by professionals and beginners.

Another drawback is the high noise level compared to other Cricut machines. This is expected because it is designed to cut with more power; in fact, the power of its cut and the speed of its cut is twice that of Cricut Explore Air.

Even with these disadvantages, the Cricut Explore Air 2 is an amazing cutting machine that will give you a huge value for money.

CHAPTER 4:

Cricut Maker

The Cricut Maker is considered to be Cricut's flagship model. This is the one that can do just about anything under the sun on just about any material you can fit into the mat guides of your machine. The one drawback of this powerhouse model is the price point. This does make this model more prohibitive unless you plan to make crafts that you can sell with this model. If this is your intention, you can rest assured that whatever you turn out with this machine will be the best of the best, every single time. If you're selling your crafts, this baby will pay for itself in little to no time at all.

With that in mind, the Cricut Maker costs $399.99. That is a large sum of money for someone who doesn't have it and even for someone who does have it. Although there's a lot you can do with $399.99, there are just as many things you can do with the Cricut Maker. My advice would be to save until you can afford it or put it on your wish list in the meantime and subtly hint to your loved ones that you'll absolutely love to have one of these bad boys. Hopefully, someone will catch on and not balk at the huge amount of dollars that it will eat up.

The Cricut Maker can be used with your images, which is a plus for those who prefer to use their own or don't want to buy a subscription or pay for individual images. It allows you to personalize your items and make your statement.

You can make personalized cards, signs, and anything your heart desires. The ability to personalize your items with multiple lines and fonts broadens your horizon, and if you make products to sell, you can offer personalization.

Cricut Maker Dimensions and Weight

Dimensions = 22.6 inches by 7.1 inches by 6.2 inches

Weight = 24 pounds

Cricut Maker color options:

- Blue

- Champagne

- Lilac

- Mint

- Rose

What Comes with the Cricut Maker?

When you buy the Cricut Maker it will come boxed with the following items:

- Cricut Maker cutting machine in the selected color
- Welcome booklet
- Power adaptor
- USB cable
- Rotary blade and drive housing for the blade
- Premium fine-point blade and drive housing for the blade
- Cricut fine-point pen in black
- 1 FabricGrip mat (pink)
- 1 LightGrip mat (blue)
- Sample materials: Fabric and cardstock
- 30-day free Cricut Access trial membership
- 25 free sewing patterns
- 25 free ready-to-make projects easily accessible online

Cricut Maker FAQs

The following is a quick product FAQs guide for the Cricut Maker, the top Cricut cutting machine. This cutting machine does just about everything and is a professional-grade machine.

- **The Cricut Maker is best for:** Serious crafters who want to take their designs to the next level or who sell their crafts.
- **How many functions does the Cricut Maker have?** The machine has 12 or more functions which include cutting, writing, scoring, and much more. It will give crafts a professional touch.
- **Can the Cricut Maker use more than 1 function at a time?** Yes, it can. The machine comes with 2 separate function compartments.
- **The Cricut Maker's maximum material width is:** 12 inches.
- **Does the Cricut Maker have commercial-grade cutting technology?** Yes.

- **The Cricut Maker uses the following connectivity:** Bluetooth and USB.
- **The Cricut Maker uses the following design application:** Design Space.
- **The Cricut Maker is compatible with the following devices:** Windows, MAC, Android, and iOS.
- **Does the Cricut Maker do continuous cuts?** No.
- **How many material types is the Cricut Maker Compatible with?** 300 or more material types.
- **Does the Cricut Maker use cut mats?** Yes, it uses the Standard Grid Cricut mats. It also uses a few specialized mats for the cutting of various materials that the other Cricut machines do not cut.
- **Can the Cricut Maker be used without cutting mats?** No, it cannot.
- **Can the Cricut Maker use tools or accessories from other Cricut machines?** Yes, it does have some tools and accessories compatible with other Cricut machines. The machine is also backward compatible with the smaller models and older model projects.

Pros of the Cricut Maker

- The Maker can cut just about any material.
- The machine has a lot of different blades and blade tips that make it versatile.
- The Maker has an extensive list of materials that it can cut. This includes leather, wood, material, and various metals.
- The machine is a professional-level cutting machine.

Cons of the Cricut Maker

- The machine is expensive.
- The machine does not have a large cutting space.
- Cutting has to be done using one of the Cricut cutting boards.
- The machine can be a little confusing for beginners.

User Manual for Cricut Maker

The Cricut Maker is a marvelous craft cutting machine that really does open up new crafting possibilities. You can get debossing blade tips, engraving blade tips, and a cutting knife that can cut materials such as wood.

It does need a bit of space as it is a standard-sized craft cutting machine much the same size as the preceding Cricut cutting machine models.

Open the Top Flap

To open the Cricut Maker, flip up the top flap, which automatically opens up the machine's front door.

Cricut Maker Machine Top, Front, and Inside Overview

The following overview of the machine starts with the front of the machine from the left-hand side when sitting in front of the cutting machine.

Tool Cups

On the machine's left-hand side, there is a dual slot for crafting tools such as a pair of scissors, tweezers, weeding tools, and so on. It has one pocket deeper than the other, each with a protective silicone base for any blades that may be stored.

Mobile Device Holder Slot

Beneath the top flap of the machine, there is a long groove that runs over the mouth of the cutting machine. This slot is conveniently designed to hold a mobile device such as a phone or tablet.

Cricut Cartridge Port

The Cricut Maker machine does not come with a Cricut Cartridge port, but it can still take cartridges with the help of a USB cartridge adaptor which is sold separately.

Top Lid

The top lid flips up and offers support for a mobile phone or tablet to lean against if they are inserted into the mobile device slot. It is also a protective cover for the machine when it is not in use.

Cricut Accessory and Blade Housing Head

In the mouth of the machine, you will find the Cricut accessory and blade housing head. This head holds the accessory and blade clamps. This housing is a double tool holder, making it easier for the machine to operate dual functions such as cutting and scoring simultaneously. This means that you do not have to change accessories halfway through a project.

This housing head moves along a housing head guide bar located a little way back from, but just above, the material feeder guide bar.

- **Accessory Clamp A:** Accessory clamp A is for the scoring stylus pen and other Cricut drawing or marking pens compatible with the cutting machine.
- **Blade Clamp B:** Blade clamp B is for blades and blade housings.

Material Feeder Guide Bar

The material feeder guide bar helps to hold the cutting mat steady so that the cutting blades can glide over the material.

Feeder Guide Rollers

The feeder guide rollers are the 2 grey rollers located on either side of the material feeder guide bar. These rollers roll the material back and forth so that the machine can cut the materials.

Star Wheels

The star wheels are small, white wheels that look like little stars. There are 4 of them, and they are located between the 2 grey feeder guide rollers. They help to keep the material steady during cutting. Some materials will require moving these little wheels to one side of the bar so that they will not make indents in the material. Some materials are too thick for these little wheels and could cause them damage.

Mat Guides

These are the 2 little plastic feet located in front of the gray feeder guide rollers. They are there to guide the cutting mats into position and mark the maximum cutting mat or material size that can be fed through the cutting machine.

Bottom Feeder Plate

The bottom feeder plate is the portion that the material will sit on while it is being cut and will rest upon when it is finished. The plate also protects the machine and folds up when the machine is not in use.

Bottom Storage Drawer

The bottom storage drawer is a secret compartment housed in the bottom feeder plate. Here, you can store your accessories such as cutting rulers, pins, scissors, scraper, drive housings, and so on. There is a long compartment, a smaller square compartment, and 2 smaller ones. One of the smaller compartments contains a great magnetic stipend for keeping blades and pins from rattling around the compartment.

Load/Unload Mat Button

On the top right-hand side of the machine, at the front, is the "Load/Unload Mat" button. This button has an up and down arrow on it to indicate load and unload. This is the button you will use to load the cutting into the machine when you are ready to cut. It is also the button that you will use to unload the cutting mat once the cutting machine has finished cutting the design.

Go Button

The "Go" button is located right next to the "Load/Unload Mat" button and is marked with a little green "C" for Cricut. This is the button you will press when you are ready to start cutting the design.

Pause Button

At times, you may need to stop cutting for whatever reason. This is when this button comes in handy. It is located next to the "Go" button and is marked with 2 lines running next to each other, much like the "Pause" button on any electronic gaming, TV, or DVD device.

Smart Set Dial

The Cricut Maker does not have a Smart Set Dial. The material selection is chosen through the Design Space software.

Power Button

The "Power" button is located just above the "Load/Unload Mat" button on the cutting machine's top.

USB Utility Port

The USB utility port is located at the bottom right-hand side of the machine. This port is used to charge mobile devices while they are connected via Bluetooth to the machine for cutting. It must not be confused with the USB port at the back of the machine used to connect the machine to a computer.

USB Port

The USB port for the machine is located at the back of the machine near the power port. This is used to update the machine's firmware and to connect to a device.

Power Port

The Cricut Maker's power port is located at the back of the cutting machine.

Material Feeder Slot

The cutter cuts materials up to 12 inches long at one time. In order to cut out these patterns, it needs to slide the mat back and forth across the blade or any accessories loaded for the project.

That is why there is a material feeder slot at the back of the machine; so, the mat can slide in and out to cut the material's full length.

Cricut Maker First Project

The next step may be to accept the gifts that come with Cricut Maker. There are a host of free fonts, images, and projects. You can also get a free 1–2-month Cricut Access membership. The Cricut Access libraries are recognizable by the green "a" marked next to them.

To get started and test the machine, once you have connected the Cricut Maker to your PC or smart device, you will be taken to the "You're Only a Cut Away" screen. This will be the start of your first mini project on the Cricut Maker, where you will be making a greeting card.

Supplies

- Cardstock—White sample cardstock that came with the machine
- LightGrip mat (blue)
- Black Cricut marker pen—The pen would have come with the machine
- Cricut stylus scoring pen (optional)

Instructions

1. Click "Continue" and accept the project to make the card.
2. Follow the instructions on the screen and click the "Make It" button.
3. The next screen is the "Prepare Mat" screen. Read the instructions and follow them by clicking "Continue."
4. On the panel on the left-hand side of the "Prepare Mat" screen, the image of the board has the words "Draw" and "Cut." This means that the project is going to use both a pen and a blade tool.
5. The next step is to set up the material for the machine to cut. The Maker does not have a dial, so this will be done through the Design Space software. Choose the material that the screen is prompting you to choose; "Medium Cardstock" 80 pounds.

6. The next step takes you through installing the accessories into the accessory clamp.

7. Use the Cricut Maker accessory clamp A.

8. The first accessory to install will be the black pen that comes with the Maker. On the pen, there is an arrow. Make sure that the arrow is facing you. Open the gray flap on clamp A. Position the pen into the slot, gently pushing it down until the arrow disappears. Once the pen is in position, close the gray clamp flap to secure the accessory in place. When the pen is loaded, press "Continue."

9. The next step will be to load the cutting mat.

10. Using the white cardstock material, stick it onto the top left-hand corner of the LightGrip cutting mat (follow the onscreen example).

11. Slide the cutting mat with the cardstock in place through the mat guides and up to the material feeder guide bar. The mat should be positioned just under the feeder rollers.

12. The Maker will load the cutting mat and position it. When it is ready, the screen on your PC will change, prompting you to click "Go."

13. When the cutting mat has been loaded, the "Go" button (Cricut C) will start to flash to indicate that the machine is now ready to start cutting. Press the "Go" button, and the Maker will start to draw the design. This will take a few minutes.

14. When the drawing process is finished, the Design Space screen will change to "Detecting Blade." If it cannot detect a blade, it will prompt for one to be loaded. Depending on the material that has been selected, the software will prompt the blade that is best suited to the project.

15. As the fine-point blade is preloaded with the Maker, it will not prompt for a blade change for this project. The Maker will start to cut out the image.

16. The screen will prompt for the pen accessory to be removed from the clamp. Remove the pen by opening the flap on the clamp. Pull out the pen and then close the flap.

17. Pull the excess card stock off of the cutting mat, leaving behind the cut-out design.

18. You can use the weeding tool to pull out bits on the card and then pull the card from the cutting mat.

19. Fold the card in half.
20. Place the blue insert into the card by inserting each of the corners into the slots on the card as indicated by the on-screen prompt.
21. Your first Cricut Maker project is done!

CHAPTER 5:

Cricut Joy

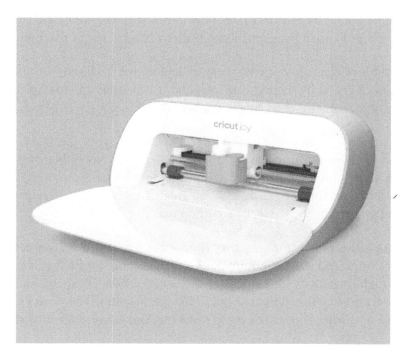

The latest of the Cricut cutting machine series is the Cricut Joy and presently the smallest. It is designed to be super simple to operate and has no button on it. It is sorely operated from the Design Space app, which you can download and install on your PC, tablet, phone, or on all 3 of them.

There are several things your latest Cricut Joy can do for you apart from its portability including supers amazing labels, long cuts, cut vinyl without using the mat, cut repeated shapes for about 20 feet long, easier ways of making cards, and more.

The Cricut Joy is the latest addition to the Cricut family. It is a compact machine that can create larger-than-life crafting projects. This little machine is designed to be used without a cutting mat, making it able to produce cuts repeated for up to 20 feet in length. It can also cut a single design up to 4 feet. This makes it an excellent little machine to cut longer projects.

It needs to use some of its accessories designed specifically for the machine due to its compact size. This means you will not be able to use the standard Cricut pens and some blades from the larger machines.

The little Cricut Joy is the best machine for children, beginners, scrapbookers, and greeting card makers. It can whip up small projects in no time, and as it is so small, it is portable too.

The Cricut Joy can cut over 50 different material types. To make your life easier with the Cricut Joy, Cricut has designed Smart Materials for use with this mighty little machine. These Smart Materials do not need a cutting mat and, as such, can be loaded directly into the cutting machine without the hassle of a cutting mat.

It should be noted, though, that the Cricut Joy is not a commercial-grade cutter, and it does require quite a few bits and bobs to get it going. Although the Cricut Joy can draw, emboss, do score lines, and cut, you can only do one function at a time. This means you will have to change tools a few times if you are cutting, drawing, and doing score lines in the same project.

Cricut Joy Dimensions and Weight

Dimensions = 5.5 inches by 8.40 inches by 4.25 inches

Weight = 3.85 pounds

Cricut Joy color options:

The Cricut Joy only comes in teal with white trim.

What Comes with the Cricut Joy?

When you buy the Cricut Joy, it will come boxed with the following items:

- The Cricut Joy cutting machine
- Power adaptor for the Cricut Joy cutting machine
- An all-purpose fine-point cutting blade
- The pre-installed Cricut blade housing
- Standard Grip 4.5 inches by 4.5 inches mat (green)
- Cricut Joy fine-point pen (0.4 mm.) in black
- 2 sample materials: Deluxe adhesive-backed paper and Smart Material vinyl
- 30-day free Cricut Access trial membership
- 50 ready-to-make projects easily accessible online

Cricut Joy FAQs

Following is a quick product FAQ guide for the Cricut Joy which is the simplest of the Cricut cutting machines and one of the smallest:

- **The Cricut Joy is best for:** Smaller everyday-type projects like cards, vinyl decals, stickers, and beginners or supervised children.
- **How many functions does the Cricut Joy have?** 2 functions: cutting and writing.
- **Can the Cricut Joy use more than 1 function at a time?** No.
- **The Cricut Joy maximum material width is:** 4.25 inches.
- **Does Cricut Joy have commercial-grade cutting technology? No.**
- **The Cricut Joy uses the following connectivity:** Bluetooth only.
- **The Cricut Joy uses the following design application:** Design Space.
- **The Cricut Joy is compatible with the following devices:** Windows, MAC, Android, and iOS.

- **Does the Cricut Joy do continuous cuts?** Yes, when using Smart Material designed specifically for the Cricut Joy.
- **How many material types is the Cricut Joy Compatible with?** 50 or more material types.
- **Does the Cricut Joy use cut mats?** Yes, it has its own special mats that are not compatible with other Cricut machines.
- **Can the Cricut Joy be used without cutting mats?** Yes, when it is being used with Smart Materials that have been designed for the Cricut Joy.
- **Can Cricut Joy use tools or accessories from other Cricut machines?** No, it cannot. Due to its compact size, most of the materials, equipment, cutting mats, accessories, and tools are specifically designed for the machine.

Pros of the Cricut Joy

- The Joy is well priced and affordable.
- This little machine is the perfect machine for beginners, teens wanting to start crafting, and supervised children over the age of 10.
- The Cricut Joy is a wireless design that makes it neat, simple, and quick to use.
- The machine does not weigh more than 4 pounds and is lightweight, making it portable.
- The machine uses Smart Materials for easy and convenient cutting without a cutting mat.

Cons of the Cricut Joy

- The Joy is mainly used for simple designs like cards, stickers, and decals.
- The Cricut Joy can only cut or write.
- The machine can only do 1 function at a time—either write or cut.
- Although you could use various materials with the machine, it tends to work best with the Smart Materials from Cricut. This makes the materials you can use with the machine limited.

User Manual for Cricut Joy

This machine is the smallest of the latest Cricut cutting machines. But it is not without purpose. as this little machine is really handy for those quick-on-the-go DIY crafts.

All the Cricut machines, including the little Cricut Joy, are electronic cutting machines that will need to be plugged into a standard wall plug socket.

Open Flap

All Cricut machines are compact and at first look, a bit like a laser printer. The Cricut Joy looks a little bit like a handbag without a handle. One of the most noticeable characteristics about this little machine is that it does not have any buttons on it.

To open the machine, simply pull down the front face cover with your hand. It folds out much like the paper tray of some inkjet printers.

Cricut Joy Machine Top, Front, and Inside Overview

The Cricut Joy does not have any buttons on it. What you will find on the front, top, and inside of the Joy includes:

Cricut Accessory and Blade Housing Head

This is the head that houses the Cricut Joy's accessory and blade housing clamp.

Cricut Accessory and Blade Housing Clamp

There is only one accessory clamp in the Cricut Joy. This clamp is for both the Cricut Joy fine-point blade and the Cricut Joy pen accessory. Only the blade and housing designed for the Cricut Joy can be used with this little machine. This is the same for the pen accessories as well as mats and materials.

The accessory and blade housing clamp run along a metal bar that sits a little way back and above the material feeder bar.

Material Feeder Guide Bar

The material feeder bar is the thick silver bar that the material and cutting mat feeds under. This bar helps to support and keep the material steady as the machine cuts out the design issued to it through Design Space.

Feeder Guide Rollers

The feeder roller guides are the thick grey rollers that are positioned on the material feeder guide bar. They secure the materials and help to roll them back and forth as the machine cuts.

Mat/Material Feed Guides and Sensors

The mat/material feed guides are the 2 plastic feet just in front of the feeder guide rollers. These sensors are located beneath the feed guides that have been designed to sense the length of the Smart Materials for the Cricut Joy.

Bottom Feeder Plate

The bottom feeder plate is the flap that is used to open and close the machine. This is the material resting plate that needs extra care. Position the machine comfortably on a table so the plate is being supported. The plate is to hold the material being fed into the machine.

Power Light

This is the little white beauty spot located on the top in the middle of the Cricut Joy. When the machine is powered up, the light will turn green. It will flash while the machine is cutting or about to cut.

What Is at the Back of the Cricut Joy Machine?

The Cricut Joy does not have any buttons on the machine. What you will find at the back of the Joy includes:

Power Port

The power port is at the back of the machine and is where you will plug in the power cable. You will notice that it is the only port, other than the paper feeder slot at the back of the machine. The Cricut Joy does not have any USB ports, but it does have Bluetooth connectivity, connecting the machine to the device with Design Space installed.

Material Feeder Slot

The long slot at the back of the Cricut Joy aligns with the paper feeder on the front of the machine. This is where the material gets fed through as the Joy cuts out the design. It is important to keep the Joy at least 10 inches from the wall to give the machine space to feed material through.

Setting Up the Joy

1. Before you plug the machine in, you will need to open the front of the machine and take out all of the safety materials that protect the blade, housing, and feeder plate during transport/packaging.
2. To set up the Cricut Joy, you will need to go to www.cricut.com/setup where you will find a step-by-step setup guide.
3. Choose "Cricut Joy."
4. In the first step, the program will tell you to position the machine at least 10 inches from the wall.

Plugging In the Joy

The power supply comes in 2 parts; the part that plugs into the back of the machine and the other part that plugs into the wall. Connect these 2 parts before plugging them into either the machine or the wall.

Plug the power supply into the wall and make sure that the wall port is off before you do this. Plug the power cable into the back of the Cricut Joy (it can fit in one place only).

Once the machine is set in position and plugged in, you can turn on the wall port.

Connecting the Cricut Joy Via Bluetooth

Make sure Bluetooth is active on your computer or smart device. The Bluetooth connection screen will pop up, and you should be able to find your Cricut machine.

Highlight your machine and connect it.

If you cannot find the machine on your device, select "Search for New Devices."

Cricut Joy Firmware Update

The first time you connect, the software will test that the machine has the latest firmware on it. If it has, this part will happen fast and come back to let you know it has the latest firmware revision.

If the machine needs an update, there will be another step where it will ask you to download it. Follow the on-screen instructions to do this, as it is important to have the latest firmware revision on the machine to ensure that it functions correctly and works with any updates.

This part will also register the new Cricut Joy for you.

Click "Continue" to take you to the next setup section.

Cricut Joy First Project

To get started and test the machine, once you have paired the Cricut Joy with your PC or smart device and updated the firmware, it will move to the "Let's Test a Cut" screen. This is going to be your first Cricut Joy mini-project.

Supplies

- Smart vinyl
- Weeding tool
- Brayer or scraper tool
- Tweezer
- Transfer paper

Instructions

1. Choose one of the test cut images from the screen.
2. Click on the "Next" button at the bottom of the screen.
3. The next screen to appear is the "Prepare for Cut" screen.
4. The Cricut Joy is driven by the Design Space software. All the bigger Cricut cutting machines have "Manual Load/Unload," "Go," "Pause," and "Material Dial Settings." The Cricut Joy gets its directions and commands from the Design Space software.
5. Ensure that the correct accessory or blade is loaded into the accessory clamp of the machine. If the pen is needed for the design, this would be the place where you would be asked to load the pen. It is the blade you need to make sure that it is correctly and securely loaded into the accessory clamp.
6. Once you are happy that the blade is firmly and securely in place, click on the arrow on the right side of the screen.
7. You will notice the little light on top of the Joy has started blinking to indicate that it is ready to accept the material.
8. The next screen will prompt you to load the vinyl into the machine. Follow the instruction and slide the sample vinyl that came with the Joy beneath the guide feet.
9. The Smart Material vinyl has an extra bit of paper on the sides that feed into the cutter. This is what the machine senses as the Smart Material which does not need a cutting mat.
10. Slide the material gently up until it catches beneath the guide rollers.
11. As soon as the material hits the rollers, it will pull it in and ready it to start cutting.
12. There is no "Go" button on the machine. You have to click on "Go" or "Next" in Design Space to make it start cutting.
13. As Joy cuts the material, it will slide back and forth. If the material was longer, it would slide out of the back paper feeder.
14. When the Joy is finished cutting out the design, the screen in Design Space will change to "Test Cut Complete."
15. Click the "Next" button on the bottom of the screen.
16. Click the "Unload" button at the bottom of the next screen, and Joy will unload the material.
17. Use the tweezer tool to hook up a corner of the excess vinyl and gently pull it off of the design image.

18. Use the weeding tool to clean up the image. This is where you pull a circle out of an "o," for example.
19. Cut a piece of transfer paper and place it over the image.
20. Use either the scraper tool or the brayer tool to make sure the transfer paper is smoothed over the image.
21. You can now transfer the vinyl design to a tumbler, pencil case, lunch box, and so on.
22. To transfer the image, pull the backing sheet off of the vinyl.
23. Place the image onto the object it is to be transferred onto.
24. The transfer paper should be face up.
25. Use the scraping tool to gently make sure that the vinyl firmly adheres to the object.
26. Gently pull off the transfer paper sheet.
27. Well done! You have just completed your first mini-project.

Using the Joy Blade/Accessory Clamp

The blade and the blade housing will come already installed into the Cricut Joy. If you need to remove them to put in the pen accessory or to change the blade, you must pull back the teal clamp to release the accessory or blade.

Slide out the blade or accessory, slide in the pen accessory or blade housing, then close the clamp to secure the object. Although the clamp flap is quite hardy and durable, you will need to be careful with it to avoid damage.

Using Cutting Mats with the Cricut Joy

Three different kinds of cutting mats can be used with the Cricut Joy. These are mats specifically designed for the little Joy machine and they are not interchangeable with the bigger Cricut cutting machines.

The blue LightGrip mat and green Standard Grip mat work the same way that the larger ones do. Cut the material to the needed size and then stick it onto the mat before loading it into the Cricut Joy. It should be noted that the Smart Material designed for the Cricut Joy does not need a cutting mat.

CHAPTER 6:

Best Materials to Use with Your Cricut Machine

Cricut machines have been designed to handle a wide variety of materials. Most of the machines can work with a majority of materials, but they do have specialties among them. Read on for more information on the Cricut Explore One, Cricut Explore Air 2, Cricut Maker, and Cricut EasyPress 2 and the materials that work best with each.

Cricut Explore One

This machine only has one carriage, so you might find yourself swapping out tools more often than with the other machines. This machine can cut over 100 different materials. It can also write and score. Here's a sampling of some of the most common materials used with the Explore One machine:

- **Vinyl:** Vinyl, outdoor vinyl, glitter vinyl, metallic vinyl, matte vinyl, stencil vinyl, dry erase vinyl, chalkboard vinyl, adhesive foils, holographic vinyl, printable vinyl, vinyl transfer tape, iron-on vinyl, glitter iron-on vinyl, foil iron-on, holographic iron-on, printable iron-on for light or dark fabric, flocked iron-on vinyl, and neon iron-on vinyl.
- **Paper:** Cardstock, glitter cardstock, pearl paper, poster board, scrapbook paper, vellum, party foil, cereal boxes, construction paper, copy paper, flat cardboard, flocked cardstock and paper, foil embossed paper, freezer paper, Kraft board, Kraft paper, metallic cardstock and paper, notebook paper, paper grocery bags, parchment paper, paper board, pearl cardstock and paper, photographs, mat board, rice paper, solid core cardstock, watercolor paper, and wax paper.

Cricut Explore Air 2

The Explore Air 2 can cut the same materials as the Explore One.

The difference is that it has 2 carriages instead of one, so it's easier to swap between tools. It's also a bit faster than the Explore One. The Air machines have wireless and Bluetooth capabilities, so you can use the Cricut Design Space on your phone, tablet, or laptop without connecting directly to the machine.

Cricut Maker

The Cricut Maker has about 10x the cutting power of the Explore machines. It includes a rotary blade and a knife blade, so in addition to all the above materials, it can cut into more robust fabrics and materials. With the sharper blades, it's also better at cutting into more delicate materials without damaging them.

Cricut EasyPress 2

The Cricut EasyPress 2 is a small, convenient heat press. It works with any type of iron-on material and can adhere to fabrics, wood, paper, and more. Cricut also offers Infusible inks that are transferred to the material using heat. The EasyPress is a great alternative to iron, as it heats more quickly and more evenly.

Crafting Blanks

The objects you decorate using your Cricut can be referred to as blanks. This can be absolutely any object, and it can be something you stick vinyl to, etch, paint, draw on, write on, or anything else you can think of. They're called blanks because they provide a mostly blank surface to be decorated, though they can also have colors or designs.

Some popular blanks are cups, mugs, wine or champagne glasses, travel mugs, tumblers, and other such drinking vessels. Craft stores will usually sell these, but you can find them at almost any store. They don't need to be considered a "craft" supply for you to use. Most stores have a selection of plain cups and mugs or travel mugs and tumblers with no designs on them. As long as you can imagine a Cricut project with it, it's fair game.

Drink wares aren't the only kitchen or dining-related blanks. Get creative with plates, bowls, and serving utensils. Find blank placemats or coasters at most stores. Decorate Mason or other types of jars. Dry goods containers, measuring cups, food storage containers, pitchers, and jugs—anything you can put in your kitchen can serve as a great blank for your projects.

Clothing is another popular choice for Cricut projects. T-shirts are easy to make with iron-on vinyl, and you can find cheap blanks at any store or a larger selection at craft stores. In fact, craft stores will typically have a large selection of clothing blanks, such as T-shirts, long sleeve shirts, ball caps, plain white shoes, plain bags, and so on. Thrift stores or consignment shops can be an unusual option as well. You could find a shirt with an interesting pattern that you'd like to add an iron-on to or something similar.

Glass is fun to work with and has a ton of project options with your Cricut machine. Glass blocks can be found at craft or hardware stores. Many stores that carry kitchenware will have plain glass cutting boards, or you can find them online. Craft stores and home goods stores could sell glass trinkets or décor that you can decorate. You can even buy full panes of glass at your local hardware store and have them cut to your desired size.

There are plenty of blanks related to electronics, as well. Electronics stores, online stores, and some craft stores offer phone and tablet case blanks. They might be clear, white or black, or colored. Portable battery packs are another option as well. These blanks are often significantly cheaper than already decorated ones, or you can buy them in bulk for a lower price. Get your phone case for a lower price and customize it how you like.

Book covers make great blanks, as well. Customize the cover of a sketchbook, notebook, or journal. Repair the cover of an aged book. Or, create a new book cover for a plain one that you have. If you have old books that you aren't going to read, create a new fake cover for them and use them as décor.

CRICUT

CHAPTER 7:

Comparisons Between All Printers

Cricut Joy vs. Cricut Maker

The Cricut Maker and Cricut Joy are 2 amazing craft machines in the market; however, these 2 machines have a few differences which focus mostly on their work capability and size, yet each of the machines has its unique capability; let's take a look at the differences between these 2 machines.

The Cricut Joy machine is quite small and portable; it then has lightweight, which makes it possible and easy to carry about; if you are someone who wants something small yet efficient and effective, the Cricut Joy should be good to go.

The Cricut Joy does not feature any single button. However, you can just plug it into a power outlet each time you need to turn it on, while the Cricut Maker features buttons and storage spaces in it, on the Cricut Maker, you can press a single button to power on your machine.

To store and place your important tools in the storage spaces around the machine, the Cricut Joy has this portable bag that comes in handy and organized, in this bag, there are compartments for keeping your important tools safely. The Cricut Maker has a double tool holder, which is the opposite of the Cricut Joy.

The Cricut Maker has diverse types of colors, so you can select your preferred type of color when you work in a store, while the Cricut Joy features a single white and blue color that I find attractive and nice.

The Cricut maker possesses more cutting capability than the Cricut Joy; nevertheless, it can cut additional thick and dense materials including the matboard and balsa wood.

The rotary blade of the Cricut maker cuts thorough fabrics, and you can still acquire a knife blade to cut thicker materials; furthermore, a wide cutting rate would let you create larger projects as well as more designs. The Cricut Joy is nearly opposite to the Cricut Maker; however, because of the smaller magnitude of the Cricut Joy, it tends to cut a lower size of material with a width of 4.5 inches when compared to the Maker. The Cricut Joy can only cut +50 materials; it can't cut many heavy and dense materials just like the Maker.

One of Cricut Joy's best features is its capability to cut without a mat when you use a material known as Smart Materials. These Smart Materials are long with a thick back covering, so you can cut without a mat.

The Cricut Joy features one tool holding space which is built specifically for Cricut Joy products; the Cricut Joy blade cuts through less dense and medium dense Cricut Joy's unique materials, such as the smart iron-on, vinyl, cardstock, and paper.

The Cricut Joy machine is quite easy to use, therefore crafting and designing are much easier.

The Design Space app is a Cricut Joy machine app that can be installed on your smartphone; this is where operations and machine controls take place; just plug in your machine, open the Design Space, create a design, and let the machine do the job.

The Smart Materials still make it possible to create and cut designs easily; with the Smart Materials you can just work with ease without placing material on a mat, just feed your Smart Material into the machine after creating your pattern on the Design Space, tap the "Go" button and let the machine do its work; if the project has only one color and one material, it will save you more time and strength.

The Cricut Maker holds double tools at a time, so you can cut and write at the same time; with the Cricut Maker, you need to use a cutting mat each time you want to begin another project; however, you need to be careful so as not to rip off the designs.

The Cricut Maker is more versatile and efficient when compared to the Cricut Joy, the adaptive tool in the Cricut Maker can let you use different cutting tools, such as the knife blade for cutting heavier materials, you can deboss, engrave, score, and do much more with the Cricut Maker.

The Cricut Maker is usually used by crafting professionals and experienced designers. In disparity, the Cricut Joy is used for cutting; however, this doesn't mean it can't do much.

Cricut Joy vs. Cricut Explore Air 2

The size of the machine is the most obvious difference. The Joy is a small travel machine, while the Explore Air 2 is a large tabletop plotter.

The cutting area, of course, is also linked to the size of the machine. In the case of the Joy, we have the mat that comes with the machine, which is 11 by 16 cm. (more or less), the large mat of 11 by 30 cm., and the card mat, which allows us to make folded cards of 11.4 by 16 cm. In the Explore case, we have a more traditional cutting area—30 by 30 cm. with the mat that comes with the machine and 30 x 60 cm. with the large mat.

Each one also has its tools, and they are not interchangeable. In other words, the blade and pens of the Joy are not compatible with Explore and Maker, and vice versa. In the case of Joy, we still only have a normal blade and pens. While the Explore has the basic blade, the deep cut blade allows us to cut thicker materials such as Eva Rubber or some cardboard, and also have pens and a folding pencil to mark the cutting lines.

In the case of the Joy, the car is simple; that is, we can only put one tool at a time. Therefore, if we want to draw and then cut, we will have to switch tools midway. The Explore carriage is double, so we can put the pen and the blade at the same time and do it all at once.

The Joy is a travel machine, and therefore, has as few cables as possible, so it connects only via Bluetooth. The Explore, on the other hand, has the option of connecting via Bluetooth but also via USB for those computers that do not have Bluetooth.

As for differentiated functions, in the case of the Joy, they have added the option of cutting without a mat. This can only be done with vinyl and textile vinyl. Designs can be up to 1.2 m. long, and we can pull them repeatedly cut up to 6 times, more than 7 m. long. In the case of the Explore, it is not possible to cut without a mat, but instead, it allows us to print and cut. We can print our designs on the printer and then cut around with the machine. This is not possible with Joy.

So far, these are the main differences between the 2 machines.

Explore Air 2 vs. Cricut Maker

If you are a newbie in the field of cutting devices, I would take a Cricut Explore Air 2; however, if you are highly smart and require a high-end cutting device with the capability to decolorize and etch (which I typically require), then the Cricut Maker is for you. Inside the box are a cutting board, a scoring tool, and a couple of other tools for cutting and embroidery.

The Cricut Explore Air 2 can cut and compose 2 times and cut 2 times such as compose and etch or print and embroider.

If you desire a screen-printed feel to your T-shirts, this is a terrific alternative to vinyl, and the Explore Air 2 makes it simple for you to understand your imaginative vision. If you have an interest in graphic style, graphics, or other innovative tasks, and you're trying to find an item to assist you to get more innovative or simply begin creating more tasks, you can't fail with Cricut.

You might have forgotten this present; however, you could be an enthusiast who wishes to enhance your abilities, or you may wish to utilize it to begin an innovative company.

A Cricut is a cutting device that can cut various products with cartridges, computer-drawn stamps, and images. Depending upon the design, a Cricut Maker can cut, draw, inscribe and cut. Basically, it is an electronic cutting maker that allows do-it-yourselfers and enthusiasts to produce professional-looking tasks in your home. You can develop a range of various kinds of stamps and images that can be cut, drawn, or cut.

It can cut a range of various kinds of stamps and illustrations such as paper, ink, paper clips, plastic, metal, wood, glass, and even paper.

Like the Cricut Explore device, the Maker can cut magnetic products; simply charge the device with window clips and develop your style.

Other Alternative Printers

- Cricut Explore Air

- Cricut EasyPress Mini

- Cricut EasyPress 2

- Cricut Cake

- Cricut Create

- Cricut Imagine

- Original Cricut

CRICUT

CHAPTER 8:

Machine Beginner Setting

You have all of your materials on hand, which is great, but how do you use a Cricut machine? Well, that's what you are about to find out. If looking at your Cricut machine makes you feel a little confused, read on—here, we'll tell you how to use your new Cricut machine in a simple yet effective way.

Machine Configuration

First, we recommend that you set up your Cricut machine. To start, make a space for it. A craft room is the best place for this, but if you don't know where to put it, I suggest arranging it in a dining room if possible. Make sure you have an outlet nearby or a reliable extension cord.

Then, read the instructions. You can often jump right in and start using the equipment, but it can be very boring with Cricut machines. The best thing to do is to read all the material you get with your machine—as we go through the setup in this book, if you're still stumped, take a look at the manual. Make sure you have ample free space around the machine itself because you'll be loading the mats in and out, and you'll need that little bit of room to maneuver.

The next thing to set up is, of course, the computer where the designs will be created. Make sure whatever media you're using has an internet connection, as you'll need to download the Cricut Design Space app. If it is a pre-Explore Air 2 machine, it will need to be connected directly, but if it is a wireless machine—like Air 2, you can simply plug it into your computer and from there design what you need design.

Now, once you've initially set up this bad boy, you should learn how to use Design Space—and that's what we'll talk about next.

Imputing Cartridges and Keyboard

The first cut you'll make involves keyboard input and cartridges, and these are usually done with the "Enjoy Card" project you get right away. Then, once everything is set up, choose this project, and from there, you can use the tools and accessories within the project.

You will need to set up the smart dial before you start making your designs. This is on the right side of the Explore Air 2 and is basically how you choose your materials. Turn the knob to whatever type of material you want, as this helps ensure the right blade settings. There are also half settings for those in-between projects.

For example, let's say you have lightweight cardstock. You can choose that setting or the adjacent half. Once chosen in Design Space, the machine will automatically adjust to the correct setting.

You can also choose the fast mode, which is located in the "set, load, go" area on the screen, and you can then check the position of the box below the indicator for the position of the dial. Then, press this and make your cut. However, the fast mode is incredibly loud, so be careful.

We mentioned the cartridges. While these are usually no longer used in Explore Air 2 machines, they are useful with beginner projects. To do this, once you have the Design Space software and everything is connected, go to the hamburger (3 bars) menu, and you will see an option called "ink cartridges." Press that bad boy and from there choose the Cricut device. The machine will then tell you to insert the cartridge. Do this, and once it is detected, it will tell you to plug in the cartridge.

Remember, though, that you can't use it with other machines once you plug this in; it is the only limitation to these cartridges.

Once confirmed, you can go to the pictures and click on the cartridges option to find the ones you want to create. You can filter the cartridges to get what you need, and you can check the image card for any other purchased or loaded cartridges. You can get digital cartridges, which means you buy them online and choose images directly from the available options. They are not physical, so no connection is required.

Loading and Unloading the Paper

To load paper into a Cricut machine, you should make sure the paper is at least 3 by 3 inches. Otherwise, it won't cut very well. You should use plain paper for this.

Now, for this to work, you need to put the paper on the cutting mat. You should have one, so get it right away and remove the attached foil. Place a corner of the card in the area where you are headed to line up the corners of the card. From there, push the paper directly onto the cutting mat for proper adhesion. Once done, load it into the machine, following the arrows. We recommend that you keep the paper firmly on the mat. Press the "Load Card" button. If it is not necessary for some reason, press the "Unload Paper" button and try again until it appears.

Now, before making any cuts for your design, you should always have a test cut in place. Some people don't, but it's incredibly useful when learning how to use a Cricut. Otherwise, you will not get the correct pressure in some cases, so make a habit of doing this for your pieces.

Is there a difference between vinyl and other products? The main difference is the cutting mats. Depending on what you are cutting, you may need a grip or lack of grip. If you feel that your material is not sticking completely, take some Heat N 'Bond to help you out as often, the problem with cutting fabrics comes from it not sticking. But you may also need a bit thicker mats to get a better grip on these.

Selection of Shapes, Letters, and Sentences

When you create your pattern in Design Space, you usually start by using different letters, shapes, numbers, or fonts. These are the basics, and they are incredibly easy.

To create some text, just press the text tool on the left side and type the text. For example, write the word "Hello," or "Joy," or whatever you want to use.

You can change the font size by pressing the drag and drop arrow near the corner of the text box or by going to the side panel at the top to choose the actual font size. You can also choose different Cricut or system fonts. The Cricut ones will be in green, and if you have Cricut Access, this is a great way to start using it. You can order these, too, so you don't end up accidentally paying for a font.

The Cricut ones are supposed to be made for Cricut, so you know they will look good. Design Space also allows you to put them closer together so they can be cut with a single cut. You can change this by going to "Leading" and adjusting as needed. To correct certain letters, go to the advanced drop-down menu to separate the letters so everything is separated as needed.

Cricut also offers several different writing styles, which is a great way to add text to projects. The way to do this is to choose a font created with a specific style, choose only the Cricut ones, and then go to writing. This will narrow down your choice so that you can use a good font for writing.

Adding shapes is also quite simple. In Design Space, choose the shapes option.

Once clicked, the window will pop up, and you'll have a wonderful range of different shapes that you can use with just one click. Choose your shape and from there, put it into space. Drag the corners to make them larger or smaller.

There is also the score line, which creates a folding line for use. Personally, if you are thinking of trying to make a card in the beginning, I suggest you use it.

You can also resize your options by dragging them to the right side, and you can change the orientation by choosing that option, then flipping it. You can also select exact measurements, which is good for those design projects that require everything to be accurate.

Once you've chosen your design, it's time to start cutting, and we'll discuss this next step below.

How to Remove the Cut from the Cutting Mat

Removing the cut from the mat is easy but complicated.

I ran into the problem that it was more complicated with vinyl projects as they love to stay there. But we will tell you how to create great cuts and also remove them.

The first point to remember is to make sure you are using the right mat. The ones with light grip are good for very light material, with the pink one being one of the strongest and can only be used with the Cricut Maker. Once the design is cut out, you'll probably be eager to remove the design directly from the mat, but one of the problems with this is that often the design will be ruined if you're not careful. Instead of pulling the project off the mat itself, fold the mat with your hand and push it away from the project, as this will loosen it from the mat. Fold it both horizontally and vertically so that the adhesive releases the design.

Remember the spatula tool we told you to get with your Cricut machine in the beginning? This is where you use it. Use this putty knife to pull the vinyl lightly until you can grab it by the corner and lift it. Otherwise, you risk curling it or tearing the mat, which is what we don't want.

Now, with initial cuts, such as paper cuts, it will be incredibly easy. Believe me, I was surprised at how little effort it took, but one of the biggest details to remember is that with Cricut machines, you have to go slow when removing material. Do it slowly and don't rush towards the end. Taking your time will save you a lot of trouble and also save you money and stress!

You will notice that Cricut mats are incredibly sticky, and if you don't have a Cricut spatula on hand or don't want to spend the money, metal spatulas will work too. You can put the paper on a flat surface and then remove it slightly. But always be careful when removing these items.

Cricut machines are quite easy to use, and the great advantage is that with the right understanding and ideas, you can make any object you want.

CHAPTER 9:

A Few Projects to Try On with Your Cricut Machine

How to Make Custom Graphic T-Shirts

First, you will need to determine what you want your shirt to say. It is best to stick with just one color when you start. But as you get better at creating with your Cricut, you can move on to more color options in one design. Next is to pick which shirt you would like to use. This can be a preexisting shirt from your closet or it could be one that you purchased specifically for this project. The shirt needs to be a material that can be ironed.

Supplies

- Cricut machine

- Vinyl for the letters

- Your Cricut tools kit

Instructions

1. Start by choosing the image you want to use. It can be done in Photoshop, or you can place your text directly into the Design Space.
2. Next, open the Cricut Design Space. Choose the canvas you wish to use by clicking the canvas icon on the dashboard, located on the left-hand side. Select the canvas that you will be using for your vinyl letters. It can be anything within the categories they offer.
3. Then, select the size of the shirt for the canvas. It is located on the right-hand side of the options.
4. Now, click "Upload" for uploading your image, which is located on the left-hand side. Select the image you are using by browsing the list of images in your file library. Then, select the type of image that you have picked. For most projects, especially iron-on ones, you should choose the "Simple Cut" option.
5. Click on the white space that you want to be removed by cutting out. Remember to cut the insides of every letter.
6. Next, be super diligent and press "Cut Image" instead of "Print" first. You do not want to print the image. You cut it as well.
7. Place the image on your chosen canvas and adjust the sizing of the image.
8. Place your iron-on image with the vinyl side facing down on the mat and then turn the dial to the setting for iron-on.
9. Next, you must click the "Mirror Image" setting for the image before hitting go.
10. Once you have cut the image, you should remove the excess vinyl from the edges around the lettering or image. Then use the tool for weeding out the inner pieces of the letters.
11. Now you will be placing the vinyl on the shirt.
12. And now, the fun part begins. You will get to iron the image onto the shirt. Using the cotton setting, you will need to use the hottest setting to get your iron. There should not be any steam.
13. You want to warm the shirt by placing the iron on the shirt portion to hold the image. This should be warmed up for 15 seconds.

14. Next, lay the vinyl out exactly where you want it to be placed. Place a pressing cloth over the top of the plastic. It will prevent the plastic on the shirt from melting.
15. Place your iron onto the pressing cloth for around 30 seconds. Flip the shirt and place the pressing cloth and iron on the backside of the vinyl.
16. Flip your shirt back over and begin to peel off the sticky part of the vinyl that you have been overlaying on the shirt. This will separate the vinyl from the plastic backing. It should be done while the plastic and vinyl are hot. If you are having trouble removing the vinyl from the plastic backing, then place the iron back on the part that is being difficult. Then proceed to pull up, and it should come off nicely.
17. This should remove the plastic from the vinyl that is now on the shirt. Place the pressing cloth on top of the vinyl once again and heat it to ensure that it is good and stuck.

How to Make Vinyl Wall Decals

Supplies

- Adhesive vinyl

- Cricut machine

- Weeding tool

- Scrapper tool

Instructions

1. Log in to the Cricut Design Space.
2. Create a new project.
3. Click on "Upload Image."
4. Drag the image to the design space.
5. Highlight the image and click on "Flatten."
6. Click on the "Make It" button.
7. Place vinyl into the cutting mat.
8. Custom dial the machine to "Vinyl."

9. Load the cutting mat into the machine.
10. Push the mat up against the rollers.
11. Cut the design out of the vinyl.
12. Weed out the excess vinyl with a weeding tool.
13. Apply a thin layer of transfer tape on the vinyl.
14. Peel off the backing.
15. Apply the transfer tape on the wall.
16. Smoothen with a scraper tool to let out the air bubble.
17. Carefully peel off the transfer tape from the wall.

How to Make Recipe Stickers

Supplies

- Cricut cutting machine
- Sticker paper
- Cutting mat

Instructions

1. Use your Cricut ID to log in to the Design Space application. Then click on the "New Project" button in the top right corner of the screen to start a new project and view a blank canvas.
2. Click on the "Images" icon on the Design panel and type in "Recipe Stickers" in the search bar. Select the image that works for you, then click on the "Insert Images" button at the bottom of the screen.
3. The image that you have selected will appear on the canvas and can be edited to your preference. You will be able to make all kinds of changes, for example, changing the color and size of the image (the sticker should be between 2–4 inches wide). The image selected for this project has the words "Stickers" inside the design, so let's delete that by first clicking on the "Ungroup" button and selecting the "Stickers" layer, and clicking on the red "X" button. Click on the "Text" button and add your recipe's name, as shown in the picture below.
4. Now, move the text to the middle of the design and select the entire design, including the text. Then click on "Align" and select "Center Horizontally" and "Center Vertically" so that your text will be uniformly aligned right in the center of the design.
5. Select all the design layers and click on the "Group" icon on the top right of the screen under the Layers panel. Now, copy and paste the designs and update the text for all your recipes. (Tip: You can use your keyboard shortcuts like "Ctrl + C" (to copy) and "Ctrl + V" (to paste) instead of selecting the image and clicking on "Edit" from the Edit bar to view the drop-down option for "Copy" and "Paste.")

6. Click on "Save" at the top right corner of the screen and enter a name for your project, for example, "Recipe Stickers," then click "Save."

7. Your design is ready to be cut. Simply click on the "Make It" button on the top right corner of the screen. All the required mats and materials will be displayed on the screen. (Tip: You can move your design on the mat by simply dragging and dropping it anywhere on the mat to resemble the cutting space for your material on the actual cutting mat).

8. Once you have loaded the sticker paper to your Cricut cutting machine, click "Continue" at the bottom right corner of the screen to start cutting your design.

9. Once your Cricut device has been connected to your computer, set the cut setting to "Vinyl" (recommended cutting the sticker paper since it tends to be thicker than regular paper). Place the sticker paper on top of the cutting mat and load it into the Cricut device by pushing it against the rollers. The "Load/Unload" button would already be flashing, so just press that button first, followed by the flashing "Go" button. Viola! You have just created your very own recipe stickers.

PART 3:

TOOLS, MATERIALS, AND ACCESSORIES

CHAPTER 10:

Materials You Can Use in the Machine

T he machines can use many different materials for any project you desire, and we will be breaking down which machine can use what materials. Something that you should know is that there are materials that the Maker can cut that the other machines cannot; as a matter of fact, they include over 100 different types of fabric. The Cricut machines' official website periodically upgrades in what they say the machines can cut, so as a result, you will need to check their website often. In doing so, you will realize what you can still cut even if it may have been taken off the list.

In this section, we will go over several of them in detail to get a better understanding of how truly remarkable the Cricut machine really is! Get inspired by a collection of diverse, high-quality materials, all designed to cut perfectly with Cricut machines. Material finishes ranging from fun and flashy to polished and rich. These materials make it easy to achieve the exact look you want. Once you get more comfortable using the different types of materials, you will easily create projects with multiple materials in one. Utilize resources such as this book to refer to when you have questions relating to what type of material to use and when. The more you learn, the better your project will be!

Vinyl

Adhesive vinyl for Cricut cutting machines comes in a wide variety of colors, designs, and uses. The adhesive properties can either be semi-permanent (easily removable with adhesive remover) or permanent. Semi-permanent is typically used for indoor projects; such as wall decals or window clings. Permanent vinyl would be used for outdoor use, such as holiday decor and tabletop designs.

Those are perfect for making stickers, indoor and outdoor items, and even "printing" on mugs and T-shirts. Once you get into it, it is truly addictive to acquire different colors and types. For example, you can get chalkboard vinyl, which is awesome for labeling, or outdoor vinyl, which will look great on your car window. These materials can be purchased at virtually any craft shop, and they are not too expensive if you do a little canvassing. Double-check that it is indeed the type of vinyl you are looking for.

Vinyl is the most used material for Cricut projects outside of paper because it is one of the most versatile materials to work with. Adhesive vinyl is a great starting point for creators who are new to Cricut but want to branch outside of paper crafting. It is a material that will need to be weeded, as designs are typically cut out of the vinyl, and the negative space will need to be removed to see the design.

Paper

A wide variety of paper products can be cut using the Cricut machine. Some varieties include cardstock—which is one of the most popular—corrugated cardboard, foil embossed, Kraft board, scrapbooking paper, pearl, sparkle/shimmer, and poster board. Paper products can come in a wide range of sizes, with 12 by 12 inches being the most common and easily applied type as it fits perfectly on a 12 by 12 inches cutting mat.

Paper is most commonly used in card projects, but it can also assist in wall decor, gift boxes, cake toppers, and lantern projects. Most crafters familiar with the Cricut recommend starting with a paper project first to handle the different options Cricut cutters have. Paper allows you to create intricate designs and get familiar with the cutting blade depth at the same time. You should remember that you need something to practice on, and a cheap printer paper works wonderfully for that. You will not feel bad for making mistakes because the material does not cost much. If you are feeling more creative than usual, you may get the colored paper too. This way, when you get the hang of cutting, you can create letters for cars or stencils.

The following materials can only be used with the Cricut Maker machine.

Chipboard

The Cricut website sells a variety of packs of this type of material, which is great for getting to know the material and what projects to use it for effectively. It is suggested to be used on projects such as sturdy wall art, school projects, photo frames, and more. Since this material has a 1.5 mm. thickness, it can only be cut using the Cricut knife blade. Chipboard is great for any type of project that requires dimensions, such as gingerbread or a haunted house around the holidays!

Fabric

The fabric is great if you have the Cricut Maker. The chances are that you will want to cut some textile with this machine on hand; that is why you should stock up on that and get extra just in case. You can obtain some cheap, scrappy fabrics to practice before moving on to the projects' proper fabrics.

This simple, yet classic material, is another favorite among Cricut Maker users. Many use fabrics to create custom clothing, home decor, and wall art. Imagine all the times you went out looking for the perfect top, or skirt only to come back home empty-handed after many hours of searching. It would be ideal to find exactly what you want when you want it! Now, without the help of a bulky and outdated sewing machine, you can make simple and affordable clothing exactly the look and feel you want! Fabric is also a great material to make homemade gifts for friends and family. Lots of people enjoy curling up on the couch during the winter months, with a cozy quilt and a favorite movie.

Felt

Blended fibers between natural and synthetic are also common among craft felts. Felt is commonly used to help young children distinguish among different types of textiles. Felt is also commonly used in craft projects for all ages. The felt is easily cut with your Cricut machine; no deep-cut blade is required! Felt can be used for: fun decor, kid's crafts, baby toys, stuffed shapes, and more! When starting on the Cricut Maker, this is one of the best materials to start out with. This material is very forgiving and will allow you to keep the gift-giving spirit going! This material is also great for creating faux flowers. You can bring the outside indoors, without maintenance or worrying about children or pets getting into a mess!

Cardstock

If you plan on making cards or labels, cardstock is a must. The more, the better. It is really awesome to have a large pile of it and just be able to cut to your heart's content. It will also help to practice once you have perfected cutting normal printing paper.

Fondant

Fondant is for those bakers out there. There is a possibility that you already have extra fondant lazing about in your home. However, it never hurts to have more. The awesome thing about fondant is that you can reuse it to an extent, depending on how well it freezes or how big the need is to freeze it before cutting. Of course, it is useful to have backup materials for the days you are in a crafty mood. Most materials are available on the Cricut website, so you can order them along with your Cricut machine. Everything will be delivered at once, and you will not have to buy anything again for a while.

It also depends on what sort of material you will be interested in for creating something awesome. If you are going to cut wood, for instance, you will have to stock up on that as you will be going through it quite fast if you are an enthusiastic and excitable crafter.

The Explore series can only cut certain items, and we are going to list them now.

The Explore series can cut these items:

- Tattoo paper

- Washi tape

- Paint chips

- Wax paper

- Faux suede

- Wrapping paper

- Washi paper

- Posterboard

- Parchment paper

- Sticker paper

- Construction paper

- Photo paper

- Printable fabric

- Magnetic sheets

- Paper grocery bags

- Craft foam

- Window cling vinyl

- Cardstock

- Flannel

- Vellum

- Duck cloth

- Wool felt

- Corkboard

- Tissue paper

- Duct tape

- Matte vinyl

- Iron-on vinyl

- Leather up to 2.0 mm. thick

- Sheet duct tape

- Oilcloth

- Soda cans

- Stencil film

- Glitter foam

- Metallic vellum

- Burlap

- Transparency film

- Chipboard that is up to 2.0 mm. thick

- Aluminum metal that is up to .14 mm. thick

- Stencil vinyl

- Glitter vinyl

- Glossy vinyl

- Faux-leather up to 1.0 mm. thick

- Fabrics, when used with the Explore series, need to be stabilized with Heat N Bond. Examples of fabrics are shown on the list below:

- Denim

- Felt

- Silk

- Polyester

Other items that the Explore Series can cut are listed below:

- Chalkboard vinyl

- Adhesive vinyl

- Aluminum foil

- Cardboard

- Stencil film

- Dry erase vinyl

- Printable vinyl

- Outdoor vinyl

- Wood birch up to .5 mm. thick

- Corrugated cardboard

- Shrink plastic

- Metallic vellum

- White core

- Rice paper

- Photo framing mat

- Pearl cardstock

- Cereal boxes

- Freezer paper

- Iron-on

- Printable iron-on

- Glitter iron-on

- Foil iron-on

- Foil embossed paper

- Neon iron-on

- Matte iron-on

The Maker can cut everything that the Explore series can cut, but it can cut so much more because the Explore series operates with 3 blades, but the Maker has 6. The fact that they have 6 blades, enables them to cut more as well as thicker fabric. They also differ from the Explore series because the Maker does not have to use Heat N Bond to stabilize fabrics. This is a great thing because it means that you can go to a fabric store, choose a fabric, use it for a project with no preparation, and no additional materials.

The Maker can use the rotary blade as well. This type of blade is new, and it differs from the others that the Explore machines use because this blade spins and twists with a gliding and rolling motion. This rolling action is going to allow the Maker to cut side to side, as well as up and down. Having a blade able to cut in any direction is going to help you with the ability to craft great projects. The Maker is even able to cut (up to) 3 layers of light cotton at the same time. This is great for projects that need uniform cuts.

The Maker is also able to use the knife blade, which is a more precise option and cuts better than the others before it. This blade can cut up to 2.4 mm. thick fabric. This machine is also able to use 10 times more power to cut than the others as well.

With that being said, the Maker can cut over 100 different fabrics that others cannot. We will be listing some of those fabrics below:

- Waffle cloth

- Jacquard

- Gossamer

- Khaki

- Damask

- Faille

- Heather

- Lycra

- Mesh

- Calico

- Crepe paper

- Gauze

- Interlock knit

- Grocery bag

- Acetate

- Chantilly lace

- Boucle

- Corduroy

- EVA foam

- Tweed

- Tulle

- Moleskin

- Fleece

- Jersey

- Muslin

- Jute

- Terry cloth

- Velvet

- Knits

- Muslin

Remember that this is just scratching the surface of what the Maker can cut. There are many other materials as well since the Maker is the ultimate machine and the best out of the 4. The Maker is also great for sewing, and there are hundreds of these projects on Design Space. Having a machine that can have access to these projects and the ability to cut thicker materials means that you have a machine that opens your crafting skills to a whole new level.

CHAPTER 11:

Cricut Tools and Accessories

Tools for Cutting

We will start with the tools that you can mount on your Cricut devices to achieve the perfect cut, scoring, and writing for a variety of your projects.

Deep-Point Blade

The Cricut deep-point blade facilitates the effortless cutting of a wider range of products. You can use chipboard to build customized wall calendars, cut personalized stamps using rubber sheets, and even create unique magnets.

With this blade, any 1.5 mm. thick material can be easily cut, such as poster boards, heavy cardstock, and much more. This blade can be used with the Cricut Maker and the Cricut Explore line (including the Explore, Explore One, Explore Air, and Explore Air 2). It is recommended to be used for these materials: Magnet, chipboard, stamp material, thick cardstock, stiffened felt, foam sheets, cardboard. You can buy the deep-point blade with the housing for $34.99.

Premium Fine-Point Blade

The premium fine-point blade can deliver highly durable precision cutting to ensure your DIY projects are a total win. This high-strength blade has been built with German carbide steel with a special design to allow cutting of even the most intricately designed graphics with the Cricut machine.

It is resistant to regular wear and tear and is capable of cutting through the lightest and medium-weight materials such as iron-on, vinyl, and cardstocks. This blade can also be used with the Cricut Maker and the Cricut Explore line (including the Explore, Explore One, Explore Air, and Explore Air 2). It is recommended to be used for these materials: faux leather, iron-on, vinyl, cardstock, poster board. It is also available for purchase with the housing for $34.99.

Bonded-Fabric Blade

The bonded-fabric blade as the name suggests it is specifically designed to cut through bonded fabric and fabrics with iron-on by ensuring that the blade is capable of precisely cutting and will stay sharp for a long time. It is constructed with premium carbide steel from Germany and is developed to bring your intricately designed graphics to life with the Cricut Maker. It allows the creation of fantastic DIY projects such as personalized applique and sewing projects that will take your fabric crafting skills to the next level. Although, this blade can be used with the entire Cricut Explore line (including the Explore, Explore One, Explore Air, and Explore Air 2) and not just the Cricut Maker. It is also available for purchase with the housing for $34.99.

Rotary Blade

The rotary blade is a uniquely designed sharp blade that can cut exquisite designs from soft textiles for your dream sewing projects much faster and easier than ever before. You will be able to effortlessly cut silk, cotton, denim, canvas, and even burlap. With this blade, you will also be able to cut through delicate materials such as crepe paper and create parts to make stunning quilts, plush toys, bags, accessories, decorations, among others. It is recommended that when you start noticing uncut threads or if the material configurations on Design Space are not as precise, you should replace your rotary blade to keep getting high-quality results. This blade can only be used with the Cricut Maker and doesn't support the Cricut Explore line or any older models. The rotary blade replacement kit is available for purchase at $16.99.

Knife Blade

The knife blade is designed with extra depth to easily and safely cut through thick and dense materials up to 2.4 mm. (3/32). It is good to use if you are interested in adding dimensions to your project. It can be used for a broad spectrum of practical and artisan materials such as chipboard, balsa wood, basswood, mat board, craft foam, garment leather, and tooled leather. You can easily create puzzles, models, dinosaur skeletons, dioramas, wood decor, leather goods, toys, and much more. But it is not recommended to cut images or designs smaller than 0.75 inches. This blade can only be used with the Cricut Maker and doesn't support the Cricut Explore line or any older models. The knife blade with drive housing is available for purchase at $45.99.

Scoring Wheel Tip

The scoring wheel tip can be used to transcend creative barriers and create in-depth scoring lines. This tool is designed to help you create professional-looking and high finish tags, cards, and gift boxes to marvelous wearable art, 3D home décor, and structures by generating professional-level precision on every crease-and-fold project that comes to your mind. You can create crisp creases and perfect folds without struggle; all marked with a flawless finish. The patented design of the wheel can effectively work on basic materials while generating 10 times more pressure than the scoring stylus. This blade can only be used with the Cricut Maker and doesn't support the Cricut Explore line or any older models. It is available for purchase at $29.99 and the scoring wheel tip with drive housing for $49.99.

Maker Tools

Every craftsman has a distinctive approach to bringing their ideas to life, and you may want to supplement your artistic tools by employing one or more of the tools listed below to create stunning projects.

Engraving Tip

The Cricut engraving tip will help you generate customized texts and monograms. You can design ornamental embellishments and flourishes as well as inscribe any famous quote of your choice on a keepsake. This tip is made with high-quality carbide steel that will allow engraving on Cricut aluminum sheets and anodized aluminum, so you can highlight the silver underneath for a professional-looking effect. This tip can be used only with the Cricut Maker machine. The Cricut engraving tip will help you create intricate dog tags with personalized engraving, customized nameplates, engraved art and decoration, jewelry, monograms, wood sculptures, and mementos. It is recommended to be used with aluminum flat, soft metals, leather, acrylic, plastic, among others. You can buy the Cricut engraving tip for $24.99.

Fine Debossing Tip

The fine debossing tip (2.0 mm.) is the ultimate tool to create elegant papercrafts by incorporating professional finish and elevation to the base material. It will help you achieve crisp debossed designs with fine details. This tip is uniquely designed with a rolling debossing ball, that will provide you the freedom to create customized and personalized designs with exceptional intricacy, unlike standard embossing folders available in the market that limit you to a predefined layout. You can easily create dimensional wedding cards, monogrammed "thank you" notes, or attached flourish to the gift boxes and gift tags, and much more. You can also create an amazing effect on coated paper, shimmer and glitter paper, and foil cardstock. This tip can be used only with the Cricut Maker machine. It is recommended to be used with cardstock, foil poster board, foil cardstock, foil kraft board, poster board, and kraft board. You can buy the fine debossing tip for $24.99.

Basic Perforation Blade

The basic perforation blade is uniquely designed with 2.5 mm. teeth and 0.5 mm. gaps to quickly generate smooth tears with accurate and consistent perforation cuts for all your craft projects. For all your perforated design needs, this blade will allow you to create models with finely perforated and uniform lines that would eliminate the need for folding the paper prior to tearing it up and is very handy particularly for shapes with curves.

You can effortlessly create tear-out booklet pages, raffle tickets, homemade journals, or any project requiring a tidy tear, such as Christmas decorations, paper dolls, tear-away cards or gift coupons, advent calendars, and much more. It is recommended to be used with fabrics like paper, cardstock, foam, acetate, and foil. This blade can be used only with the Cricut Maker machine. You can buy the basic perforation blade for $29.99, exclusively through HSN.

Wavy Blade

The wavy blade will help you create decorative edges much faster than a drag blade for a broad range of projects with smoothly molded cuts. This uniquely designed blade made from stainless steel is perfect to create original vinyl decals, iron-on designs, envelopes, cards, gift tags, and collage projects, or when you are looking to add stylish accents with a whimsical wavy edge to your craft. It is recommended to be used with iron-on, vinyl, paper, cardstock, and fabric. This blade can be used only with the Cricut Maker machine. You can buy the wavy blade for $29.99, exclusively through HSN.

Craft Tools

Cricut also offers a variety of crafting tools such as rulers, fabric shears, seam rippers, thread snips, knives, trimmers, rotary cutters, measuring tape, and much more. All the tools are carefully designed to help you take your crafting skills to the next level resulting in professional-looking crafts with a premium finish. For instance, the True Control Knife Kit contains 5 replacement blades along with a storage cartridge to help you monitor and discard the used blades. This knife is designed with a razor-sharp edge, piercing tip, and superior blade lock system to provide you better control and stunning finishes every time. It can be used to create precision cuts on paper, cardstock, thin plastics, canvas, and various other material. Their patented hands-free blade changing system means you can safely change your blades without needing to touch them and accidentally hurting yourself. It also boasts an anti-roll design to ensure that the knife will stay in place when not being used along with a padded grip for a comfortable handling experience.

Weeder Tool

So, the following tools are from the Cricut company, and one of the things that you might want to get for yourself is a weeder tool. A weeder tool is one of the most essential tools that you can have because while the spatula and the tweezers that come with the machine are beneficial, the weeding tool is necessary if you're trying to lift vinyl off of your mat. There are a lot of different tools that people can use for weeding, and they all work to raise the vinyl from the backing sheet in a safe way so that the project doesn't get ruined and your mat doesn't get ruined.

However, if you want a tool that's direct from the company itself, you can use the weeder tool, or you can buy the weeder toolset because it has finer points, and it might be able to do more for you.

Some of the other popular tools that people use for weeding are dental picks, but the handles may be uncomfortable; however, you can also use an Exacto knife, but you'll have to be very careful not to damage the project or cut yourself open. They also use an old gift card or a credit card, but you should be aware that this might scratch the project, so you'll have to be very careful with this as well.

Spatula Tool

The next tool we're going to talk about is the spatula. The spatula is for lifting material from the cutting mat when you don't want to worry about tearing the fabric. It will take care of this by lifting the material from the mat as easily as possible, and it can also be used with a scraper tool to keep the mat clean and debris-free. Cricut sells the scraper and spatula together for a very reasonable price as well.

Scraper Tool

Now that we talked about the spatula let's talk about the scraper tool. A clean mat is essential for getting a good project done and making sure that your material isn't moving around during the cutting. The last thing you need when you are spending a lot of money on the material is to have it move halfway during the project, and then you have to start completely from the beginning, and you wasted all that money as well. Other tools remove that issue, but the scraper tool is much faster, and it ensures that you have a nice clean mat. There are different sizes, but most people prefer the extra-large as it's easier to hold, and it's faster than the smaller one, which means that it can also help get the bubbles out of your vinyl.

Extra mats are always something that is recommended because there's nothing more irritating when you're working on a project than realizing that your mats are no longer sticky. There are definite ways to re-stick your mat, and they can save you money, but just in case, it is still always a good idea to have a couple of extra mats on hand just in case you need them. The mats do different things for different projects, such as the following.

- The pink that's for fabric is, of course, only for fabric.
- A strong grip, which is purple, would be better for thicker projects like leather, poster board, or thicker card stock.
- A standard green would be for iron-on and vinyl.
- The light blue would be for paper and card stock projects.

Toolset

They also offer an essential toolset that has almost every item that we're talking about it. The toolset includes the following items.

- Tweezers.
- Weeder.
- Spatula.
- Scraper.
- Scissors.
- Scoring stylus.

By buying this, you can cut down on a lot of money instead of buying the items individually if you just buy the set instead.

Bright Pad

A Bright Pad is great for many different reasons because it makes weeding so much easier. After all, it makes the cut lines much more visible, but if you have anything more than a simple cut, this is really going to help you out because you'll be able to see exactly where the lines are, and you could even use it for adapting patterns and tracing.

EasyPress

An EasyPress is great as well. If you're still using the iron for heat transfer vinyl, the EasyPress makes things so much easier than iron because there's no peeling after 1–2 wares, and it takes out all the guesswork of the right time and temperature as well. If you have space, you can get a real heat press for just a little bit more if you can afford it, but we would recommend considering a beginner heat press first, especially if you're doing anything in a large quantity or for commercial purposes.

Brayer Tool

A brayer tool is good for larger vinyl projects or working with fabric; then you should use a brayer. This fixes the problem of not fully stabilizing your material before cutting. A brayer makes the material stick to the mat but without damaging it.

Trimmer

A paper trimmer is super handy if you want to get a straight cut. You do not have to use scissors, and you don't have to use a ruler. As such, it makes cutting a lot easier on you, especially if you're working with vinyl. The company also sells their trimmer; however, there are other places where you can get a trimmer as well. If you go with a shortcut paper trimmer, it has the option for scoring to get a perfect fold, so that may be something that you would want to look into.

Scissors

Scissors make a world of differences well. The company scissors are made with stainless steel, which creates an even cut while remaining durable, as stainless steel is one of the most durable materials that we have. The scissors are quite sharp, and they come with a micro-tip blade, which means that working on the fine details in a smaller area is easier and clean right down to the point. It also has an interchangeable colored cap, which is protective as well; therefore, your scissors can be stored safely.

Tweezers

The tweezers are super helpful, and many people have more than one type. They usually have one for small items and one for vinyl. This tool is in the Cricut toolset, but if you want to go for something else, there are Pazzlee needle point tweezers, and they have a very sharp point, which makes them excellent for vinyl. The points are also sharp enough to pick fine pieces from the mat without using the edges or any other little trick, and they can also pick up the tiniest small scraps. If you don't want to get the company's tweezers, you can go with this other company instead.

Pens

Pens are a big part of the Cricut world as well, and you can purchase these pens in a variety of places. However, you can use other pens that you can find just about anywhere and for really cheap prices.

Other

There're other tools you can get for yourself if you find that you are a busy person and that you go to other people's houses or you go on business trips or things of that nature, such as a tote bag to carry all of your Cricut supplies and machine. The company sells a great tote for a reasonable price, and you would be able to use it for your benefit because you will be able to keep everything organized and neat the way it needs to be. If you don't like their price point, there are actually a lot of other places where you can get a great tote as well.

You can also get rotary blades or a control knife. A control knife is basically like an Exacto knife, so you'll have to be careful with this because even though it adds precision and accuracy to your projects, you could end up cutting yourself pretty badly. You'll have to make sure to be careful.

If you need rulers because you feel like you're not accurate enough, they have these as well, and they have all different types and kits that have all the tools you need so that you don't have to buy everything individually. This is a great thing to look into so that you can see everything that you need. There are many different websites on the Internet where you can find tools for your machine, and each of them claims that their materials are better than the rest.

Cricut offers everything you would need on their site, and they offer very reasonable prices, but you can also do some additional searching if you feel like their stuff isn't what you would want, and you would want something else. As we've already listed examples from other companies, this will help you get an idea of what we're talking about. If you decide to get these additional tools, you'll find that your projects will be able to go a lot easier, and you'll be able to have more precision and more accuracy with them as well. Many people who like the Cricut and their company recommend getting these items just for that purpose.

Mats

There are 3 different categories of mats offered by Cricut which are compatible with different Cricut machines and heat presses, as described below:

Machine Mats

The Standard Grip machine mat is 12 by 12 inches and compatible with all the Cricut machines. These mats are designed to hold the material firmly in place while you cut through it and then easily remove the material when ready. It is recommended to be used with cardstock, patterned paper, embossed cardstock, iron-on, and vinyl.

They also offer the LightGrip machine mat, which is also 12 by 12 inches and specifically designed for the adhesion of lightweight and delicate materials such as standard paper, light cardstock, and vellum.

Self-Healing Mats

Cricut offers a wide variety of self-healing mats and claims them to be twice more self-healing than their competitors. They are designed with larger numbers on a 1-inch-wide border, for easy readability. These mats cannot be used inside the Cricut machines. Some of these offerings include Decorative Self-Healing Mat—Mint, Decorative Self-Healing Mat—Blue, Decorative Self-Healing Mat—Lilac, and more.

EasyPress Mats

The Cricut EasyPress mat is uniquely designed to work with the Cricut EasyPress for impeccable heat transfer projects. The long-lasting cover offers even thermal conduction and uniform distribution of the heat. The interior liner can easily absorb moisture resulting in clean and dry heat. The foil membrane can reflect heat onto the material, preventing the transfer of moisture vapors, while the silicone foam insulates the surface and protects it against heat damage. They come in 3 different sizes, namely, 12 by 12 inches, 20 by 16 inches, and 8 by 10 inches, and special Decorative Polka Dot Mats in blue/mint and rose/lilac in 14 by 14 inches.

Storage

There are 3 different categories of storage bags specifically designed for Cricut machines and tools as described below:

Machine Totes

These premium storage bags are 26 inches long, 9.25 inches wide, and 9.25 inches tall and carefully designed so you can organize and store your Cricut machine at home and easily transport it if needed. The bag has side pockets and compartments to allow storage of craft tools and supplies and comes with a sturdy double-snap handle. These bags have soft padding to provide additional protection and shock absorption. You can buy these bags in different colors (purple, navy, tweed, and raspberry) for $149.99.

Rolling Craft Tote

These bags are equipped with rollers for easy portability and storage at home. They are 26 inches long, 10.25 inches wide, and 14.38 inches tall but remember these bags are designed to store your craft supplies and will not fit any Cricut machines. These bags are also available in different colors (purple, navy, tweed, and raspberry) for $199.99.

EasyPress Tote

These bags are specifically designed for storage of Cricut EasyPress along with its safety base, mat, and other small accessories at home or on the go. They are made from robust and heat-resistant material to protect your device against bumps and scratches while you work through your heat-transfer projects.

A convenient shoulder strap and powerful gripped handle will allow for easy carrying around with the Velcro strap to secure your device for travel. A back pocket and front pocket are added to store the mats and iron-on accessories.

Cricut BrightPad

The Cricut BrightPad is an electronic crafting pad that looks like a tablet. You can use this to light up your paper designs for easier drawing, tracing, weeding, quilting, and lower the strain on your eyes in the process. It is thin, lightweight, and sturdy for comfortable use and portability, with 9 by 11.5 inches of the uniformly LED-lit area and 5 different brightness settings. It is made of a 6H Hardness Surface, which makes it highly resistant to scratches. You can use it to weed vinyl or iron-on designs and paper piecing quilt blocks. Bas well as for models, jewelry, needlepoint. You can buy a Cricut BrightPad in a rose or mint color for $79.99.

Cricut Cuttlebug Machine

The Cricut Cuttlebug is a machine to cut and emboss a range of different materials. With clean and crisp cuts as well as uniform and deep emboss for professional quality results. Cricut also offers an entire line of compatible Cuttlebug embossing folders and cutting dies, while you can still use other folders and dies that are offered by other leading brands. You can use this machine to not only cut and emboss paper but a variety of other materials, including tissue paper, foils, acetate ribbon, and thin leather. You can buy a Cricut Cuttlebug machine in rose or mint color for $89.99. A variety of accessories for this material are also offered, including cutting spacers and embossing folders.

Cricut Accessories

Generally, almost all machines need specific accessories to function properly; the same goes for Cricut machines. There are some accessories you need to possess to use a Cricut machine effectively. Although the accessories you will need will be dependent on the nature of the project you want to work on, and how you want to work on it. Several different accessories work with Cricut machines; however, some are more important than others. Below are accessories you must have when using a Cricut machine, no matter what you are planning to create.

Cricut cutting machines come with quite a few accessories that you can purchase to add to your machine's functionality. There are some accessories that most of the machines can use and others that are designed only for a specific machine.

The newly designed Cricut Explore Air 2 machine comes with all the tools you need to get started for your regular cutting project. Every project will determine what tools you will need, and apart from the Cricut Explore Air 2 and the starter guide.

PART 4:

CRICUT DESIGN SPACE

CRICUT

CHAPTER 12:

What Is Cricut Design Space?

Cricut Design Space is the software powering the Cricut cutting machine variety. It also houses a vast library of pictures, projects, fonts, and designs, all of which can be trimmed on a Cricut machine by pressing a button. That's pure magic, don't you think?

Of course, you can also create your projects from scratch, but if you're short on time or ideas, then from Design Space you can choose from over 60,000 plans and pictures.

You'll need a Cricut for these activities. The Explore Air 2 is also an incredible cutting machine. Once set up, it's just a case of buying the designs and following the directions to create them. You are free to combine it by adding the designs to separate colored T-shirts, or even jumpers and hoodies.

Before digging in, let's understand the meaning of the Cricut Design Space Canvas Area. This is where all the process occurs before cutting your projects.

Investing in a Cricut is fruitless if you don't know how to master the Design Space because to cut any project, you will always make use of this software. In my own opinion, Cricut Design Space is an excellent tool for beginners. If you don't have experience with any design programs such as Photoshop or Illustrator, you'll find it overwhelming in the beginning, but it's pretty simple. There's nothing to fear; you just need to get the hang of it.

On the other side, if you have expertise with any of Adobe's Creative Cloud applications or Inkscape, you'll see this program's a breeze. It's primarily to touch up your projects and produce minimal designs with shapes and fonts.

By logging into your Cricut Design Space account and starting or editing a new project, you'll do everything from a window called Canvas. Cricut Design Space's Canvas Area is where you do all your edits before actually starting to cut your projects.

Downloading/Installing or Uninstalling

Do you know where to get the Cricut Design Space? Well, if you are on a desktop or personal computer, navigate to https://design.cricut.com. If you are using an iOS device such as an iPhone or iPad, find your way to your App Store and input "Cricut Design Space" on the search space.

If your smartphone runs on Android OS, enter the Play Store and use the same search term. Remember that downloading or installing this is completely free of charge. Also, bear in mind that you will need a Cricut ID to sign in. This you can also get for free, even if you do not have a Cricut. Simply follow the prompts provided.

Once you have entered your email and gotten your ID, you will at once be taken into the main domain of the Cricut Design Space, the place where all of the magic happens. A quick tip: bookmark this page to your web toolbar so you can find it easily whenever you want to.

The Canvas you will be shown after, similar to a painter's whiteboard, is the big space where all your designs and progress will reflect; this space has a full grid by default to allow you to see everything about a single work without having to pinch-zoom and un-pinch. Nevertheless, you can choose the appearance and measurements of the grid.

Install on Windows/Mac

- Click on your browser and navigate to www.design.cricut.com.
- If you are a first-time user, you need to create a Cricut ID otherwise sign in with your Cricut ID. Ensure that the page is fully loaded before carrying out this activity to avoid the error.
- Select "New Project."
- Select "Download Plugin" from the prompt.
- Wait for the download to finish and then select the downloaded file to open/run it.

- Click "Next" when the Cricut installer opens.
- Read the Terms of Use and accept the agreement.
- Click "Install" to begin the installation.
- Click "Done" at the end of the installation.

Install Cricut Design Space App on iOS

- Tap on the App Store icon on your device.
- Search for Cricut Design Space.
- Tap the "Get" button to download. Please confirm the download with your iTunes password if prompted. The app will launch and display the necessary options that will be used to complete the process.

Install Cricut Design Space App on Android

- Tap Google Play Store App on your device to open it.
- Search for Cricut Design Space.
- Tap on the "Install" button.
- Tap on the Cricut Design Space icon to open it when the installation is complete.
- Sign in and start designing your project.

Uninstall the Cricut Design Space on iOS

- Press and hold the Design Space icon on your iOS device till it vibrates.
- Press the "X" button to delete it from your device. This is very easy, right?

Uninstall Cricut Design Space App on Android

- Go to Settings.
- Tap on "Apps" or "Applications."
- Swipe to the "Download" tab or "Application Manager."
- Search for the App you intend to uninstall.
- Tap the "Uninstall" button to finish, and the app will be gone for good.

Uninstall on Mac

- Move to "Finder" and open the "Applications" folder.
- Search for Cricut Design Space.
- Drag it to trash.
- Right-click on the Trashcan and select "Empty Trash" to remove the application.

Uninstall on Windows

- Click on the "Start" button.
- Select "Settings."
- Select "Application."
- Look for Cricut Design Space and choose "Uninstall."

Changing the Display

Most people would want to, first of all, change the display pattern to a partial grid. Some others will even like to choose no grid at all, which means there will be no background. You can do this by clicking on the blank space that appears between the zeros. You will find this option at the top left corner of your rulers.

If you are using an app version, whether Android or iOS, to remove the gridlines, select the "Settings" option in the bottom toolbar, then toggle "Grids." Many people do this, especially when they want to take an accurate screen of something, without having to deal with the grid sticking out its seemingly ugly head in the background.

All projects, skills, and preferences are respectively not created equal, and that is why the Cricut Design Space has made it possible for you to change the measurement of your grid. If you are using the desktop version, navigate to the hamburger (3 lines) menu which you will find in the top left corner. There, you will see the "Settings" option, select it, and then choose from inches and centimeters as you please. On the mobile version of the space, click on the "Settings" option you will find in the bottom toolbar and then toggle on "Metric Units" on or off. When you do this, whether, on a computer or a smartphone, it will surely look and sound cool, enough for a quick smirk.

Smart Guides and Shortcuts

Quick one: Smart Guides are a feature of the Android and iOS app versions of the product. They are designed to help you when you want to position things concerning other things. But that could not turn out or position the way you want it to. If you want to turn this off on the app version, go to "Settings" at the toolbar's bottom areas and toggle the Smart Guides off.

Meanwhile, there's something about the desktop version of Cricut Design Space that makes it somewhat cool; it has some keyboard shortcuts that will come in handy. If you want to see them at any point of use, tap on the question mark key on your keyboard "Shift." Shortcuts that will prove useful to you include the "Show/Hide" menu, "Toggle Grid," and "Select All" options.

Other shortcuts also allow you to "Save" and "Save the Project As."

Other also useful are "Redo," "Cut," "Copy," and "Paste."

What's more, "Bring Forward," "Send Back," "Bring to Front," "Send to Back," and, of course, "Delete."

If you are the kind of technophile who's more used to the keyboard than clicking on a mouse, you will find these shortcuts super useful.

How to Position Items on the Cricut Canvas?

Not to discourage anyone, but it can take you several months of using the Cricut Design Space almost every day before you will find this useful, and probably a little more time before you can get used to it.

Well, this little nugget informs you on how to move and rotate your items on the mat preview. This is done to position your cuts and write when you want or feel the need to.

You know when you are working on a project and just want to flip things up fast? This feature lets you do so quickly and effortlessly well, almost (insert smirk emoticon here).

This comes significantly handy when you want to use up scraps and just spread them all over your canvas. If you are working on an addressed envelope, for instance, you can use this tool so that your letters reflect on the "write" side of the envelope. You may also want to reposition by tapping and dragging an item on your canvas to a new location. Simple enough, isn't it?

On the desktop version, move the objects to another mat and conceal them. Just click on the 3 dots; they are not hard to find since they are virtually in your face. Now you know how to best position those items to make your design easier; now, on to the next on our list.

Do You Want to Sync Your Colors?

Even the newbie designer knows the essence and impact of colors. In Cricut Design Space, you need to make sure your colors are happy and in harmony, just like every other artwork.

If you have ever worked on a design that had up to 5 different pink shades that all needed to be cut out on separate pieces of paper or vinyl, you would understand what we are talking about. If not, you will understand soon too.

Well, in case you do not know or probably forgot how it feels, it can be very frustrating. It becomes ironic when you develop a red face that matches terribly with the moment.

Thanks to the syncing color feature, you can get all these shades and tint to match one another. Use the Color Sync option in the desktop version by simply clicking on "Color Sync," which appears at the top of the panel on the right side.

When you do this, Cricut Design Space will show you all the colors being used in your project, and then you will be able to manage them in the best possible way.

For Android and iOS users, tap on the Sync icon in the lower toolbar to have access to the same set of options. Color syncing makes your work looks more unified and professional, by the way.

Showing Others What You Are Working On

You would want others to have a sneak peek at your design in Cricut at some point in time. If you have followed design freaks and enthusiasts, you would want to show them what you have been able to whip up, probably to tell you what you should add and remove.

Well, sharing is very possible, as long as the canvas on which you are currently working does not contain any uploaded files such as SVG files. Also, make sure that you have not disabled the "Public" option.

If all these details are in place, then absolutely nothing stops you from sharing your design, except, of course, you change your mind.

First, make sure you have saved the project. Navigate the Cricut Design Space to your "Saved Projects" location. Find the project you want and click on the "Share" option.

This will automatically provide you with a link you can send to people you want to see the project. It is just like the conventional info gram share option everyone is using nowadays. You can share your design with others only on the desktop and iOS versions.

We are still waiting for the developers to include the same option in the Android app version of the design. But before that, sharing is easy, and I am sure Android's child will be too.

How to Center Your Designs to Cut in Cricut Design Space?

- Sign in to the Cricut Design section. Click on the "New Project."
- Click "Download."
- Click "Upload Picture."
- Click "Browse."
- Save your picture.
- Select the saved image and insert an image.
- Select the picture. Click on it.

- As you can see, the picture is automatically moved to the upper left corner.
- To prevent this, you can fool the software by placing the image in the center of your design area and the mat. This is useful if you want to create openings in the middle of a page.
- Click on the "Shape" tool.
- Create a shape of 11.5 by 11.5 inches.
- Select the square and change the setting to cut it in the drawing.
- The square now appears as an outline.
- Click "Align" and "Center" with the selected pattern and square.
- Click the arrow of your square's size and resize it without moving the top left corner to reduce the size of the square.
- Select the square and pattern, then click "Attach." Click on it.
- As you can see now, the design is centered.

How to Write with Sketch Pens in Cricut Design Space

- Sign in to the Cricut Design section. Create a "New Project."
- Click "Download."
- Select upload a picture.
- Click "Browse."
- Open your file. Then save. To get a good effect, use a file with thin lines and no large spaces.
- Click on the pattern and paste it.
- Select the pattern.
- Change the drawing to draw.
- You will now see the drawing as an outline drawn.
- Click on it.
- Your drawing will now be displayed on the cutting screen. Click on "Continue."
- If you change your drawing to draw, the software automatically selects the pen tool. Insert the pen or marker into the recommended clip. Insert paper and click on the "Start" icon.
- The pen now draws your pattern.

How to Upload PNG File in Cricut Design Space

After you've converted your PDF document to PNG file format, there are some ways to clean up the file before printing and then crop it with Cricut Design Space.

- Click "Create New Project."
- Click "Upload Picture."
- Click on the image to upload.
- Click "Browse."
- The "Open File" dialog box will open. Select the PNG file you want to upload and click.
- An example of a picture can be found in Cricut Design Space. Since we want to edit this file, we select "Complex Image" and click "Next."
- The PNG file is loaded into Cricut Design Space. Select and delete.

How to Convert a PDF File to PNG Format

After downloading the PDF document to your computer, open your browser and go to png2pdf.com.

- Click on the upload files.
- The "Open File" dialog box starts. Locate the PDF file to convert (probably in the Downloads folder), click the PDF file and click "Upload." You should see a progress bar. Once the file has been uploaded and converted, a "Download" button will appear below the uploaded file's small image.
- Click on the "Download" button. The file is then downloaded as a ZIP file and will appear in the status bar at the bottom of the screen. Just click on the filename to open the ZIP file.
- The "Open File" dialog opens, and the downloaded file should be displayed. Since the file is still in ZIP format, you must first unzip it. Just click "Extract All Files."

- The "Open File" dialog opens, and your newly converted PDF file should be displayed in a PNG file. You can open the file with a double-click if you only want to see what the file looks like. Close the window now by clicking on the red "X."
- After you have converted your PDF file to PNG format, you must upload the PNG file to Cricut Design Space so that you can use the "Print" and "Cut" functions.

CHAPTER 13:

How to Start Cricut

The Cricut system is a really renowned invention. It's helped scrapbookers and lots of individuals with their demands, not just restricted in the scrapbook creating planet but also to other aspects too. It's to be mentioned; however, that it's helped us on the scrapbooking kingdom. From the fantastic old dark ages, even if you weren't proficient at carvings or in case you didn't understand how to compose, your favorite moment goes down the drain.

Those two would be the sole means of maintaining the memories back afterward. It might appear crude and ancient to us back then; it was that they needed. Now, we've got everything set up to preserve someone's memories and, we owe it to Father Technology.

When a scrapbooker decides to make a scrapbook, the layout is almost always a key consideration. Before picking a design could cause migraines of epic proportions but today is another story. According to a particular pattern or layout, the Cricut system to be mentioned is only accountable for cutting-edge newspapers, vinyl, and cloth. The design or pattern can be made or edited using a software application known as the Cricut Design Space.

If you're searching for simple and well-recognized designs which are already built-in, you can use the Cricut Design Space. There's no limit to everything you could think of using the layouts that are already set up. The golden rule would be to allow your creativity to go crazy. This really is a tool that any aspiring scrapbooker must possess. So, how much is it? The prices generally start at $299 and will go up based on the version which you pick.

It might appear to be a substantial sum of money; however, the expense is well worth it. But if you wish to employ the additional effort to learn to locate a fantastic deal, you're more than welcome about this. The worldwide web is almost always a wonderful place to get some excellent bargains; you simply have to look. There is Amazon, eBay, so a lot more.

The Cricut machine has lots of uses besides being a cutter of layouts to get a scrapbook. The layouts themselves may be used to make different things like greeting cards, wall decorations, and more. You simply have to believe creatively. There are no limitations, and when there are, they're only a figment of your imagination.

The Cricut Machine: A Short and Intimate Appearance

When you think about building a scrapbook, the very first thing that comes to your head is exactly what pictures to put. That is fairly simple as all you want to do would be to pick images that highlight a particular event or moment in your lifetime. After this was completed, at this point, you should think of the layout of the scrapbook. Again, this can be quite simple as everything that you have to do is base your choice on whatever occasion has been depicted in your pictures. Let us take, for instance, a wedding day.

Pick a design that will transfer that audience back in time and relive everything that transpired throughout your wedding day. Common sense is everything you may need here. The next step is to produce the layout. How can you take action? Can you do it? "No" is the reply to those above queries. You do so through the usage of a Cricut machine.

The Cricut machine is a fantastic creation. This little baby is able to help you cut paper, cloth, and vinyl sheets to whatever pattern you would like. These designs' actual production may be achieved via software tools like the Cricut Design Space or via capsules using pre-engineered designs assembled into them. Therefore, if you're an enthusiastic scrapbooker, this system is a must-have. eBay is a good place, to begin searching for one of these machines.

Recall nevertheless, that carrying purchases through eBay can take dangers so that you need to be certain you check out each of the vendor's profiles which you may want to participate in. If you're the fantastic conventional shopper who'll never devote to internet purchasing, you could do this old-school and then buy from a mall through earnings or anything else similar.

The Cricut machine has additionally many applications which extend far beyond the domain of scrapbooking. Given the number of layouts that might be in your cartridge or software application, you may always use them to make Cricut calendars, hangings such as partitions, and greeting cards for special events. Your creativity is the one thing that may limit you.

Cricut Suggestions: Tips that May Help You Get Started

Capturing memories onto a virtual camera, even an HD camera, or a voice recorder makes life much more purposeful. When there's a unique moment you would like to catch and be in a position to return to at any certain time, you can certainly do this so easily with the assistance of these instruments. However, pictures continue to be the favorite medium by the majority of people. So, if you wish to put together those images and compile them onto distinctive memorabilia, then you flip into scrapbooking.

Scrapbooking is a technique of preservation of thoughts that's been in existence for quite some time and it's evolved up to now better. Previously, the invention of a single scrapbook was a monumentally crazy job. But now, with the creation of devices like the Cricut cutting edge machine, matters are made simpler. If you're looking to developing a scrapbook, this baby is the instrument for you. There are lots of good Cricut projects out there you can make the most of.

Scrapbooks are only some of many Cricut projects on the market. If you understand how to optimize it, this instrument makes it possible for you to create items that go past scrapbooking, for example, calendars. If you buy a Cricut cartridge, then there is a slew of layouts uploaded in each.

With calendars, you can design every month to represent the weather, the disposition, and exceptional events connected with that. The Cricut machine will take care of this. But in case one cartridge doesn't have the layout that you search, you can always go and purchase another. It's that simple!

Make Your Cricut Mat Sticky Again

Are you aware you don't have to obtain a new mat every time your mat reductions it is stickiness?

When your mat reaches the point at which nothing will adhere and your newspaper only moves around if you attempt to reduce, then it is time to take care of your mat. This is a really straightforward procedure, and you'll be stunned at how well it's working!

1. Carry your mat into your sink. Use some hot water, a couple of drops of dish soap, and a green scotch brite washing machine. Scrub your mat beneath the tepid water. You will begin to find the small newspaper pieces, and filthy sticky grime begins to come off. You might even use the scrapper which came on the Cricut tool kit that will help you scrape away some of the gunk. Keep scrubbing before all of that additional layer of gunk is eliminated. Based upon your mat, then this can strip it all of the ways to the vinyl with no stickiness left or right there can still be a little quantity of stickiness. Either way would be fine.
2. You then need to let it air dry or use your hairdryer. Do not use a towel to wash it since it is going to leave lint.
3. Dry with air for approximately 1 hour. It is ready to be put back again. I've done this on my mats over and over again.
4. Then, have a wide-tipped ZIG 2-way glue pen and use paste in lines around the entire mat.
5. Let it dry for 1 hour before implementing the translucent sheet back.

Cricut Sale: Enhancing Your Abilities

If a man was great at something, could he do it at no cost? Sometimes, the response will be "yes." However, if it's a skill that you feel can deliver food onto the table, you want to capitalize on it. Therefore, if you've got a Cricut cutting tool, a program, and a knack for managing layouts and patterns, this may be a better opportunity for you to measure and begin earning. This is where it is possible to find a Cricut sale.

The Cricut machine may be used to cut the layouts you pick from the applications tool. With the support of this Cricut-style studio, it is possible to eventually discover the layout that you search for a great deal of stuff. However, before we proceed any further with the idea of ways to acquire a Cricut purchase, let's understand the various applications of the designs and patterns we get from our applications.

Greeting cards are among the most frequent items that the layouts are used for. The cover is easily the most likely recipient of those designs or layouts. Therefore, if you currently have an issue in your mind, plug in your personal computer, activate the program, and search for your layout. In case the cover copes with a Christmas motif, then search for a layout that will tell the story of Christmas. It's that simple. Consequently, if you understand those who desire their gift cards customized, this is definitely the most opportune time to allow the company person to talk.

CHAPTER 14:

Setup or Software for Your Cricut

Cricut Basic

It is a program or software designed to help the new user get a smooth start on designing new crafts and DIY projects. This system will help you with image selection to cutting with the least amount of time spent in the design stages. You can locate your image, pre-set projector font, and immediately print, cut, score, and align with tools which are found within the program. You can use this program on the iOS 7.1.2 or later systems as well as iPad and several of the iPhones from the Mini to the 5th generation iPod touch. Since it is also a cloud-based service, you can start on one device and finish from another.

Design Space

Design Space is for any Explore machine with a high-speed, broadband Internet connection that is connected to a computer or an iOS device. This more advanced software allows full creative control for users with Cricut machines.

This program allows you to connect with your software and provides you with much more functionality as far as shapes and fonts are concerned. There are various options for tools that provide you with resources for designing more creative images. You will be able to flip, rotate, weld, or slant the images and fonts. However, you will still be limited in the amounts or types of fonts you can use based on those available in the cartridges. There is a higher level of software features that allow for customization.

Craft Room

Some machines, such as the Explore and Explore Air, cannot use Craft Room, but many other models can. Craft Room users also have access to a free digital cartridge, which offers images that all Cricut machines can cut.

CHAPTER 15:

Overview of the Cricut Design Space App

A s a Cricut user, knowing the basic tools and functions of the Cricut Design Space is essential. Not knowing them means you can't handle even the simplest of projects on your own, which doesn't look too good. To ensure you have the right foundation, a foundation that can build you to attain mastery, here we will take you through all the fundamental tools and functions of the Cricut Design Space. Don't worry about making use of these tools and functions now, simply ensure that you know how they work. This is all that learning is about; knowing how things work and making exploits with them.

Cricut Design Space Navigation

If you are using this platform for the first time, welcome to the Cricut world! It is an exquisite tool and really easy to use. You should not worry if you do not know anything about design systems. Here we are getting to know the use of some of its functions so that you will become familiar, and thus, see your crafts projects and artistic business grow.

The Cricut Design Space software has a few things to remember:

- You can create a template using more than one cartridge; when you are ready to cut, you will need to have all the cartridges available.
- For your projects, you can still create various layers, like shadows and other elements.
- Although you can display and configure the software with any cartridge out there, you can only use the machine with the cartridges that you currently have. The great thing is that you will get a far better idea of what cartridges you want to get next after designing different items on the PC and, for later use, you can save your designs.

- Having an off-day creativity-wise? Do you need inspiration for something new? Check out the message boards for Cricut or search the web to access the fun and innovative files created by other Cricut Design Space users. This is often an easy way to add different styles to your designs, but also to inspire you with new and fresh ones.

Likewise, the official Cricut application called Cricut Design Space is a type of programming particularly intended to make cutting pictures easier. Using an easy thumb drive device (USB), you will have the prompt advantage of delivering all the formats that you want to be cut using a Cricut gadget. This is often the quickest and handiest connection that you can ever need for your PC and Cricut.

With this Cricut program's assistance, you can create numerous plans for any activity that you are considering making. You will have the upside of welding, resizing, reshaping, mixing, as well as turning photos of your choice. These properties alone can offer you more autonomy and adaptableness that you have accepted conceivable. Additionally, you do not need to be a master to be able to achieve and make your specialties creative.

Cricut Design Space is expected to provide all craftspeople incalculable points of interest. Among those points of interest include how the appliance was restacked with every single cartridge accessible for your Cricut cutters.

This implies around 1,000,000 unmistakable plans and examples that you can use since they consolidate with each other to make all the more dazzling, particular, and lavish cutting formats. Think about the unending potential outcomes, it is conceivable to imagine the many formats you will have to choose from. It is conceivable to do blend-ins with your buddies.

Presently, you might have second thoughts about getting yourself this program since you may consider moving toward new examples. Dismiss this idea! Among the most significant and cleverest focal points of the Cricut applications are that you essentially should check for the latest updates from time to time after you have purchased the machine using their official site. When there is a fresh out of the box new overhauled daily practice, you do not need to buy another program to get a hold of this, you merely just update your present programming, and you are good to go. The number of structures you produce will be cut and made with the containers you have access to. Be that as it may, you shouldn't be stressed because the Cricut will request that you fit the required cartridge you have to use for your growth schedules.

Imagine the number of occupations that you are able to perform with Cricut applications. As expressed, beforehand, you do not have to be an expert in computerized design to use this program. This is fabulous news for beginners who struggle to use interesting types of creating applications. The absolute best feature about this specific program is that it is an interface easy to understand. You can undoubtedly get the hang of it before you know it; you will be snared on using the applications with every project you can think of. There are no impediments to what you can plan and deliver with this program. So, proceed, try Cricut Design Space and start your own scrapbooking experience.

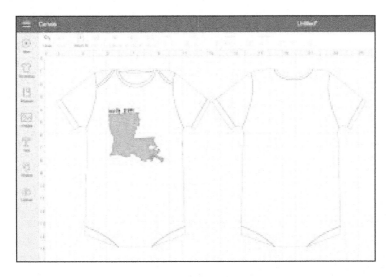

The reason for starting with the Canvas area is that all the arts and designing happen on this platform. The Canvas area is where you'll be using your tools the most. You can easily carry out the organizing of your projects and the uploading of fonts and images here.

The Design Space is parallel with many other designing and editing programs people use out there if you look closely. Programs such as Photoshop, Illustrator, and Adobe Creative Cloud are all similar to Cricut Design Space. Therefore, if you've got prior experience using programs like these, you shouldn't find it too challenging to flow with the Cricut Design Space. The Canvas area is where your designs can be edited and perfected before cutting them. Nonetheless, there're several options to explore when working on the Canvas area, and you might get overwhelmed easily. We will be discussing these options one after another, making their uses known as we proceed.

The Canvas area consists of 4 panels: the right panel, left panel, top panel, and Canvas area.

Right Panel

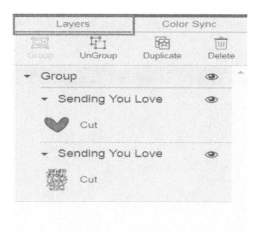

The Right panel is made up of layers; therefore, it's safe to call it the Layers Panel. Layers indicate the designs present in the Canvas area. The number of layers you'll be using will be dependent on the intricacy of your project or design. Take a birthday card, for example; you'll have different texts and decorations on it, and possibly 1–2 pictures. These are called the layers of your design. This panel enables the creation and management of layers when a design is being made. All the items on the Layer Panel will show the "line type" or "fill" you're using.

Group, Ungroup, Duplicate, and Delete

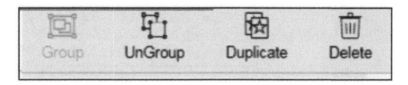

These tools enable the moving around of different designs on the Canvas area.

- **Group:** This tool allows you to join or group different layers. When many layers need to come together to form a design, then you can use the Group tool to bring everything together. For instance, if you're designing a house or building, there'll be diverse parts and sections in that building. A typical building should have a door, roof, windows, and walls. The Group tool will enable you to organize every layer and make sure that they all stay together whenever you're making the design.
- **Ungroup:** You can likewise detach a design that is made up of many layers by using the Ungroup tool. It simply does the opposite of what Group does.
- **Duplicate:** This tool is self-explanatory. It simply duplicates whichever layer you choose on the Canvas.
- **Delete:** This tool gets rid of the layers you choose. It'll delete it permanently away from the Canvas.

Black Canvas

This layer is located on the right panel. It enables you to modify the current Canvas color. If you're trying out different looks on your design, this option can be used to place your design against numerous backgrounds.

Layer Visibility

This icon in the image above indicates the visibility of your design or layer. You'll find it on all layers on the panel. It can be used when you're designing, and you observe that a certain element or segment looks odd; you can then click on the icon to get it hidden. Doing that will make sure you don't remove it permanently if you want it back later. Hidden items can be recognized with a visible cross mark.

Slice, Weld, Attach, Flatten, and Contour

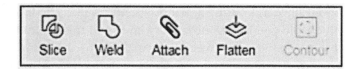

It's vital to study how to maximally use these 5 tools. They'll always come in handy, regardless of whatever you're designing.

- **Slice:** Cricut made this tool for its users to carve out shapes, texts, and diverse elements from an entire design.
- **Weld:** This is majorly used for merging shapes to form a new one. If you desire to make something different or creative with your design, you can combine different shapes.
- **Attach:** Attach is more like an advanced version of the Group tool. It joins shapes and modifies their colors to fit the background color you're using. These changes will still be in effect even after you're done cutting.
- **Flatten:** This tool will be very useful when you're about to print different shapes. To flatten different shapes, select the layers you desire to print, and then pick the "Flatten" option.
- **Contour:** You can make use of this option if you desire to hide an entire layer or a small part of a layer of design. However, this can only be done when the layers in your design can be separated.

Color Sync

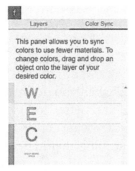

This tool is designed for balancing out your design and background colors. It can likewise be used to change diverse shades of a design color to a single color. As the name implies, Color Sync synchronizes the colors.

Left Panel

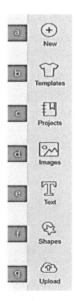

The left panel consists of every option needed for inserting. Shapes, images, texts, and even ready-to-cut projects can be added. With the left panel, you can insert everything you want to cut. The left panel has 7 options; let's quickly explore them all consecutively.

New

This option can be selected when you desire a new page, different from the page you're designing. It's better to save all your current designs before moving on to the page you just created. This is done to keep your designs in case you'll be needing them later. If you don't save before moving to the page you just created, your preceding designs will be lost.

Templates

A template allows you to preview how your design is going to look after cutting it out on a specific kind of fabric, such as a bag or a T-shirt. If you're making a bag with an iron-on design, it'll show you an image of your bag, and the design can now be placed on that template so that you can start planning the appearance of the bag in reality.

Templates will not cut out a real backpack for you, but they'll explain what the designs look like when they are cut out.

Projects

If you're ready to start cutting, then go to "Projects." You'll choose your project, make edits, modify it to suit your taste, and then click the "Make

It" option. Several projects are available for users with Cricut Access membership, and some projects are accessible by purchase only. Apart from both means, only a few projects are free.

Images

Images enable you to spice up your designs by adding a personal touch. With this tool, you can insert images which are provided on the Design Space for you. Cricut even offers free pictures each week, though some of them come with the Cricut Access.

Text

The Text tool enables you to include texts in your designs or simply on the Canvas area. Clicking the Text tool will open a little window, indicating that you should add your text. You can also customize the color and font.

Shapes

This tool is used when you wish to add a shape to your Canvas area. The Design Space provides some shapes for its users: square, triangle, hexagon, pentagon, heart, star, and octagon.

There's likewise the "Score Line" tool located under the "Shapes" option. You can use this tool for folding these shapes to form other diverse shapes, particularly when you're making cards.

Upload

The Upload tool is the last tool you'll find in the left panel. This tool enables you to carry out file and image uploads, excluding the ones provided by Cricut. With this, images and patterns can be uploaded.

Top Panel

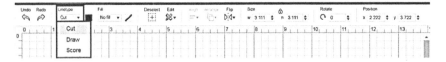

The top panel is the only panel that is always full of activities. It is used for organizing and making general editing on layers of design and elements.

First Subpanel

This enables a user to name their projects, save them, and finally cut them. You can also find the options to save, name, and send your project for cutting on the Cricut machine in this subpanel.

- **Toggle menu:** This option enables you to perform account and subscription management. This menu likewise allows you to update your Design Space, calibrate your Cricut machine, and perform some other operations.
- **Project name:** Apparently, you can use this function to name your project. The project's default name will be "Untitled," it'll

always be like that until you rename it to something unique you can identify the project with.

- **My projects:** This serves as a library for all your saved projects on the Design Space. It. makes it possible to access old projects easily.
- **Save:** This option gets your project saved into the Design Space library. You should always save your work, so you will not have issues when your browser crashes or stops responding.
- **Cricut Maker/Cricut Explore:** When using the Design Space for the first time, a question will pop up to inquire if you're making use of a Cricut of the Explore Series or a Cricut Maker. Cricut Maker stands as the most advanced machine made by Cricut, and therefore, it provides several benefits on the Design Space more than other machines you'll find in the Explore Series.
- **Make It:** Click "Make It" after you've uploaded your files so that it can start cutting. The software categorizes your projects based on their colors, and if you're making plans to cut two or more projects, you can use this tool to increment the projects you wish to cut.

Second Subpanel

The second subpanel is a menu for editing. It enables you to arrange, organize, and edit fonts and images on the canvas area.

Undo and Redo

Clicking "Undo" will revert a recent activity or action, and it's mostly used when a mistake is made or when an undesired move has been made. "Redo" does the opposite of "Undo," it brings back a deleted or reverted activity or action, and it's mostly used when something needed has been mistakenly deleted.

Linetype

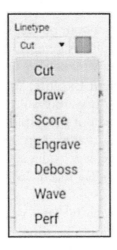

- **Cut:** You'll find this line type on every layer present in the Canvas area. After picking the "Make It" option, your Cricut machine starts cutting the designs which are on your Canvas area. This function enables you to alter the fill and colors of your layers.

- **Draw:** Cricut likewise enables you to draw and write on the designs you create. When you choose this linetype, you're given several choices of diverse Cricut pens. You can use these pens to make drawings in the Canvas area. In this linetype, whenever you click "Make It," instead of cutting, your machine starts drawing or writing.

- **Score:** This function does almost the same thing as the "Scoring Line" tool in the left panel; it's just more advanced. Selecting this function for any of your layers will make it look like the layer has been scored. After that, clicking on "Make It" will get the materials scored by your Cricut machine instead of having it cut. A scoring wheel or scoring stylus will always be needed whenever you want to score. And only the latest machine, the Cricut Maker, can work with the scoring wheel.

- **Engrave, wave, deboss, and perf:** These tools were recently released by Cricut. Therefore, only Cricut Maker users can make use of them. Additionally, it's required to have the newest version of the Design Space app before these new tools can be accessed. These tools enable you to make significant effects on many materials.

Fill

Cricut majorly designed this function to print and make patterns. However, you can only use this function when "Cut" has been selected as a Line type.

Print

This function is loved by every Cricut user. Even though you cannot do without it if you want your design to be cuttable, you'll also find this function a little bit interesting. It enables you to first have your design printed out and then cut them out. If you want to print out your design, click on "Make It" when the "Fill" option is active. After that, send the files to your home printer before you start sending them to the Cricut machine for cutting.

Edit

This function consists of 3 options on the menu list. You'll find a "Cut" option, which enables you to copy and clear elements from the Canvas, you'll find the "Copy" option, which allows you to copy the same component without getting it cleared, and lastly, you'll find the "Paste" option, which helps you insert the element you've copied or cut.

- **Select all:** Clicking this will highlight everything you've on your Canvas area.

- **Align:** There're several diverse options under this function, and it's essential for you to master all these options. Let's take a look at them:
    - o **Align left:** This function makes sure that every element is left-aligned. However, the movement will solely depend on the item at the end of the left side.
    - o **Center horizontally:** This will horizontally align every design element.
    - o **Align right:** This function makes sure that every element is right-aligned. However, the movement will solely depend on the item at the end of the right side.
    - o **Align top:** This will automatically align all the selected elements to the Canvas page's uppermost part.
    - o **Center vertically:** This will vertically align every design element.
    - o **Align bottom:** This functions as the exact opposite of the "Align Top" function. It aligns elements or layers to the bottom.
    - o **Center:** Clicking this function will center-align all elements that are either vertically aligned or horizontally aligned.
- **Distribute:** This enables you to distribute the spacing between layers or elements equally. We have two types:
    1. Distribute horizontally
    2. Distribute vertically

Flip

This function will allow you to see the reflection of your designs. You can see this function as a mirror-view of your designs. There're 2 options available for this function:

1. Flip horizontal
2. Flip vertical

Arrange

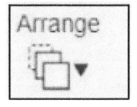

The "Arrange" function enables you to arrange elements such as designs, texts, or images to the back or front of others. There're 4 types of arrangement, and they are as follows:

- **Send to back:** This moves the design or element you select to the farthest back of other elements or designs.
- **Move backward:** What makes this function and the "Send to Back" function different is that this function moves an element or design back once. This allows you to control how further back you want an element or design.
- **Move forward:** This does the exact opposite of "Move Backward," you can control how further you want an element or design.
- **Send to front:** This moves the design or element you select to the furthest front of other elements or designs.

Size

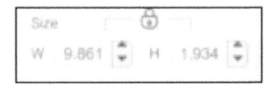

This function enables you to alter an element size or the whole design size. Whatever you create within the Canvas Area has a specified scale, and you can use this to either decrease or increase the size. This is more useful when you're following a particular format for all the elements or the entire design.

Rotate

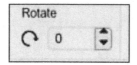

With this Design Space function, you can rotate elements or layers to your desired angle.

Position

Since the Canvas area has gridlines, just like coordinates, you can make use of this function to find and pick a certain position for the element on the X and Y-axis.

Font

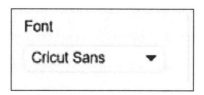

There're various types of fonts on Cricut for all users with Cricut Access membership. You can make use of your default font or purchase different fonts from Cricut if you don't have a Cricut Access subscription.

Font Size

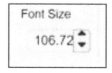

This function enables you to either decrease or increase your font size.

Line Space

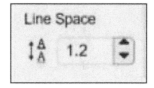

This is particularly suitable for use whenever you wish to make sure that all texts on your designs are orderly or manually spaced.

Letter Space

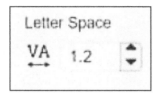

This function enables you to decide how much space you want between letters.

Style

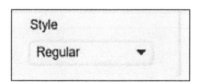

This consists of "Regular," which is already applied by default, "Bold," which makes the font thick, "Italic," which tilts the font sideways, and then "Bold Italic," which combines both the Bold and Italic function.

Curve

You can also design your texts by using the curve setting. You can curve your text upwards or inwards and also curve your text into a circle.

Advanced

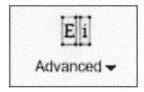

You'll find this function on the top editing panel, and it's the last function on the panel.

- **Ungroup to letters:** This enables you to detach all letters into single layers apiece.
- **Ungroup to lines:** This enables you to break paragraphs on different lines.
- **Ungroup to layers:** This option is available only on Cricut Access. It can also be purchased. It's quite tricky, though; you must be fully conscious of what you're doing.

Canvas Area

This stands as the major workspace of the Design Space. You can find all the designs and elements that you're working on this platform.

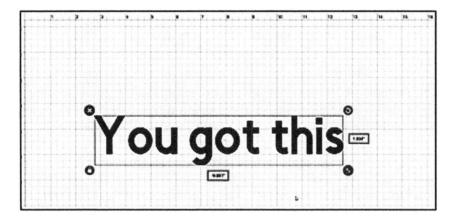

Canvas Grid and Dimensions

Gridlines are the lines that cover your Canvas area on the Design Space and divide the area into small squares. The Canvas area resembles the cutting mat, which, therefore, gives you the feeling of being designing on your actual cutting mat on the screen. You can make use of centimeters or inches, and you can also decide to turn the grid off in your settings.

Zoom Out or In

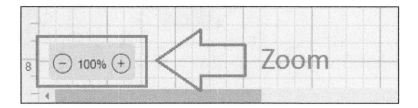

You can use this function to expand or reduce the focus of a design or an element on your canvas area. This function can be used if you wish to make your design bigger or smaller to work on it comfortably or if you just want to focus on a design or an element.

Selection

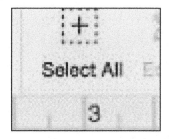

Whenever you select two or more layers, the color of the selection turns blue, and the 4 corners surrounding it enable you to adjust the layer.

You'll see an "X" in red color; click on it when you want to delete those layers.

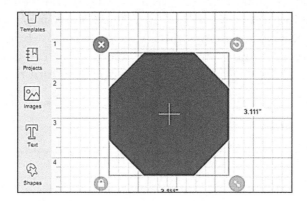

CHAPTER 16:

How to Create a Cricut Project from an Image or a Photo

S electing the image, you want to use can be fun. There are so many to choose from and you'll enjoy browsing the library.

You should start by browsing the Cricut Image Library. There you will find cartridges, called image sets, where you can choose your designs.

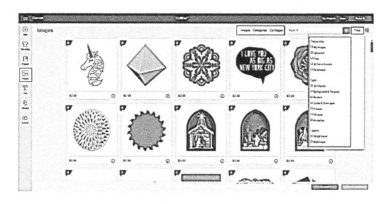

How to Browse and Search for Cartridges

To begin, select the "Images" icon in the design panel to the left of the canvas. A new window should appear with the Image Library. Next, select the "Cartridges" tab at the top of the screen to browse all the available cartridges. There are over 400 cartridges to choose from. You should see the cartridge name and a sample of the image. It will tell you if the cartridge is free or if it can be purchased individually or is a part of the subscription plan.

You don't have to search alphabetically. You can type all or parts of a cartridge's name into the search bar and click on the magnifying glass icon. You then click "View All Images" to browse your search results.

Once you've made your selection, simply click the "Insert Images" button, and they will be added to the canvas. Once added to the canvas, you can size your image(s) and move them around on the canvas. You can get an idea of where you want your image and how it will look on your final project.

It can be more cost-effective to purchase entire cartridges than to purchase individual images if your selection isn't included in the free offerings.

Searching for Cartridge with Filters

If you want to search for cartridges with filters, you simply click on the "Cartridge" icon and select the "Filters" menu in the top right corner of the screen. This will bring up all available filters.

There are 3 ways to search: Alphabetical order, cartridge type, or by a specific cartridge. When you find the filter you want, select "Apply" to transfer it to your canvas.

How to Purchase Images

- **My Cartridges.** This includes all free cartridges, linked, purchased, and part of Cricut Access. You must be a member to have access to these.
- **Free.** These cartridges can be used without a subscription or a one-time purchase.
- **Cricut Access.** These cartridges are accessible with your subscription.
- **Purchased.** These are the cartridges you've already purchased and are added to your canvas.

These are your 4 options for obtaining images. I've included how to access them for free for those who don't want to spend money on images or have their own.

It's good to check the Cricut website for any price changes and the features each subscription entitles you to.

Uploading Your Own Images

You can upload your own images in the file formats PNG, GIF, JPG, BMP, DXF, and SVG, Design Space will let you upload your images for free and will convert them into shapes that you can cut.

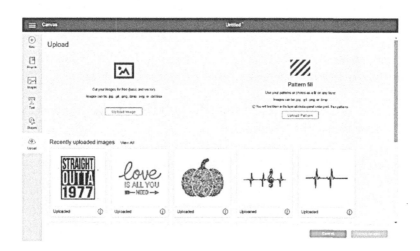

There are two different ways your images are uploaded, depending on the file type:

- **Basic images:** These are compatible with GIF, JPG, PNG, and BMP file types. When uploaded, these files can be a single layer, and you can edit the images throughout the upload course.
- **Vector images:** These include SVG and DXF file types. These files are designed before you upload them to your canvas. They will routinely be disconnected into layers afterward uploading then saving.

To begin a basic upload, click "Upload" from the Design Panel on the screen's left side. A window will open and prompt you to choose an image or pattern to upload. Click the image you want, and click the "Upload" icon again. It's that simple!

How to Edit Images Using the Slice Tool

Many Cricut users do all their editing separately because it seems too difficult to do on the machine.

Let's walk through the process, so you'll be able to do this with ease once you've had a little practice.

First, you need to include your uploaded photos to your canvas by clicking on the image then select "Insert Images." You can add one more image at this time.

You can make your image a bit bigger if you need to. Click the right-bottom corner and drag it down so you can see it better.

There's no erase option, so if something in your image you don't want, you'll have to use the Slice tool.

This can be a bit more difficult than simply erasing with the eraser tool.

You'll need to click on "Shapes" on the left side and click the square. You'll see a lock icon on the left bottom of the circle just below the square. This will unlock it and give you the freedom to move it wherever you'd like.

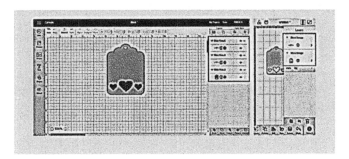

Place it over the part of the image you want to erase. This should bring up a bubble. Your square and your image should be highlighted. Make sure they are and click the Slice tool. You'll find it in the bottom-right corner. You can begin to pull away from the pieces and delete them. You may have to repeat this several times before you've erased the parts of the image that you want to go. This will depend on the size of your erasure.

Be sure to save your changes.

Editing Images in Upload Mode

This is an easy process for editing your uploaded image. But first, you need to upload an image from your computer. When it's uploaded, click on the "Complete" icon, and a window should open. Look to the top-left corner of your canvas, and you should see a wand. Place it over the part of the image you want to erase and click once. Click "Continue," and you'll need to type in a name for your image and click the "Save" button. That part of the image should be gone. You'll repeat the steps for each part of the image you want to be erased.

When you have erased everything you want, you need to make sure it's named before saving it and closing it.

Add both photos to your Cricut Design Space canvas. When you have them there, you can put them back together.

The nice thing about this feature is that you can do more than erase. If you want to change color, the same process applies.

Editing doesn't have to be a difficult task, and the more you get to know your Cricut and the Design Space, the easier it will be to upload and edit your images.

CHAPTER 17:

SVG Files and Cricut Design Space

What Are SVG Files?

An SVG file is a file format for storing rich graphics. It is completely vector-based and can be scaled to any dimension without losing detail. SVG files are basically an XML document that uses several tags inside the <SVG> tag to describe different elements.

Different tags are used for different shapes, such as circles, rectangles, ellipses, etc. But some elements act as containers for other elements or group sets of elements into a single element like <g>.

You can also add animation and interactivity with SVG files using SMIL.

How to Create SVG Files

SVG files are vector image files. They are created in programs such as Adobe Illustrator and Inkscape.

In those programs, you can draw shapes using either lines or fills, then group the shapes to create a compound shape. Once done, you can export the file as an SVG image.

SVG Files and Cricut Design Space

You can use SVG files in Cricut Design Space by downloading SVG files from your computer, uploading them into the SVG file gallery, or Dropbox or Google Drive.

Inside Cricut Design Space, you can either use them in an SVG project or add them as a graphic to cut with your mat (just like a photo).

SVG Image Sizes and Resolution

Most SVG images come in sizes of 1,000 by 1,000 pixels and 1,500 by 1,500 pixels. These images will get scaled-down when using them as a cuttable graphic on your mat (180 dpi) so that they look right when cutting on the Cricut machine. The larger this image is, the higher resolution (pixels per inch), meaning that it's going to take longer to print than a low-resolution image.

Image sizes are also dependent on the type of SVG file you create, whether it's a vector image or a bitmap image.

If you're using an SVG file that has a higher resolution, it can be scaled down to 180 dpi, which can be done by converting it into a PNG or JPG.

SVG Files and Cricut Cut Files: Creation vs. Saving

To understand how to use SVG with Cricut Design Space, we must first understand the difference between SVG cut files and SVG graphic files. If you save your SVG file as a normal graphic (JPG, PNG, GIF), the design space machine will not recognize it as an SVG file. How can this be? The answer is because instead of saving the created file in a folder called "SVG," you must save them in folders called "Cuts." This is where they get recognized correctly by Design Space as an SVGs file.

With Design Space, there are 2 options for creating SVGs for cutting: You can use brushes or use premade SVG files.

- With premade SVGs, you can save 10 SVGs in the same SVG file (separated by a semi-colon symbol). Your design space machine will recognize this as one graphic to cut, and all 10 premade shapes will be cut at the same time.
- When exporting from Illustrator or Inkscape, your file must be saved in the "cuts" folder.

How to Cut an SVG File with Cricut Design Space

To use your SVG file with Design Space as a graphic on your mat, just follow these steps:

1. Upload your design (preferably vector) into the Cricut Design Space's SVG file gallery by clicking "Use Gallery." This puts your design in the gallery for easy access by other users of Design Space.
2. Upload any graphics you want to cut into CDS using either Design Space's tools or using the "Import/Export" button that appears when pressing "Ctrl + O."
3. In Design Space, select your SVG file or graphic and choose your mat.

When cutting, each cut will be placed in a separate file and saved into its folder.

SVG Images for Cricut Projects

You can use SVG files with Cricut projects by uploading them into the gallery or by dragging/dropping them into a project's image tab. If you drag/drop an image into the project tab, it will be pinned to the artboard's top-left corner. To move it around, un-pin them and then re-pin them where you want.

To add a graphic from your computer as an image in a project:

1. Open your project in Design Space, click "Add" at the top of the window to open up the "Add an Element" box.
2. Locate "Use Files," then select "Add Images" and click "OK." This will bring up your computer's file explorer, where you can search for whatever image you want which is on your computer to add to Design Space. Click "Add" when you've selected the images you want to use in Design Space.

How to Edit SVG Files

To edit an SVG file:

1. Go to the "Library" tab and select the "SVG Files" folder from the left-hand side of your screen. This will bring up all of the items in this gallery on the right-hand side of the screen, where you can click on any item to see its details by merging it with your library view (on right).
2. Now double click on any item in the library view to open it (this action opens up a new browser window for viewing).
3. You can then edit the SVG file by opening it in the program where you created it (i.e., Illustrator or Inkscape).

CHAPTER 18:

List of Alternatives to Design Space

It is no longer news that digital die-cutting units are extremely restrictive for craft enthusiasts and people who love the Cricut die-cutting system. They mostly allow users to cut a small number of fonts, and they are not cheap at all. Thankfully, a few programs out there have managed to open Cricut to enable them to cut designs, TrueType fonts created by users, and many more.

Below is a list of the best third-party software to use with Cricut:

Make the Cut

This is an awesome third-party Cricut design software that comes with simple but highly effective design features, e.g., it packs quick lattice tools and it can convert raster images into vectors for cutting. The program has been around for some time. Some of the most outstanding features of the tool include:

- It comes with advanced editing tools, and it is quite easy to use (even for a newbie) because the user interface is effortless to learn.
- The software works with many file formats, and it also uses TrueType fonts.
- The software comes with a pixel trace tool that allows users to take and convert raster graphics into vector paths for cutting.
- For those who are interested, Make the Cut works with Gazelle, Craft ROBO, Wishblade, and Silhouette.
- Some other features include the fact that users can import the following: WPC, GSD, PS, AI9, EPS, OTF, TTF, SCUT, or PDF files and can also export shapes in SVG, PDF, Ai, EPS, PNG, and JPG formats.

Make the Cut is a user-friendly and flexible Cricut-related software that adds more utility to the digital die-cutting machine that is normally limited in terms of usage and application.

Sure Cuts a Lot

The Sure Cuts a Lot of software gives users complete control of their designs without the restrictions of cartridges featured in Cricut Design Space. Users must install a firmware update to their Cricut die-cutting machine; however, they can do this for free by downloading the trial version of Design Studio. It is a very easy task to perform.

Some of the features of the Sure Cuts a Lot software include:

- It allows users to use the OpenType and TrueType fonts.
- It is the one and only Cricut design tool available that comes with freestyle drawing tools.
- It allows users to create personal designs with basic drawing and editing tools.
- The program works with Silhouette, Craft ROBO, and Wishblade die-cutting machines.
- It is specifically designed to open up all of Cricut's cutting features and abilities.
- It allows users to edit the individual nodes that make up the path.
- It comes with an auto trace feature that converts raster graphics into vector images.
- The programs have about 200 built-in shapes and other exciting features.
- It allows users to import different file formats including PDF, SVG, AI, EPS, and WPC. The pro version allows users to import DXF and PLT.
- It allows users to select styles, including Blackout and Shadow, to easily change shapes and letters with just a few clicks of the mouse.
- It allows users to use advanced features such as layers, grouping, and the weld tool to make the most out of their designs.

To download and get the complete set of Sure Cuts a Lot of features, you can check their website.

The Sure Cuts a Lot program doesn't come with fonts; it only allows users to make use of the fonts that are already on their computers.

Getting more fonts to your computer isn't a big deal because thousands of fonts are out there. Besides, you don't have to buy any special cartridges to get more fonts for your system.

Cricut Design Space

Cricut Design Space, a product of ProvoCraft, allows users to connect Cricut to a personal computer to do much more with Cricut fonts and shapes.

For those that don't know, Provo Craft is the same company that manufactures Cricut die-cutting machines. With the aid of various tools, this Cricut software allows users to adjust fonts and shapes.

Some of the best features of the software include:

- Users will be able to weld, flip, and rotate easily.
- Users have the option of previewing and creating designs with different images from the Cricut library.
- Users will have to purchase a cartridge to cut.
- The software comes with a high level of customization to the Cricut library, and the extra features are very helpful.
- People who use this software are still limited to the same shapes and fonts from the cartridges they own, but bearing in mind the tools packed in the program, that is not an issue.

The program remains a very good option to use alongside your Cricut, and you'll be able to get the best out of its features.

To know more about the software, go to their official website.

Inkscape

Inkscape is an open-source graphics editor for Windows and other operating systems. It is a professional program that costs absolutely nothing.

Users can use the program along with Cricut to create and edit vector graphics such as illustrations, diagrams, line arts, logos, elaborate paintings, and much more.

Below are some of the features that come with the software:

- It can be used to render primitive text and vector shapes.
- It supports embedding and optional tracing of raster graphics.
- The objects can be filled with solid colors, patterns, radial, linear color gradients, and others; their borders can be stroked with adjustable transparency.
- The program can be used to create vector graphics from multiple raster sources and pictures.
- Shapes created can be manipulated easily with different transformations that include: moving, rotating, scaling, and skewing.

There are many more features present in this powerful software, and the easiest way to get acquainted with them all is to visit Inkscape's official website.

In order to maximize the use of your Cricut machine, you should consider using these awesome software applications that are compatible with Windows systems.

For the best experience possible, you should pair them up with some 2D digital pixel art tools or with some photo editors.

Depending on what you choose to do, you will easily take control of your creativity and use Cricut Design Space the way you've always dreamt of.

PART 5:

COMMON PROBLEMS + TIPS AND TRICKS

CHAPTER 19:

Common Problems and How to Solve Them

Material Tearing or Not Cutting Completely Through

This is the biggest problem with most Cricut users. When this happens, the image is ruined, and you've wasted material. More machines have been returned or boxed up and put away due to this problem than any other.

But don't panic; if your paper is not cutting correctly, there are several steps you can take to try and correct the problem.

Most important is this: Anytime you work with the blade, turn your machine off. I know it's easy to forget this because you're frustrated, and you're trying this and that to make it work correctly. But this is an important safety precaution you should remember.

Make simple adjustments at first. Turn the pressure down one. Did it help? If not, turn the blade down one number. Also, make sure the mat is free of debris, so the blade rides smoothly.

Usually, the thicker the material, the higher the pressure number should be set to cut through the paper. Don't forget to use the multi-cut function if you have that option. It may take a little longer to cut 2, 3, or 4 times, but it should cut clean through by then.

For those of you using the smaller bugs that do not have that option, here is how to make your multi-cut function: After the image has been cut, don't unload the mat; just hit load paper, repeat last, and cut. You can repeat this sequence 2, 3, or 4 times to ensure your image is completely cut out.

If you are using thinner paper and it is tearing, try reducing the pressure and slowing down the speed. When cutting intricate designs, you have to give the blade enough time to maneuver through the design. By slowing it down, it will be able to make cleaner cuts.

Clean the edge of the blade to be sure no fuzz, glue, or scraps of paper are stuck to it.

Make sure the blade is installed correctly. Take it out and put it back, so it's seated firmly. The blade should be steady while it's making cuts. If it makes a shaky movement, it's either not installed correctly or there's a problem with the blade housing.

Be aware that there is a deep-cutting blade for thicker material. You should switch to this blade when you're cutting heavy card stock. This will also save wear and tear on your regular blade. Cutting a lot of thick material will wear your blade out quicker than thinner material and cause you to change it more often.

You can try cutting a different material. Remember to adjust the setting to accommodate the new material and cut. If it works, then the problem is with your material, not the machine.

If all of these options fail, you might want to call the customer care line.

Machine Freezing

Remember to always turn your machine off when you switch cartridges. When you switch cartridges, leaving the machine on, it's called "hot-swapping," and it can sometimes cause the machine to freeze. This is more of an issue with the older models and doesn't seem to apply to Expression 2.

You know how peculiar electronic gadgets can be, so give your machine rest for 5–10 minutes every hour. If you work for several hours continuously, your machine might overheat and freeze up.

Turn the machine off and take a break. Restart it when you come back, and it should be fine. Then remember not to rush programming the machine and give it an occasional rest.

Don't press a long list of commands quickly. If you give it too much information too quickly, it will get confused in the same way a computer sometimes does and simply freeze up. Instead of typing in one long phrase, try dividing up your words into several cuts.

If you're using special feature keys, make sure you press them first before selecting the letters.

Power Problems

If you turn your machine on and nothing happens, the power adapter may be at fault. Jiggle the power cord at the outlet and where it connects to the machine to make sure it's firmly connected. Ideally, you should test the adapter before buying a new one. Swap cords with a friend and see if that fixed the problem. Replacement adapters can be found on eBay by searching for a Cricut adapter power supply.

The connection points inside the machine may also pose a problem; here is how to test that: Hold down the plug where it inserts into the back of the machine and turn it on. If it powers up, then the problem is inside the machine, and the connection points will have to be soldered again.

If the machine powers up but will not cut, then try a hard reset.

Next are a few tips, especially for Expression 2 users. Have you turned on your machine, you watch it light up and hear it gearing up, but when you try to cut, nothing happens? Or you're stuck on the welcome screen, or the LCD screen is unresponsive?

Well, here are 2 quick fixes to try:

- First, try a hard reset, sometimes called the rainbow screen to reset to recalibrate your die cutter.
- If that does not resolve the problem, you will have to restore the settings.

To help cut down on errors, try to keep your machine updated. When an update is available, you should receive a message encouraging you to install the latest version.

For those of you using third-party software no longer compatible with the Cricut, you probably already know that updating your machine may disable that software.

When you cut heavy paper and your Expression 2 shuts down, try switching to the normal paper setting and use the multi-cut function.

Carriage Will Not Move

If the carriage assembly does not move, check to see if the belt has broken or if the car has fallen off the track. Provo Craft does not sell replacement parts, which is sad, so try to find a compatible belt at a vacuum repair shop.

If the wheels have fallen off the track, remove the plastic cover, and look for a tiny screw by the wheel to unscrew it. You now should be able to move the wheel back on track.

Unresponsive Keyboard

If you are sure you are pressing the keys firmly, you have a cartridge inserted correctly, and a mat loaded ready to go, but the keypad is still not accepting your selection; the problem may be internal.

You will have to remove the keyboard and check if the display cable is connected to the keypad and the motherboard. If the connections are secure, you have a circuit board problem and repairs are beyond this book's scope.

An important reminder, please do not attempt any repairs unless your machine is out of warranty.

Weird LCD Careen

The LCD screen is now showing strange symbols or is blank after doing a firmware update. Try running the update again, making sure your selections are correct.

When the image you choose is bigger than the mat or paper size you selected, the preview screen will look grayed out instead of showing the image. Increase the paper and mat size or decrease the size of your image.

Also, watch out for the gray box effect when using the center point feature. Move the start position down until you see the image appear. The same thing may happen when using the fit to length feature. Try changing to landscape mode and shorten the length size until the image appears.

Occasionally using the "Undo" button will cause the preview screen to turn black; unfortunately, the solution is to turn the machine off. Your work will be lost, and you have to start again.

Cartridge Errors

Sometimes dust or debris accumulates in the cartridge port; gently blow out any paper fiber that may have collected in the opening. Make sure the contact points are clean and that nothing is preventing the cartridge from being read properly.

With any electrical machine, overheating can be a problem. If you get a cartridge error after using your machine for a while, turn it off and let it cool down for about 15 minutes.

If this is the first time you're using the cartridge and you get an error, I'm sure you know the trick about turning the cartridge around and inserting it backward.

If you thought you could use your Imagine cartridges with your Expression 2, think again. You will get an error message because you can only use the art cartridges that you can cut with; the colors and patterns cartridges are for printing.

Even brand-new items fresh out of the box can be defective. If you see a cartridge error 1, 2, 3, 4, 5, 6, 9, or 99 call customer service and tell them the name, serial number, and error message number, and they may replace the cartridge.

Trouble Connecting to Your Computer

All Cricut machines come with a USB cord that lets you connect to your computer and allows you to use the other products like the Cricut Design Space software, Cricut Craft Room, or the Cricut Gypsy with your machines.

Double-check your USB connection and try another port.

Check to see if you may have a firewall or antivirus software blocking the connection.

See if you're running the latest firmware. You may need to update. Older machines update via firmware (Personal Cutter, Expression, Create, and Cake) the newer (Expression 2, Imagine, and Gypsy) use the Sync program to update.

When Anything Else Fails

I know that no one wants to hear this. But there are going to be times when you may have to resort to calling customer service. This is especially true if your machine is still under warranty. You don't want to do anything that might void the warranty on a truly defective machine.

Sadly, Prove Craft is known for its long wait times and sometimes less than stellar service. Stick it out and demand that your machine be fixed or replaced.

After a while, you may notice some of your projects coming out in a condition that is less-than-crisp.

Ensure Your Machine Is on Stable Footing

This may seem pretty basic, but ensuring that your machine is on a level surface will allow it to make more precise cuts every single time. Rocking the machine or wobbling could cause unstable results in your projects.

Ensure no debris has gotten stuck under the feet of your machine that could cause instability before proceeding to the next troubleshooting step!

Redo All Cable Connections

So, your connections are in the best possible working order, undo all your cable connections, blow into the ports or use canned air, and then securely plug everything back into the right ports. This will help to make sure all the connections are talking to each other where they should be!

Completely Dust and Clean Your Machine

Your little Cricut works hard for you! Return the favor by making sure you're not allowing gunk, dust, grime, or debris to build up in the surfaces and crevices. Adhesive can build up on the machine around the mat input and on the rollers, so be sure to focus on those areas!

CHAPTER 20:

Tips and Tricks

The Blade Isn't Being Detected

In Design Space, you will see that it recommends a blade in the "Load Tools" step. This is on the Preview screen. Make sure that you have installed the right tool.

When I don't have the right tool, I just unload the mat, select the "Edit Tools" option in the project preview screen, and select a different tool. This usually does the trick. Remember to use clamp B.

You also have to make sure that the tool sensor is clean. Be very gentle about this and use a microfiber cloth. Any form of dust build-up can cause issues so best keep it squeaky clean all the time instead of struggling with it when you want to start projects.

The Machine Turns Off Unexpectedly

This usually happens when you cut metals or foil. The reason for this happening is that there is a buildup of static electricity. Dry environments can also cause this, so don't worry too much about this.

To solve this issue, you can spray some mist into the air to humidify it. Do not, under any circumstances, spray it directly onto the Cricut machine. When I go to a particularly dry area with my Cricut, I like to have a humidifier handy. This is very, very useful and it might be worth investing in if your machine continues to give you this problem.

Slow Internet Connection

You must understand that a slow internet connection is one of the main causes of Design Space problems, without saying much. Poor internet connection translates into problems for the software because it requires consistent download and upload speed to function optimally. A lot of Cricut users have this problem with the Design Space. There are a lot of complaints that the platform is slow or not working. However, this is, most of the time, not true. Before you start getting frustrated at Cricut, ensure your internet connection is working efficiently.

Several websites only require good download speed, e.g., YouTube, thus users on these sites can do away with slow upload speeds. However, unlike those sites, Cricut Design Space requires good upload and download speed to function optimally because users constantly send and receive information as they progress with their designs.

If you want to work smoothly on the Design Space, you need to have a consistent and steady internet speed. The upload and download speed of your internet must be good enough for the Design Space to work perfectly. A poor connection will only lead to issues like freezing or dragging. If you realize that your connection is always slow, adjust or move your device closer to the modem or contact your internet service provider. If you're using a modem, you're likely to have a more stable connection if you move closer to it.

Getting Free Images and Fonts

To get free pictures in the image library on the Design Space, make use of the "Filter" tool and click the "Free" option. Doing this will display all free images available on the Design Space.

It is likewise possible to get free fonts on the Design Space. Go to "Font Squirrel" and get free fonts downloaded, then start applying them whenever you're designing on the Canvas area.

Every application, including Cricut Design Space, is prone to crashing, freezing, or other challenges. There are some reasons why these problems can happen.

The Search Function

To use the search function to search items more efficiently, always be specific. Don't use plural words. For example, if you're searching for images on the search bar, don't pluralize the images' names by putting "s" or "es" at the end. If you are looking for shapes that look like a star, don't search for "Stars," search for "Star" instead. Removing the "s" will produce more results.

Similarly, if you are unable to find a certain image, try searching for the image synonym instead. For instance, when you're making a birthday card, search for love, heart, flower, etc.

Using the Right Browser

To enjoy the Design Space to the peak, always ensure your browser is up-to-date. The name or type of browser doesn't matter, given that it's the latest version of its kind. And if you find that the Design Space is not working with a specific browser, then switch the browser to another one; this usually works.

Using the Right Device

You should be conscious of the kind of system or device you're using to access the Design Space. It could also create issues sometimes. For the Design Space, there're some standard requirements for every device that wants to access the platform. The minimum requirements for some devices are as follow:

Apple Computers

For Mac computers, the following are the minimum requirements:

- A CPU with a 1.83 GHz processor.
- A minimum of 50MB free space.
- A minimum of 4GB installed memory (RAM).
- Must be Bluetooth-enabled with a USB port.
- The Operating System must be at least X 10.12.

Windows Computers

For Windows computers, the following are the minimum requirements:

- An AMD processor or Intel Core series.
- A minimum of 50MB free space.
- A minimum of 4GB installed memory (RAM).
- Must be Bluetooth-enabled with a USB port.
- The Operating System must be at least Windows 8 or more advanced.

If these requirements are met by your system, and you're still having trouble working on the Design Space, then there must be some other issues with background programs. You can try clearing your history and cache, update your antivirus and your Operating System, upgrade your computer features, or contact the Cricut Help Center.

With these few basic tips and techniques, you are no more an amateur in the Design Space. You can now handle the elementary operations on the Design Space. However, we're not stopping here or settling for the basics. We are going in much deeper into the software to ensure that we clear all the beginner traits you may have. The following chapters will educate you more about how things work in the Design Space. You will master the platform in no time, and you will find yourself teaching other Cricut users who are having struggles with the platform; like a professional, yes, you'll be a professional user!

PART 6:

MINDSET FOR MAKING OF CRICUT A BUSINESS

CHAPTER 21:

How to Leverage Mindset on Making Cricut

Now, if you were to buy any of these machines during a holiday sale with a bundle deal that comes with a variety of tools, accessories, and materials for a practice project as well as free trial membership to Cricut Access, you would already be saving enough to justify the purchase for your personal usage. The cherry on top would be if you can use this investment to make more money. You can always get additional supplies in a bundle deal or from your local stores at a much lower price. All in all, those upfront costs can easily be justified with the expenses you budget for school projects that require you to cut letters and shapes, creating personalized gifts for your loved ones, or decorating your home with customized decals, and of course, your jewelry creations. These are only a handful of the reasons to buy a Cricut machine for your personal use.

Let's start scraping the mountain of Cricut-created wealth to help you get rich while enjoying your work!

At this stage, let's assume that you have bought a Cricut cutting machine and have enough practice with beginner-friendly projects. You now have the skillset and the tools to start making money with your Cricut machine, so let's jump into how you can make it happen. The ways listed below have been tried and tested as successful money-making strategies that you can implement with no hesitations.

How to Turn Your Designs into Money

So many people have asked the question, "How do I make money using my Cricut?" or "Should I buy a Cricut? Is the market too full? Can I still make money? How do I start?" Sometimes, it is hard to answer all these questions because some of the people using Cricut do not want to tell you how to make money from this craft. They do not want to share their secrets. But this book is here to give you all the inside information you need to know if you want to make money with Cricut.

When a lot of people are starting out and they are venturing into a craft—maybe they have a Cricut or another vinyl cutting machine, or perhaps they do not have one, and they want to get one—they have all these questions about how to get started, and it is overwhelming at first. It can be confusing and complicated, and then sometimes you will reach out to those that have one, and they do not want to share their secrets; they are afraid that you might become their competitor. But the truth is that everyone can succeed if you will build each other up there is room for us all to succeed. Let us start with the first question.

Let's now see how we can make money from all the knowledge we have gotten. Someone rightly said, "if you cannot make money from the knowledge you have gotten or if you have the knowledge and it is not useful to you in any way, then the knowledge is useless to you and the society." In order for this knowledge to be useful to you, I will show you how to make money from it. I'm not saying that the knowledge is useless if you use it to only make crafts for your family and friends; if you use it for that reason, then the knowledge is still useful.

Several of us are on Facebook, we go to marketplaces; you may have visited Etsy, and you've seen so many shops selling signs, selling shirts, selling one thing or the other, you probably wonder, "can I still make money with craft?" The simple answer to the question, "Yes, you can, and it is not that hard." With everyone specializing in a specific area where they know how to do better, the market can never be saturated. Take, for instance; someone might major only in the making of T-shirts, while another on making cups, another on woodwork design, and many more. The truth is that you will not find many people that are good in one particular area. So, the market can never get filled.

Now you are ready, you have gotten your Cricut, and you are wondering, "where do I start?" The easiest place to start is literally by making items for your friends and family. There are so many products you can make for your friends that they will appreciate and pay you for. Some of them are stickers, design their name on their T-shirts, and write motivational words on their T-shirts. You can brainstorm on some objects you think your friends would like and start designing for them. You can also make a design for your children and your spouse. When you are done with those designs, paste them on Facebook; you might get people who would want you to do the same design for them. This is the easiest way to start without investing so much money, and no one is buying it from you.

CHAPTER 22:

+100 Cricut Projects to Sell and to Make Money

1. Calligraphy wall art
2. Customized lap desk
3. "Breakfast-in-bed" tray
4. Coffee bar sign
5. Cookie jar
6. Crafting stamps
7. Planner stickers
8. Custom calendar
9. Journal pages
10. Welcome mat
11. Wine gift bag
12. Silhouette art
13. Art storage
14. Labeled laundry baskets
15. Customized travel mugs
16. State silhouette signs
17. Forest themed nursery décor
18. Candleholders
19. Custom shot glasses
20. Wedding favors
21. Book tote bag
22. Patterned wood letters
23. Quilled art
24. Team T-shirts
25. Teacher appreciation mug gifts
26. Photo booth props
27. Personalized bottle cap catcher
28. Wine cork box
29. Paper succulents
30. Patterned scarf
31. Designed umbrella

32. Mandala hoodie
33. 3D stars
34. Doll clothing
35. Custom jigsaw puzzle
36. Glitter tumblers
37. Labeled pantry bins
38. Kitchen conversions chart
39. Family center
40. Paper straw party decorations
41. Headbands
42. Personalized tea towels
43. Stained glass wind chime
44. Ring dish
45. Monogrammed throw pillow
46. Giant bows
47. Kitchen mixer decals
48. Custom onesies
49. Car window decals
50. Hanging planter
51. Bumper stickers
52. Paper flower wreath
53. Nursery mobile
54. Food pun dish towels
55. Customized beach towel
56. Drink cooler
57. Pendant necklace
58. Leather tassel earrings
59. Finger puppets
60. 3D puzzles
61. Charity shirts
62. Glass cutting board
63. Wooden family name sign
64. Notebook covers
65. Flip flops
66. Decorative hand mirror
67. Makeup storage
68. Pop up paper animals
69. Felt flowers
70. Quilts

71. Vinyl banners
72. Custom potholders
73. Thank your cards
74. Leather purse
75. Dry erase weekly menu
76. Cookies for Santa plate and mug
77. Family tree wall art
78. Photo magnets
79. Window clings
80. Felt headband
81. Tupperware for food gifts
82. Sleep mask
83. Microwaveable rice pack
84. Leather cuff bracelet
85. Custom ballcaps
86. Decorated dog bandanas
87. Tooth fairy bags
88. Coloring books
89. Pop up cards
90. Polka dot vase
91. Winter shadowbox
92. Drink koozies
93. Custom drawer pulls
94. Photo board
95. Planner pages
96. Balsa wood jewelry
97. Etched pet tags
98. Water measurement bottle
99. Etched measuring glass
100. Countdown sign
101. Workout tank top
102. Large wall decals
103. Embossed cards
104. Chipboard letters
105. Striped coffee mug
106. Teabag holder
107. Decorative tea light holders
108. Foam stamps
109. Llama mask

CHAPTER 23:

Cricut Business

Are You Ready to Go into Business?

Far too often, people who are extremely creative jump into a business before they have actually thought about the business end of the situation. If you are using a Cricut Maker often and people are giving you tons of feedback about your crafts and gifts, it might be a signal that you should go into business with your Cricut Maker. Hundreds of users are doing just that. But what can make you unique and keep you in business for a much longer time?

You should have a clear idea of why you want to go into business with your Cricut. Make a list. There may just be one clear reason, or there could be 3–4, but regardless of how many reasons, define why you want to be in business.

You might want to be at home with the kids. Have you ever tried to work at home with kids around? Or, perhaps you are making quite a bit with your Cricut Maker already and have so many orders you cannot keep up on evenings and weekends.

Working outside the home is just not your thing. You have always wanted to be in business for yourself. You enjoy marketing. In fact, you have a marketing degree, and you are champing at the bit to be your boss and use that degree to market your own projects. You think you can take this Cricut business to the top!

Finally, crafting with your Cricut maker feeds your soul. There isn't anything else you would rather do with your life for a job. You can work on projects almost 24/7, and it doesn't bother you. Even when you are not working, you are thinking of projects you could do if you were working. This is your passion. You have found a way to make the world brighter and a better place.

Make sure you are self-motivated. To be in business, any business, you have to be self-motivated. You may be extremely creative using your Cricut, but if you are not motivated to network and get customers consistently, that's going to be a problem in the long run. Also, you might have to work on projects when you don't feel like working because people need their purchases. Are you motivated enough to be able to keep up the pace a business sometimes throws your way? Also, are you ready to deal with "that" customer? We are talking about the customer who just is never happy. You need a plan for the bad penny that just will not go away.

Make sure your personal finances are in order. And then consult with an advisor and an accountant before going into business and take their advice. According to the financial advisors you can weather any storms that come along because of low tides in the business world. You don't want to ruin your love for your Cricut by ending up in financial trouble because you were not financially prepared to go into business in the first place. There is truly nothing worse than thinking you have found your dream and ending up in a daytime nightmare.

A good question to ask yourself is where will I get my clients? Etsy? Pinterest? Word of mouth? Will you market on Facebook? How are you going to get your customers? Are you planning to go to craft fairs? Think about your options and what marketing is going to cost. Are you ready to beat the pavement? Are you ready to go to schools, churches, hit up the little leagues, and everyone and anyone who needs something done by a Cricut?

Everyone who goes into business should have a solid business plan. A business plan is a road map of where you are and where you are going. How many things might potentially cost and the potential income? With a Cricut Maker, you don't have as many outside variables, and most of the success depends on your hard work and persistence. But you still need a business plan and a good one! Let's get started!

Once these 5 steps have been addressed, you are ready to get started with your new Cricut Maker business. How exciting!

Where Do I Start?

Like any start-up business, initial questions need to be addressed to overcome possible difficulties. For example, addressing issues like defining my clientele, the products that might be of interest, where to find them, and making a profit margin of your sales are important to tackle from the start. In other words, you will need a good and well-defined business strategy to start with.

Choosing Your Client

You can target 2 avenues to sell your products: either by looking at how you can approach the market locally or online. It is advisable to concentrate efforts on one approach to start with as your target is to generate profits as soon as possible. Never forget that your goal is to grow benefit and reinvest it so that your business expands. The quicker you increase your sales, the more likely you will reinvest in new tools or new products, making, in turn, a stronger financial turnover. Understanding your marketing strategy is key to your success.

You Need a Business Name and a Logo

Now that you know your machine and decide to take the plunge into owning your own business with your Cricut, you need to think of a name for this business and a symbol of you. Your name for your business needs to identify you and also be a catchy name that tells people what you do. Pick a name you plan to stick with for a long time. It's costly to change a name and logo, etc. A logo isn't necessary, but they are fun to design, and you have a Cricut Maker, so play around with your new name and design.

What Kind of a Business License Will Do You Need?

One of the steps you will have to do is contact your home state because every state is different in obtaining a state business license. A license or permit gives you the permission you need to open and operate a business. Registration allows you to claim the name of the business and the business itself as yours. Insurance is another matter and is usually not mandatory with a crating business, but it does cover costs in case of an accident.

According to state law, your business probably will need a license to operate legally; even if you are operating a small sole proprietorship and running this business out of your home. This is something you need to investigate immediately and get those details in order first. An accountant or financial advisor will be able to help you. Usually, these people can help for a minimal charge or do not mind answering questions for free. You can also go to your city or county business office and ask questions. Often, there are people there who can answer questions and even help you fill out the necessary paperwork. If your state capital is not far, you could do the same by going to your state capital's licensing division.

Also, consult with other people who are in the crafting business. Note, we said consult. This does not mean to take everything they say as the law. You still need to check the laws in your county and state, but at least if you check with others in the crafting business before you take the plunge, you will have an idea of the cost and paperwork.

And speaking of taking the plunge, are you ready to jump right in, or is this going to be a part-time gig for a while to see how you do? Most people do start part-time. Again, talk to others and get some ideas. No one can choose for you, but this is one business you could do part-time for a while in the evenings and weekends before quitting your day job. These things are all important discussions to have before you decide what to do about getting into business using your Cricut Maker on a full-time basis.

Website

The next order of business is to work on a website. You will need to find a host. Many people like Bluehost. And, while you are at it, print yourself some business cards on your Cricut. How fun is it to design and print your cards on your Cricut Maker?

Business cards are important because they are your little billboard. They are a way to advertise every time you give one out or pin one on a bulletin board in a restaurant or a coffee shop. Your phone number is on the card, and an idea of what you will create for your customers is on your card. You also will put your business email address on your business cards.

CHAPTER 24:

Making Money from Cricut

I t is a well-known fact in the world of business that to make money, you first need to invest money. With that being said, if you already own a Cricut cutting machine, then you can jump to the next paragraph, but if you are debating if it's worth the investment, then read on. As mentioned earlier, Cricut has a range of cutting machines with distinctive capabilities offered at a varying price range. The Cricut Explore Air 2 is priced at $249.99, and the Cricut Maker is priced at $399.99 (the older Cricut Explore Air model may be available for sale on Amazon at a lower price).

Is the Market Too Full?

You can target 2 avenues to sell your products: either by looking at how you can approach the market locally or online. It is advisable to concentrate efforts on one approach to start with as your target is to generate profits as soon as possible. Never forget that your goal is to grow, benefit and reinvest it so that your business expands. The quicker you increase your sales, the more likely you will reinvest in new tools or new products, making, in turn, a stronger financial turnover. Understanding your marketing strategy is key to your success.

Selling the Craft You Have Made with Cricut

We have already pointed out a lot of items that you can start doing and selling to your friends and neighbors. You don't have to convince your friends to buy many of those products because I know they will like it if you make personal designs for them. What you have to do is to find out what your friends like and make such designs for them. For example, if you have a friend who likes football and has a team, you can design the team's logo as a sticker for such a friend and write something good about the team for them. You might also have a friend that sees clothes and likes what they do. You can make a lovely design with their business name for them. Also, you can make a sticker of their logo for them to put on every dress they make.

You can also make money with your design to look for people who would want you to iron-on their clothes for them. There are a lot of people out there looking for someone that would design their clothes for them. Look for the people that sell in boutiques and sell your designs to them. This is how it is done. You can offer to do a free design for someone that sells plenty of plane T-shirts for them to see what you do. If they like what you have done for them, you can then charge the person how much you would like to receive for designing each piece of clothing for such a person. So, look for local sellers around you that you think might need your design.

Another very easy way you can make money with it is through selling to groups. You can walk up to a group of people who wear a uniform and have a group name and ask to design for their group. This is easy to get because each person in the group would like to be identified as a group member and would like to pay you for your work.

Examples of some of these groups are clubs, choirs, associations of friends, etc. The best way to go about this is to offer to do a free design for the group leader first. The idea behind this is that, if you can convince the group leader with your design, you can easily sell your work to every member of the group.

Secondly, the group members will be seeing the design of the leader and would be asking where they did the design. Some will even suggest doing the design for everyone. Then they will be forced to ask you to do the design for every member of the team. Get the leader interested, and you will penetrate the group easily.

Becoming a Cricut Affiliate

This includes being paid to make tutorials video by the Cricut company. These videos are uploaded to the internet for the netizen to make use of. To become a Cricut affiliate, you need to have a strong internet presence. You must also have a tangible number of followers on your social media accounts.

Making Money Through Teaching

This has nothing to do with being an affiliate; rather, you create a blog for videos and upload tutorial videos, and get paid through the generated traffic.

Other Places Where You Can Sell Your Craft

You can make any of the crafts you find or create and post pictures of them online, announcing to those on your list that it is for sale. This works better because whoever is buying gets to see the picture of whatever they are getting before ordering it. Personalized crafts should also be included in your order of business.

Follow the Holiday

Another way to make money is with the Cricut machine. You create an iron vinyl design and sell to people. Iron vinyl can take the form of text or a pattern. You can also do it for any season or celebration, be it Valentine's Day, Halloween, Christmas, or Easter. Buyers can also order what they want.

Selling Pre-Cut Customized Vinyl

Vinyl is a super beginner-friendly material to work with and comes in a variety of colors and patterns to add to its great reputation. You can create customized labels for glass containers and canisters to help anyone looking to organize their pantry. Explore the online trends and adjust the labels. Once you have your labels designed, the easiest approach is to set up an Etsy shop, which is free and very easy to use. It's almost like opening an Amazon prime membership account. If your design is in demand, you will have people ordering even with no advertising. But if you would like to keep the tempo high, then advertise your Etsy listing on Pinterest and other social media platforms. This is a sure-shot way to generate more traffic to your Etsy shop and to turn potential customers into paying customers. An important note here is the pictures being used on your listing. You cannot use any of the Design Space images and must use your own pictures that match the product you are selling.

Create a package of 5–6 different labels like sugar, salt, rice, oats, beans, etc., that can be sold as a standard packager and offer a customized package that will allow the customer to request any word that they need to be included in their set. Since these labels weigh next to nothing, shipping can easily be managed with standard mail with usually only a single postage stamp, depending on the delivery address. Make sure you do not claim the next day or 2-day delivery for these. Build enough delivery time so you can create and ship the labels without any stress. Once you have an established business model, you can adjust the price and shipping of your product, but more on that later. Check out other Etsy listings to make sure your product pricing is competitive enough and you are attracting enough potential buyers. Now, once you have traction in the market, you can offer additional vinyl-based projects like bumper stickers, iron-on, or heat transfer vinyl designs that people can transfer on their clothing using a standard heating iron. Really, once you have gained some clientele, you can modify and customize all your listings to develop into a one-stop shop for all things vinyl (a great name for your future Etsy shop, right!).

Selling Finished Pieces

You would be using your Cricut machine for a variety of personal projects like home décor, holiday décor, personalized clothing, and more. Next time you embark on another one of your inspiring journeys leading to unique creations, just make 2 of everything, and you can easily put the other product to sell on your Etsy shop. Another great advantage is that you will be able to save all your projects on the Design Space application for future use, so, if one of your projects goes viral, you can easily buy the supplies and turn them into money-making offerings. This way, not only your original idea for personal usage will be paid off, but you can make much more money than you invested in it, to begin with. Again, spend some time researching what kind of designs and decorations are trending in the market and use them to spark up inspiration for your next project. Some of the current market trends include customized cake and cupcake toppers and watercolor designs that can be framed as fancy wall decorations. The cake toppers can be made with cardstock, which is another beginner-friendly material, light in weight, and can be economically shipped tucked inside an envelope.

Personalized Clothing and Accessories

T-shirts with cool designs and phrases are all the rage right now. Just follow a similar approach to the selling vinyl section and take it up a notch. You can create sample clothing with an iron-on design and market it with "can be customized further at no extra charge" or "transfer the design on your own clothing" to get traction in the market. You can buy sling bags and customize them with unique designs to be sold as finished products at a higher price than a plain boring sling bag.

Consider creating a line of products with a centralized theme like the DC Marvel characters or the Harry Potter movies and design custom T-shirts, hats, and even bodysuits for babies. You can create customized party favor boxes and gift bags at the request of the customer. Once your product has a dedicated customer base, you can get project ideas from them directly and quote them a price for your work. Isn't that great?!?!

Another big advantage of the heat transfer vinyl, as mentioned earlier, is that anyone can transfer the design on their desired item of clothing using a standard household iron. But you would need to include the transfer instructions with the order letting them know exactly how to prep for the heat transfer without damaging their chosen clothing item. And again, heat transfer vinyl can be easily shipped using a standard mailing envelope.

Marketing on Social Media

We are all aware of how social media has become a marketing platform for established corporations and small businesses and budding entrepreneurs. Simply add hashtags like for sale, product, selling, free shipping, the sample included, and more to entice potential buyers. Join Facebook community pages and groups for handcraft sellers and buyers to market your products. Use catchy phrases like "customization available at no extra cost" or "free returns if not satisfied" when posting the products on these pages as well as your personal Facebook page. Use Twitter to share feedback from your satisfied customers to widen your customer base. You can do this by creating a satisfaction survey that you can email to your buyers or include a link to your Etsy listing asking for online reviews and ratings from your customers.

Another tip here is to post pictures of anything and everything you have created using Cricut machines, even those that you did not plan to sell. You never know who else might need something that you deemed unsellable. Since you will be creating these only after the order has been placed, you can easily gather the required supplies after the fact and get crafting.

Target Local Farmer's Market and Boutiques

If you like the thrill of a show-and-tell, then reserve a booth at a local farmer's market and show up with some ready-to-sell crafts. In this case, you are relying on the number of people attending and a subset of those who might be interested in purchasing from you. If you are in an urban neighborhood where people are keenly interested in unique art designs but do not have the time to create them on their own, you can easily make big bucks by setting a decent price point for your products.

Bring flyers to hand out to people so they can reach you through one of your social media accounts or email and check all your existing Etsy listings. Think of these events as a means of marketing for those who are not as active online but can be excited with customized products to meet their next big life event like a baby shower, birthday party, or wedding.

One downside to participating in local events is the generation of mass inventory and booth displays, topped with expenses to load and transport the inventory. You may or may not be able to sell all of the inventory depending on the event's size, but as I said earlier, you can still make the most of this by marketing your products and building up a local clientele.

CHAPTER 25:

Brand Positioning, Digital Mindset, and Branding for Your Business

There are countless items you can make with Cricut. Likewise, there are countless products you can make which are marketable. Independent entrepreneurship is easier than it's ever been, thanks to the Internet and web platforms that make selling your products a breeze.

You've likely already heard of some of the platforms that make it easy to start a shop of your own. Etsy is probably the most well-known of these platforms, and setting up a shop with them is so simple, it's almost impossible not to be interested in starting one for yourself!

With the Cricut, making countless items of every type and theme is the name of the game for any occasion. Doing these projects can be a huge source of joy for the avid crafter, but if you're spending the money on the materials for your projects, it might make sense for you to start generating a return on those, depending on how much you're doing and spending.

We'll cover some of the basics of what it means to go into business for yourself when you're the sole manufacturer of the goods in your store. Without providing a brick-and-mortar space for your shop, overhead can be so much lower than starting a shop or store, which is viable for people who might not have a lump sum of startup capital ready to hand.

How Do You Know When It's Time to Start a Shop?

If crafting is your passion, if you prefer to spend your time making items with your Cricut than out or doing any other activity in your downtime, it could be the right time. Suppose you're finding that your crafting room is getting full of projects you've made but haven't gotten to use for that special occasion yet. In that case, you might find that you could sell those items to others, make back what you spent on the materials, as well as get paid for the time it took you to put the project together in the first place!

Should I Quit My Day Job and Go All In?

The thing about selling the products you create is that, since there's no brick-and-mortar location to manage, no store hours to keep to, you can manage your sales and your projects in the spare time that you have. It is best to start your store while you have a stable source of income. This way, as your store grows, you can scale back where it's necessary to do so in your usual work schedule to allow for more time to spend on your shop.

How Can I Make Sure People Will Buy My Products?

There is a variety of ways to market a business in today's digital age. Get social media presence, search engine optimization, and more; you can put your name everywhere it needs to be to generate interest. However, you might find that it will be easiest to pick items that are not custom when you're starting out. Make a couple of each type of item, take stunning product photos, upload them to your store, then sell those as off-the-rack items.

As you start to generate more business, you may find that taking on the occasional custom order or commissioned item will benefit you. By and large, you will find that custom orders will take you more time and cost more to produce for less of a return. Be watchful of this, and if you find that making 100 of a general design and selling all of those is the best use of your time and resources, stick with that! There's absolutely nothing wrong with going that route.

Do I Need to Make Enough of Each Item in My Shop to Keep an Inventory?

The short answer to this is no. You don't have to make any more of any items that are being ordered at any given time. With the way Etsy works for sellers, you can determine how much time you have before shipping out an order. You can make the items as they're ordered, so you can be certain you're never wasting product or letting it sit in your craft room for too long.

The only time it would be best to make any sort of inventory would be if you intend to rent a space or booth at a tradeshow or convention. Having a presence at craft fairs, conventions, tradeshows, etc., can generate impulse buys from passing patrons that could be great for your business.

If at all possible, it's best to wait to go to such an event until you're able to narrow down your best sellers.

Once you have a smattering of items you can make that are your hottest items, you can make several of each of those and keep them at your booth or table, ready for immediate purchase!

Do I Need to Create a Shop to Make Money with Cricut?

To be candid, no, you don't need to create a shop if you don't want to. There are always different ways of going about things, and making money with your Cricut is as customizable as the Cricut projects themselves. If someone else runs a craft shop, you might ask them to list your items for you in exchange for a share of the profits.

You could create a partnership with a local school, community center, farmer's market, or another establishment to sell your items for you to their patrons.

There are so many ways to go about getting your unique crafts into the hands of the public and to make money off the beautiful projects you make with your Cricut system.

Making an online store for your Cricut items might be the most direct, hands-on way to generate a stream of income from the items that you make. However, this does not mean that it's the only way or that it's the best way for you to go about it. Test the waters, see what's available, and pick a path that is most workable for you and the business you're working to create.

Which Are the Best Platforms to Sell My Crafts?

This question is a little bit loaded and, what it boils down to is which platform is the most convenient, workable, and reliable for you. The business you want to create will take up a lot of your time and attention, so you must be using a platform that fits all your needs, meets all your expectations, and solves more problems for you than it causes.

We can tend to be forgiving of quirks in new systems when we're learning them. However, take a little extra time to read the experiences and reviews of people who have used that platform for an extended period. This will give you a look into what your future could be like with that platform, and it's the only gauge you have to go by when it comes to how that platform will serve you.

You should spend a little extra time looking into which platforms are available, what costs are involved (if any), how they treat their sellers, what percentages of your sales are taken, and what the sellers on those platforms think of them.

Here are some of the top platforms you should check!

- Etsy
- Amazon Handmade
- Facebook Marketplace
- Folksy
- Artfire
- Craftsy
- eBay
- Craigslist

CHAPTER 26:

Setting the Price of Your Cricut Projects

It bothers me to see people selling their beautiful super elaborate creations at so low prices. Those people are not even valuing their own time. They are not taking into account their talent, materials, or other important points when setting prices.

How Should I Price My Items?

This, like everything else, is entirely up to you. One pricing method is to decide on a rate you would like to be paid per hour spent on a project, multiply that rate by how many hours you spent on that project, and add it together with the costs of all the materials you used to make your project. For instance, I would never take a full-time job that paid me less than $15 per hour. We'll use this as our artisan rate to start. You can always adjust your prices as you get better with your craft, as you generate more of a following, and as you get faster at completing each of the projects you sell! So, with this $15 hourly rate, we'll put together a little project. Let's say I'm taking a sheet of printable vinyl and printing an image that I own onto it. From there, I'm layering that vinyl onto a cardboard backing. Once that's done, I'm going to run it through my Cricut and make a jigsaw puzzle out of it. Once I've made my jigsaw puzzle, I'm going to use more cardboard to make a box, which I will then decoupage. The box will be filled with puzzle pieces, wrapped with a satin ribbon, and sold in my online store. Let's run the tally!

- Cricut printable vinyl: $9
- Cardboard sheets: $6
- Decoupage glue: $2
- Satin ribbon: $1
- 1 hour of labor: $15.00
- Artisan jigsaw puzzle: $33.00

Do not sell yourself short on your labor costs, and do not charge less than you spend on your materials, ever! That's no way to run a business, and it's no way to live. Value your time properly and charge every penny that you're worth. With how beautiful your products are, you will find people will pay your rates, and you will get rave reviews every time!

Monetizing Your Art

You have practiced, perfected, and established a style of that art that you like to do so much. You have decorated cards, personalized objects, created pictures with motivational phrases. With pride, you have shared your work on social networks.

- Own studio or on-site?
- What will be your minimum charge for small jobs?
- Your time + energy

This is where the wellness factor comes in, where you need to think about how much your time is worth to you. It's worth a lot more than buying the cheapest combo at McDonald's, but there the questions come… "How much exactly? How do I find out?" It is difficult to answer these questions, but there are certain guidelines that I can tell you that can help you.

One method is to put yourself a monthly salary with which you feel comfortable. I will speak in an imaginary way based on some local statistics of the Dominican Republic to speak with numbers and understand. Let's say (I made it up) that, on average, a monthly salary in my country is 15,000 Dominican pesos, and this is the number with which you value your time and energy.

This number will be divided by 4.3. This number is established as the average of weeks in the year since months have 30 days, another 31, and February 28. Are you already starting to see the difference? Now try to use that math to calculate your hourly rate.

Start with the monthly salary you feel comfortable with:

_____

Divide that number by 4.3 and put it here: _____

Now divide this other number by 44 (remember that this number may vary). So, this result is your hourly rate that you will put here: _____

Cost of Materials

Are you using cheap store markers or artist-quality paints? Do you use expensive papers and prepared inks? Are the special items you need? Do you have to order online specific to some part of the world or available near you?

The value increases with the quality of your tools and materials, as well as your knowledge of them. If you answer, "What kind of paint do you have/do you use?" With an "I don't know... I've had it for a long time and the label it has is no longer visible" or "a friend gave it to me, and I don't know where it got it." Your work will not be as valuable as that of someone whose answer is "I use Winsor and Newton's lightweight, water-resistant watercolors." Artist-quality materials cost more, so you must know your materials' cost in case they run out.

Project Size

This is probably one of the first factors to value your project. How big is it? Creating something, for example, a lettering composition is an 8.5 by 11 inches sheet with 10 words that will take much less time and fewer materials than those same 10 words on an 8 by 10 feet board. You can have a price for measurements, let's say square inches, or better use your hourly rate that we work above.

Delivery/Shipping

You must indicate in your budget if the delivery is included or if is an extraordinary payment. That means you need to know where the piece is going. You may have to purchase parcel shipping quotes outside of your city based on the weight size and service you need. I recommend that you investigate the rates of the shipping companies and, thus, have a standard shipping cost.

Original or Continuous Use?

Will your client use your art once (like a wedding card), continuously (like a business card or blog), or multiple times (like a T-shirt to resell)? It is always a good idea to ask this question in advance. The answer will help you determine how valuable your artwork is to the customer if it will be used continuously to promote or generate direct income for your client; the value increases.

Deliverables

What should you deliver to your customer as a finished product? An original art? Or is it digital? Both of them? What file formats? JPG, PNG, TIF, EPS, AI? Do you have experience digitizing, and do you have the best tools to do it?

Spending time digitizing and preparing multiple files takes time and experience, and therefore, should be priced accordingly. There are also those printed from digital art. Will you mail the file? In a memory? Digital start, and then you delivered it printed? All this must be taken into account, considering the time and effort it took to do it.

Note: A digital job is even more expensive since it can be reproduced. Using specialized programs requires previous experience and learning, which I suppose also costs you to acquire.

Location (In or Out of Your Studio)

Your hourly rate will also largely depend on where you will be doing the work.

When you have the luxury of your own space, you can perform several tasks simultaneously. That is, you can be working on 2 projects at the same time. This makes it easy to access all of your supplies and materials. The most convenient way for you to work in your place, at your own pace with everything you need at hand, you should not worry about traffic.

If the job requires you to be somewhere outside your study (let's say a restaurant, for example), the value of your time will increase significantly.

You will have to travel to and from the place (which needs to be included in your work time), carry all your materials with you, and only commit to that work during the assigned hours. That also means that you will be in an uncontrolled environment. This includes distractions, noise, and curious people. It can be a lot of fun working on site, and it can be a real headache.

Sometimes a combination of time in your studio and on-site works best. You can carry out all the designs and preparatory work in the studio so that you are ready to carry out your duties once you arrive on site. This would be shown as 2 different hourly rates in the quote, breaking down your activities so your client knows how they invest their money in you.

Project Term

Only you know what time is most comfortable for you to work. If not, I recommend measuring the time you take doing your work to estimate and space if something unforeseen occurs. If a client comes out of nowhere with a crazy panic because they are the most important in the world, always add a fee for speed, clarifying the time it takes you in normal time for similar works, and that you will make an exception for them. Normally these prices vary between 50–100% of the labor price.

It is best to avoid these types of jobs and only accept these cases if necessary because you start to get used to these types of clients.

CHAPTER 27:

How to Become a Successful Crafter

How to become a professional Cricut crafter? First things first, you need to be motivated to turn your crafting into a profession, which means that you need to be confident that you can actually make a profit with your works of art. If you consider becoming a professional crafter and earn your "bread and butter" in the comfort of your crafting room, read on and find out what needs to be done before you can officially become a professional crafter.

Commandments for successful Cricut Crafters

You have your knowledge, skills, talent, practice, and now you have added motivation to become a professional crafter. Sharpen your confidence and read on to find out more about taking the essential steps towards becoming a professional in crafting, or as we like to call these essentials: "Commandments for professional Cricut crafters." Starting a business and making a change in life is never as easy as we would like it to be, while we are often afraid, even of positive changes. That is why we are set to make this transition easier for you with our essentials of becoming a pro in arts and crafts.

Crafting Is Not My Hobby

If you want to become a professional crafter, one of the first things to do is stop considering yourself as a crafting hobbyist. "Crafting is a hobby" and "anyone can craft" might as well be true; however, the more realistic statement would say, "Crafting is not just a hobby" and "not everyone can craft like me." You want to stand out from crafters who are working with arts and crafts as a hobby—crafting as a hobby is more than enjoyable and can even relieve pressure and remove stress. However, if you feel like you are over crafting as a hobby, you need to make a change in your mindset and decide to act. Crafting can be a hobby, yes, but it is likewise a fruitful profession that can bring you both profit and joy. We spend most of our adult lives working, from day to day, from month to month—before you know it, you are ready to retire. So, why not have a profession you would be difficult to leave to retire, why not have a business of your own, and why not have a job you enjoy and love? There are no reasons! If you find one, however, that might be the lack of confidence speaking on your behalf. Some of the essentials that separate hobbyists from professionals are aim, conduct, and unique qualities that give character to your arts and crafts. You need to set your goals straight, work on a unique character for your projects, i.e., your brand, and make sure you can deliver following your goals and plans. You will learn more about the details such as promotion, branding, and planning in the following commandments.

Conduct with Competency

You need to be aware of what you know versus what you don't know— more specifically, you need to be aware of your strengths and weaknesses when it comes to crafting and working with Cricut machines and tools. Conducting with competency means that you are running your business with the support of your knowledge, experience, skills, and qualifications. The way you are running your business tells a lot about who you are and what you expect to get in return for investing efforts, imagination, skills, and expertise in your work. The way you communicate with your customers and potential buyers also describes the conduct of your business. You need to be polite, open, and honest— you need to have integrity so that you could make sales, be recommended, and have happy customers that would return for more products. Don't ever try to sell something you are certain you can't make or deliver—the attempt will come back to you like a boomerang and probably cost you a positive review. Only commit to what you can truly deliver, and when you can deliver. Clients respect honesty and appreciate polite sellers/crafters, so make sure to treat your potential customers as you would like to be treated by a seller. "Please," "My apologies," "Thank you," and managing misunderstandings with clients need to be done with utmost politeness as you are the face of your business. Your work will always tell the story of your business and your conduct; however, the way you treat your clients will most certainly reflect on your sales.

In Quality We Believe

Make sure to present your projects for what your crafts represent—do not try to sugarcoat things to make a quick sale. Always strive towards producing quality arts and crafts; that way, your clients are more likely to get back to you and recommend you to other potential buyers. Sugarcoating shouldn't be mistaken for marketing and the general promotion of your business. You need to know how to sell your products, yes, and we will discuss that point in detail several commandments away from our third commandment. However, you need to allow your products to speak on your behalf—by creating quality and functional products, as stated in your product descriptions, made out of quality materials, and with utmost care and skill, you are potentially scoring more sales. You are also ensuring that your brand is associated with quality. If you add uniqueness to quality, you have a winning combination there. Aside from the quality of products, the quality of service is also accounted for. You need to be able to deliver customized projects the way you promised and under the agreed deadline. Quality in business means that you are ready to commit and deliver. Quality in business means that you are reliable and accountable. Everything you do in your business needs to be done with utmost care towards your products, brands, and customers—that is the only way you can run a successful crafting business or any business for that matter.

Plan, Plan, Plan!

We have already mentioned before, planning is essential when you are working on crafting projects. Planning is likewise essential in running an arts and crafts business. You need to be able to plan ahead and for the future of your business. That means that you need to make a business plan as well. In case you wish so, you can even get the needed documentation for you to officially become a business owner, which comes at a cost as well, paying taxes and running financial books. You also need to be able to make a financial plan, accounting for the starting amount you have for starting a business, funds to buy materials and additional tools and accessories for Cricut and crafting in general, while you also need to plan how much money you need to make in terms of pricing your products to be able to make a profit. In case you are making bulk orders with multiple units of the same product, you also need to make a plan on conducting production, i.e., crafting, so you would be able to meet your deadlines and prepare the products in time. For example, many repetitive tasks can take more time to complete and are not as fun as designing and using Cricut—take the weeding for example. Weeding often takes a lot of time, depending on the amount of excess vinyl you need to remove. If you are making a dozen products, for instance, more or less, make sure to do repetitive tasks such as weeding all at once for all products. That way, your production will go faster—all thanks to efficient planning. With making plans, there come recording plans. Make sure that you can record your expenses, income, orders, and other essential plans that concern your business.

Package and Price Like a Pro

A solid brand needs a memorable and recognizable package as well. Since you already know how to find your way around crafting all sorts of projects and designs, you can design your packages such as branded boxes and tags with your name or the name of your brand. You can also make promotional material—however, we will go through that part later on as we are going through the commandments of professional crafters. Having professionally made branded tags and boxes will make your business advertisement with little to no effort (except for the part where you need to invest your time to make the tags and packaging for your products). A fine package with branded tags will encourage your customers to return for more goods and recommend your brand with a positive review. Pricing is also essential—you don't want to go over the top and inflate your prices so that not many people think that your products are both quality and affordable. As you are starting out, it is not recommended to set your prices above your competitors who already have a reputation for professional crafters. You need to start off with moderate modesty when it comes to pricing. However, you don't want to sell your products for anything either. That is why it is important to take a sneak peek into the pricing of your competitors. Make sure to involve in comparison shopping, checking out the product pricing of competitors in the area of your interest. You don't want to undersell your products by keeping the prices low, but you also want to be competitive and earn your place on the top of the business ladder. Remember that every product has its own value, and that value can be priced—then value, however, includes your time and talent, so you want to be fair with pricing without undermining your time, skill, and talents. Always check out the competition in case you are having doubts about the pricing. Moreover, you need to follow up with the costs for making a product and make sure that the price you put on the product needs to assure profit returns so that your business keeps running.

Deliver

If you have promised to deliver within an agreed deadline, then you should give your best to honor the agreement. By failing to deliver at the agreed deadline, you are risking a potential returning customer, not getting an excellent review, and wasting a perfectly good sale. Set the standards for your brand and always try your best to honor these standards. When it comes to delivering, the product being sold and delivered should fit the description on which the buyer decided to purchase precisely that item. Always deliver with quality and promptly. Make sure to deliver in branded packages so that your work speaks on behalf of your talent and your professionalism. Moreover, if you are shipping your products, your deliveries need to be neatly organized so you know which product should be shipped and where. Keep track of your deliveries, recording the time of order and the time it takes for the product to arrive from your craft shop to your customer. The next commandment in line will help you deal with some of these things as deliveries require organization as well as your business.

Organize

Before, we have emphasized the importance of organizing your crafting space and your working station. When it comes to running a crafting business, everything needs to be organized. Every aspect of your business requires a thorough organization. Starting from inventory and supplies to shipping and delivering your products—you need to think ahead and be prepared. Start with organizing your working space. Know where your materials, tools, and accessories are, and make sure to keep all your essentials neatly and safely stored. Make sure to keep track of your inventory, including tools and extra blades for your Cricut machine(s). Organize your projects and the type of products you want to make a part of your offer. The organization also means that you are able to keep track of all your orders and deliveries. Once every aspect of your business is organized, you will find it easier to focus on your projects and manage your business at the same time with success. Use planners or planning apps to help you organize—alternatively, you can find some apps suitable for a business organization that should help you keep track of your business operations. When it comes to organizing production, you should note and remember; the less time you spent on making one project, the more profit you are making. Organization can help you in terms of making your production more efficient and effective. Organize tasks for production before starting your Cricut machine to make the most of your crafting time. Since you will be working on many different projects—from quilts to stickers, there will be a lot of materials and material scraps piling up on your working station. Make sure to keep your desk organized, scraps stored for test cuts and possible use, materials neatly stored in labeled boxes, and throw away everything you don't need. Proper organization in the crafting business is half the work done.

Invest

Invest in your business. Calculate how much you are planning to make in your first month. As you are starting off, there might be only a few sales in the beginning until your brand is heard of and marketed. However, you should be able to meet the demand through supplies and materials even if you are not expecting to double your sales. Invest in your business by investing in remodeling your working space if needed, buying materials in bulks, buying extra tools and supplies that you use more often, and invest in different blades and mats for your Cricut machine.

To make efficient purchases of materials and supplies, you can make bulk orders—that way, you will be able to save some money and stockpile the materials you need the most. Do not exaggerate in the assessment of expenses for supplies, consider buying at least a third of materials and supplies over the expected amount, just to be on the safe side and assure there won't be material shortages while you are working on crafting your products. To gain access to more professional Cricut designs and images, you can invest in a monthly subscription to Cricut Access. Cricut Access offers premium images and art for your crafting designs, which can be very useful when you are crafting in bulks and want to offer a wide range of versatile designs to your clients. Investing in your business also means investing in tools and accessories that make your work better, more efficient, and faster—such as using Cricut EasyPress and EasyPress Mini, for example.

Promote Your Business

If the organization is the core value that will make professional crafting more efficient and far easier, then advertising is the key to getting your product "out there." Advertising doesn't only mean paying for an ad to be displayed on social networks and Google search engines—although these options could do a great job in the promotion of your business. Advertising and marketing your products also include creating a memorable and recognizable brand alongside making packages and tags for your products. Promotion of your business also needs to be planned—you need to know where to find your targeted audience, i.e., buyers who love arts and crafts. You need to know where you can promote your business and where you can find your potential customers. You won't advertise your handmade decals in a sports equipment magazine or on a website that has nothing to do with crafting, Cricut, or your targeted audience.

You can also start a blog or just become more actively involved with potential buyers on social networks as a business. You can combine more than several ways of advertising your business as long as your campaign is effective and brings more customers to your shop, virtual or physical. To make advertising more effective and to reach more potential customers, you should definitely combine paid ads on the internet, small ads in magazines specialized in arts and crafts, blogs and websites dealing with Cricut crafting and arts and crafts in general, as well as paid Google ads and social media activity.

Create Value

Creating value for a business regardless of the type of business—in this case, crafting with Cricut—is not a task one can complete in a day or a week even. The value of your business is shown through your products' quality and the way you are running your business, communicating with your potential buyers, and delivering your goods. The value of your business is also seen in the way you are creating and affirming your brand. You define the value of your business and your work, not only through pricing but also by the way you are treating your deliveries, commitments, and your customers. By setting prices for your work, you are creating a physical value reciprocal to your time, skills, creativity, expertise, experience, and talent. However, the overall value of your business can represent your own set of standards while your customers will pay attention to all aspects of your business—delivery, communication, quality, brand, exposure—not only the pricing of your products.

Dare to Be Different

You have to be yourself, unleash your quirkiness and creativity.

Those that have been in the Cricut crafts world for some time know all about the knockout name tiles. They became a hit, and in no time, everyone was producing and selling them.

In the crafting world, that is the norm. Thus, you could be among the earliest people to jump on a trend to ride the wave until the next hot seller surfaces. Mind you, that strategy of selling Cricut crafts can become costly and tiresome if you are not careful.

The basic idea here is to add your flair and personal style and not to completely re-invent the wheel. For example, let's say you come across 2 name tiles on Etsy; one looks exactly like the other +200 on sale on the site, while the second one has a few more tweaks and spins on it. The second product seller will possibly charge more and accrue a higher profit because their product is unique and stands out from the rest.

When you design your products, don't be afraid to tweak your fonts because even the simplest of tweaks and creativity can make your product stand out from the rest.

Remember this; if you create a product that looks exactly like others, you are only putting yourself in a "price war," where no one usually wins.

Keep It Narrow

Many crafters believe that creating and selling everything under the sun translates into more patronage and more money, but that isn't how it works. On the contrary, it might only result in a huge stock of unsold products, more burn out, and high cost. Rather than producing materials here and there, you should focus on being the best in your area of craftiness so that when people need specific products in your area, they'll come to you.

It can be very tempting to want to spread your tentacles because it might seem like the more you produce, the more options you'll provide for your clients, but that might be counterproductive.

Take out time to think about your area of strength and focus your energy on making products that you'd be known for. It is better to be known as an expert in a particular product than to be renowned for someone that produces a high number of inferior products.

Thus, you should keep it narrow and grow to become the very best in your area of craft.

Be Consistent

If you intend to become successful, you have to work on your Cricut craft business consistently. Some people work once a week or thereabout because they sell as a hobby; however, if you intend to make in-road in your business, you have to work every day.

If you have other engagements and can't work every day, then you should create a weekly schedule and stick to it. If you shun your business for weeks and months at a time, then you will not go anywhere with it.

Apart from consistency in work and production, you also have to be consistent with your product quality and pricing. When your customers are convinced about your products, they will easily recommend you to their friends, family, business partners, and many others.

In business, there are ups and downs; thus, you shouldn't reduce your work rate because things are not going as planned. Success doesn't come easy, but one of the surest ways of being and maintaining success is by consistently doing the things you love.

Be Tenacious

It is not easy to run a business because it involves a lot of hard work, sweat, and even heartbreaks. Thus, you have to bear in mind that there will be days when you will feel like throwing in the towel. There will be days when nothing goes as planned. There will also be days when customers will tick you off. You will feel like a drowning boat because you're working hard, but nothing is working out.

However, you have to look at the bigger picture because the crafting business is not a rich, quick scheme. Remember, quitters never win, so quitting isn't an option. Keep doing the things you love, and keep improving. Successful people never give up. They suffer many setbacks, but they don't stop.

Thus, for you to be successful in your craft, you have to be tenacious and resilient. Be willing to maneuver your way through tough times, and do not forget to pick up lessons.

Learn Everyday

Be willing to learn from people that have been successful in the business. You don't necessarily have to unravel everything by yourself because whatever it is you are doing; others have already done it in the past.

Whether you intend to learn how to build a successful Facebook group or how to go up the Etsy ranks, remember that people have already done all that in the past and are giving out tricks and tips they know.

Make it a tradition to learn something new about your business every day because, at the beginning of your business, you will have to do more marketing than crafting.

When you wake up in the morning, browse through the internet, gather materials, and read in your spare time, the more you learn, the better your chances of success. They say knowledge is power, and for you to become successful as a craftsman/woman, you have to constantly seek new knowledge in the form of tips, tricks, software upgrades, marketing, design ideas, tools, accessories, and many others. All I am saying is that you should learn without ceasing.

CHAPTER 28:

Best Printer and Laptop for Your New Business

- Acer Aspire E 15
- Lenovo Flex 14
- Dell Inspiration 15 5000
- ASUS Vivo Book
- Microsoft Surface
- Apple MacBook Air
- Acer Switch 7
- Acer Predator Helios
- Lenovo Yoga

Where to Buy Wholesale Goods

Here are some of the top platforms you'll want to check into!

- Etsy
- Amazon Handmade
- Facebook Marketplace
- Folksy
- Artfire
- Craftsy
- eBay
- Craigslist

You will mostly find that there are no items you can make with your Cricut, which will not appeal to someone who wants to buy one. If you sell even one of each item you ever make, you're still coming out way ahead of the game, right?

A lot of items can be purchased at a low rate from retailers, then customized using your design expertise, Cricut magic, and beautiful vinyl appliques that have sayings monograms, or appealing designs on them. The choice is yours!

CHAPTER 29:

Most Profitable Businesses in 2021

Selling for Profit

You have turned into a specialist crafter by using the imaginative structures of different Cricut cartridges. Your imaginative scrapbooking is the discussion of your companions. Your superbly made customized welcome card accumulations are the result of your imaginative Cricut thoughts. Companions disclose to you that your creation can contend with any financially delivered welcome cards or scrapbook sold in your neighborhood stationery shop.

All in all, have you thought of making cash out of your astounding and unique art creation? Here are incredible approaches to profit while doing what you cherish.

Although many crafters appreciate using their Cricut to kick the bucket cutting machine, they have not exactly aced the product to work how they anticipate that it should. Accepting this opens the door to offer your administration of taking custom requests and cutting records that your clients can use. Art gatherings are open doors for you to see what other individuals need and, after that, make those cut records and sell them on the web, explicitly on eBay.

Show your specially designed cards and solicitations in neighborhood expressions and artworks stores. They can offer them to their clients. Numerous individuals couldn't imagine anything better than to have a custom card or message made for specials events like birthdays, commemorations, dedicating, and other extraordinary occasions. Your creation can be boundless and one of a kind as a result of unending Cricut thoughts.

There are perpetual themed parties for children. Guardians love to praise their kid's birthday with topics like a Disney character outfit gathering or Pokémon party. You can, without much of a stretch, make some cash by making adornment bundles for such occasions. Print and cut out various stylistic themes, make modified IDs, or play cards the children can gather and exchange with each other even after the gathering.

Since scrapbooks are increasingly well-known each day, using the Cricut machine to kick the bucket cuts of scrapbook page formats will sell out to scrapbook lovers. As enthusiastic as you are with scrapbooking, you will have huge amounts of plans and thoughts.

Inside decorators can likewise procure your administrations on the off chance that you present them with your altered home designing activities. Your divider decals can be of any structure, craftsmanship word, animation character, or images that you made using Design Space and vinyl sheets.

With your perpetual Cricut thoughts, you can use your aptitudes and experience to make additional money with Cricut programming and simultaneously advancing with enthusiasm and side interest making delightful artworks for everybody to appreciate for a long time.

If you are into scrapbooking by any means, you have certainly caught wind of Provo Craft's Cricut cutting machines. They are astonishing machines that remove a ton of work from huge amounts of activities, they don't require a PC to be used, and they are so instinctive and clear to adapt; even we can get them! If you've used one at any point, you most likely have perceived what amount of fun they can be, yet have you pondered how you could make cash doing what you adore?

Profiting from your energy is a fantasy of many; however, they might suspect it's excessively hard and surrender as a rule. In all reality, doing this isn't too troublesome! As far as possible is your creative mind and what you can make. Here are a few plans to kick you off with pondering how to profit with your side interest:

Beautify Themed Parties

Children love to host themed gatherings. Regardless of whether it's a Pokémon party, a Bakugan birthday party, a Disney character ensemble party, kids revere them. Without much of a stretch, you could make some cash by making adornment bundles for these sorts of occasions. Print and cut out a lot of various estimated designs, make altered IDs the children can stick on, even make playing a game of cards or character cards the children can gather and exchange with one another.

Custom Cards and Invitations

Who doesn't love a redid note to say "thanks" or "welcome"? It demonstrates that a ton of ideas and love have gone into them. If you love doing this, why not offer a portion of your manifestations to profit simultaneously? It is stunning what number of individuals might want to have a custom card or welcome made for their birthday celebrations, commemorations, parties, and extraordinary occasions. Regularly, your nearby expressions and specialties store will even put your creations in plain view and offer them to their clients. They normally take a cut; however, it spares you the hour of going out and discover individuals yourself.

CHAPTER 30:

More Ideas of Businesses You Can Start

With Cricut, the ideas for projects are so vast; you will be amazed at how much you can do. So, what are some ideas that could work for you? Here are a few that you can consider and some of the best project ideas for those who are stumped on where to begin:

Custom Shirts

Custom shirts are incredibly comfortable. The beauty of this is that you can use the Cricut fonts or system options, and from there, you can simply print it on. Personally, I like to use iron-on vinyl because it is easy to work with. Just take your image and upload it into Design Space. Then, go to the canvas and find the image you want. Once you have selected the image, click on the whitespace that will be cut—remember to get the insides, too. Make sure you choose a reduced image, not print from a cut image, and then place it on the canvas to the size of your liking. Put the iron-on vinyl shiny side down, turn it on, and then select iron-on from the menu. Choose to cut, and make sure you mirror the image. Once done, pull off the extra vinyl to remove the plastic between the letters. There you go! A simple shirt.

Vinyl Decals

Vinyl can also be used to make personalized items, such as water bottle decals. First, design the text—you can pretty much use whatever you want for this. From here, create a second box and make an initial or whatever design you want. Make sure that you resize this to fit the water bottle, as well.

From here, load your vinyl, and make sure that you use transfer tape on the vinyl itself once you cut it out. Finally, when you adhere the lettering to the bottle, go from the center and then push outwards, smoothing as you go. It takes a bit, but there you have it—pure water bottles that children will love! This is a beautiful, simple project for those of us who are not really that artistically inclined but want to get used to making Cricut items.

Printable Stickers

This is super simple and fun for parents and kids. The Explore Air 2 machine works best.

With this one, you should use the print-then-cut feature since it makes it much more comfortable. To begin, go to Design Space and download images of ice cream or whatever you want, or upload pictures of your own. You click on "New Project," and on the left side that says "Images," you can choose the ones you like and insert more of these on there.

From here, choose the image and flatten it since this will make it into one piece rather than just a separate file for each. Resize as needed to make sure that they fit where you are putting them.

You can copy/paste each element until you are done. Once ready, press "Save," and then choose this as a print, then cut the image. Click the big button at the bottom that says "Make It." Make sure everything is right, then press "Continue," and from there, you can load the sticker paper into the machine. Make sure to adjust this to the right setting, which for sticker paper is "Vinyl." Put the paper into there and load them in, and when ready, press the "Go" button—it will then cut the stickers as needed.

From there, take them out and decorate. You can use ice cream or whatever sticker image you want!

Personalized Pillows

Personalized pillows are another fun idea and are incredibly easy to make. To begin, you open up Design Space and choose "New Project." From here, select the icon at the bottom of the screen itself, choosing your font. Type the words you want, and drag the text as needed to make it bigger.

You can also upload images, too, if you want to create a large picture on the pillow itself.

From here, press the attach button for each box, so that they work together, and both are figured when centered, as well.

You then press the "Make It" button—and you must turn to mirror on, since this will, again, be on iron-on vinyl. Next, load the iron-on vinyl with the shiny side down, then press the "Continue" button, follow the prompts, and make sure it is not jammed in, either.

Let the machine work its magic with cutting, and from there; you can use the weeding tool to get the middle areas out.

Set your temperature on the EasyPress for the right settings, and then push it onto the material, ironing it on and letting it sit for 10–15 seconds. Let it cool, and then take the transfer sheet off.

There you have it! A simple pillow that works wonders for your crafting needs.

Cards

Finally, cards are a great project idea for Cricut makers. They are simple, and you can do the entire project with cardstock.

To make this, you first want to open up Design Space, and put your design in. If you like images of ice cream, then use that. If you want to make Christmas cards, you can do that, too. Basically, you can design whatever you want on this.

Now, you will add the text. You can choose the font that you want to use, and write out the message on the card, such as "Merry Christmas." At this point, instead of choosing to cut, you should select the right option—the "Make It" option. You do not have to mirror this but check that your design fits appropriately on the cardstock itself. When choosing material for writing, make sure you select "Cardstock."

From there, insert your cardstock into the machine, and then, when ready, you can press "Go," and the Cricut machine will design your card.

This may take a minute, but once it is done, you will have an excellent card in place. It is super easy to use.

Cricut cards are a great personalized way to express yourself, creating a one-of-a-kind, sentimental piece for you to gift to friends and family.

3D Puzzles

3D puzzles are made up of flat pieces that fit together to make a 3D object! Creating patterns for these that can be sold and assembled by your customers is a great way to capture your target market!

3D Wall Art

Art that pops off the wall to greet you as you enter a room is a great way to create a dynamic décor that keeps people talking. Marketing art that jumps out at your target market is a great way to make an impression with people who are looking to you to provide a unique focal point for their interior design.

Aprons

Cooking enthusiasts love to have an apron that speaks to who they are as chefs or bakers. Blank canvas aprons are very affordable and, with iron-on vinyl available on the market today, from printable vinyl to glittery iron-on, there is no design you can't create to capture those creative cooks!

Banners

Creating banners for booths, tables, small businesses, product displays, and parties is a great way to break into the custom products market; if that is something you're planning on doing. If you would like to create banners but aren't looking for the custom angle, you can create banners with basic exclamations like "Sale!" "Happy Birthday!" or "Surprise!" These are sure to be a seller for those in the market for party supplies.

Beanies

During the winter months, few things can bring the same warmth and comfort as a knit cap. With adorable designs ironed or emblazoned on them, people can bundle up without obscuring their quirks and personalities from the world! Beanies can be purchased in bulk or on a retail basis at a fairly reasonable cost, making them a great candidate for your merchandise.

Beer Steins

Occasionally in stores like Target or Dollar Tree, you will find very large, blank beer glasses or steins which are available for sale at a very low price. Adding a decal onto the side of one of these immediately turns it into "Witch's Brew," or a mug with a great design on the side! Get creative with projects like these, and you'll find that people will flock to your store for them. They make such great gifts!

CHAPTER 31:

Where to Sell Cricut Items

Approaching Local Markets

You can explore selling your products from "business to business." In this configuration, the volume of sales is of importance as the larger the production, the lower the production cost per item is. This is the most challenging balance to reach for a new Cricut-based business. The advantage of obtaining contractual work means you can negotiate to buy a large quantity from vendors. However, such "golden" opportunities are hard to find since such contracts are opened to competition. Yet, as a new start-up business, you can present your products specifically tailored for business customers. A custom work approach offers positive aspects as businesses always look for originality and good products. By creating such a relationship, your business is likely to become a point of reference for future other contacts, hence launching many opportunities for upselling. However, it is important to bear in mind that finding such a niche is hard as competition is very stiff!

Another approach to consider for selling your products is from "business to customer." In this model, though the volume of sales remains important, your objective is to present your products to retail customers willing to buy them. Creativity and imagination will be keys to your success, as well as what type of media and medium you want to work in (e.g., T-shirts, mugs). Equally important is a retail space you will need to choose to offer your items. Experiencing different locations and products is all part of the efforts of a new start-up business. Also, a custom work approach for local customers will present advantages since the startup costs are the lowest of all the different strategies described. However, as a new business in the field, starting can be difficult. Word of mouth can be your first step, as well as producing good products at an affordable price.

Selling Online

If you are adept at higher technical knowledge, you can generate great benefits by providing either quality custom work, bulk offering, or information network. It is advisable to concentrate your efforts on one approach to start with. If you choose, for example, a custom work approach, you increase the chances to find potential customers looking for your products as they turn to a search engine like Google to find what they are looking for. Websites like Amazon Handmade or Etsy provide a good platform to allow you to sell custom design services. Equally efficient is the launch of your site. This strategy is worth looking at. Selling online comes with advantages such as low startup costs and access to the global market with millions of potential customers. Furthermore, online custom prices tend to be lower than those on the local market. However, access to the global market means that competition is stiff, pushing products to be competitively priced. Selling online requires certain knowledge in logistics as far as shipping and packing your products are concerned, a cost factor that needs to be taken into consideration in your pricing.

Suppose the approach of bulk offering or volume sales is the one that you prefer. In that case, the advantages are similar to those discussed under "Approaching Local Markets," namely reducing the cost per unit produced. eBay and Amazon have become the largest platforms. On the other hand, if an online retail business approach is more what you may be inclined to do, this approach will allow you to determine the demand for the designs you offer and plan the production accordingly. But selling online means challenging the existing competition!

Finally, if you prefer to sell your products online through an information network, then you become an authority in the field, creating the opportunity to generate profit with your Cricut designs. By offering blogs on technical know-how or inspiration work, you become selective on the posts you want to take on.

Starting a new business requires foremost a business strategy, the foundation for your future success. Asking yourself questions such as who your potential customers would be, what kind of products you can sell them, and how are the first steps of a future startup business.

Tips and Tricks to Know When You Want to Sell Your Own Creations

Personalized gifts are among the most well-known styles on Pinterest, and you can create incredible presents to market along with your Cricut machine (Cricut Joy, Cricut Explore Air 2, Cricut Maker). Now we have got a listing of amazing projects to get your creative juices flowing so that you may begin earning cash with Cricut!

Can You Market Cricut Layouts?

Yes! The Cricut Angel Policy permits you to sell around 10,000 layouts annually with discounts created with Provo Craft solutions. There's definitely room for you to increase your company and sell layouts made using Cricut products. Just be certain that you read over the total Angel Policy to make certain you are working inside.

What Are the Most Lucrative Cricut Companies?

The most rewarding Cricut companies are people who provide unique products that clients wish to purchase. Why waste your time creating products that nobody is considering? Rather spend your time exploring your competitors. Learn what other crafting organizations are doing well and where they're making errors. This could enable you to locate a space in your marketplace so you can create things with lesser competition.

Could I Sell Cricut Pictures on Etsy?

Yes! Don't forget to check out the Angel Policy. You can sell items using non-licensed images in the Cricut library, or you could design your graphics using Illustrator or Photoshop. You can't sell accredited pictures... Disney, Marvel Comics, etc.... These pictures are very popular, and you'll see Etsy stores selling these kinds of pictures, but these stores can be closed down or perhaps sued for selling accredited pictures.

What Can I Create to Market Using a Cricut Maker?

First, let us consider the audience that you would like to function. You can create and market your Cricut designs to folks who wish to DIY their particular crafts or you can even create crafts to make and sell on Etsy, at craft fairs, and stalls.

If you choose to sell your designs, it might be useful to know how to create SVG documents and use illustrator or photoshop. This may develop into a passive revenue choice, as you could set the files on the internet, and people could immediately download them.

Making craft jobs to market is your next alternative. You can use online tutorials to make your crafts. To stick out from your opponent's, you'll have to make exceptional items. This may mean using special materials, layouts, or markets.

You will find endless crafts to produce and sell using a Cricut machine. Do you know you could #monogram everything? (at least at the south). Intelligent quotations, educator gifts, and even infant items can allow you to get your plastic company started. You are going to be earning money with Cricut shortly with those Cricut inspirations!

Private Use vs. Industrial Use

If you'd like additional pictures, you can get them from online stores. Don't just download pictures from Google and use them to create products—you'll nearly definitely be violating copyright.

If you purchase from online vendors, make certain to read the conditions of usage of their cut file! Most pictures you could buy include only a personal use license. You can't make items to market with documents that are only for private use.

You might have the choice to buy a commercial license. Some documents may come using a commercial permit. Again, read the conditions!

Licensed Pictures

You might find pictures of characters that are licensed (such as Elsa of the Frozen or Iron Man from Marvel) on Etsy and at other stores. All these are usually breaking copyright, and also, you can get in trouble for using them. My advice? Stay away from accredited fonts and images!

And again, you cannot use accredited pictures from Cricut Design Space to market, though it's possible to use non-licensed pictures per their Angel Policy.

Beginning a Cricut Craft Business

Alright, now that we have obtained those legal details out of the way, let us discuss the way to really make money with your Cricut!

Narrow Your Own Cricut Craft Niche

Among the worst things you can do is choose to simply make whatever folks ask you to create. A tumbler here, a house decor hint there, birthday T-shirts then. You are going to wind up with lower margins, wasted merchandise, along a confused crowd.

Rather, narrow your product down to 1–2 things or topics and then nail it. I suggest choosing something in the junction of everything you love to create and what's rewarding. That you wish to appreciate what you are creating—and you would like it to be worth your time.

When you are trying to decide what items to create and market along with your Cricut, think about "added value," this may include both enhancements to a product or actually niching down. This way you may charge a premium for your goods.

A lot of people are making homemade hints; for example—possibly your "item" is adding paper succulents or hand-painted glitter accents. Perhaps you hand the letter and flip your decoration into stickers for tops.

If you are making tumblers, perhaps they're specifically targeted to teachers and have a gift cardholder. Perhaps your onesie store is filled with cute things, especially for preemies.

If you are among the only people doing something, you are able to charge more! It also makes it much easier to target your advertisements.

Note: The bigger the item, the more difficult and costlier it is going to be to ship. You might choose to save those massive home decor hints for your regional craft fair.

Purchase Materials in Bulk

If you have nailed down your market, you can purchase your materials and supplies in bulk. You can obtain more tumblers or eyeglasses, or vinyl at a more affordable price if you purchase in bulk. If you are still making "one-off" items, it is far more difficult to keep them in bulk.

If you are making holiday T-shirts, as an example, rather than purchasing routine rolls of iron vinyl in a craft shop, you can purchase in bulk to lower prices.

CHAPTER 32:

Where to Find Materials

One of Cricut Design Space's exciting parts is that the materials are not hard to find; they are all around you. There are online stores where you can easily get the materials you want. Although different e-stores have varying prices, the point is to get the ideal quality.

There are 4 popular online stores where Cricut machine users—both beginners and professionals—get materials for their Cricut projects, and they are Cricut.com, Amazon, Joann, and Michaels. These stores provide almost every supply and bundle you will be needing. They have the materials, tools, and accessories, and even the Cricut machines needed. Feel free to visit each store and compare their prices before purchasing.

Also, you can look around for stores in your local area where they sell the most common types of materials that can be used on Cricut machines, mostly paper products.

At this stage, we have been able to cover most of the basics of Cricut machines, materials, tools, and accessories. You should now know their functionalities and purposes to some extent.

PART 7:

CRICUT PROJECTS

CHAPTER 33:

Cricut Projects to Start With

Planner Stickers

Supplies

- Cricut printable sticker paper
- Cricut Explore Air machine or Cricut Maker
- Cricut standard cutting mat grip
- Printer with ink

Instructions

1. Choose the sticker designs. You can choose from the Design Space shop or upload your own.
2. Start by opening the Design Space program and click on the "Image" option. Then, head to the search function and locate the planner stickers. Locate which one you want to use.
3. Place the choices on the canvas and arrange them in the order that you would like them to be.Click the "Make It" option. Design Space will direct you to begin printing the image. Follow the directions to print the images.

Glass Etched Watercolor Wall Art

Supplies

- Glass and frame
- Stewart Glass Etching Cream
- Painter's tape
- Vinyl cut out with positive space removed

Instructions

1. Use the Cricut Explore Air 2 to cut vinyl. Then use the vinyl and glass painter's tape.
2. Use the Etching Cream and add the vinyl letters directly to the glass.
3. Allow the cream for 15 minutes to sit on the glass. Then use a tool for removing the cream tool. You can put the cream in the bottle or discard it again.
4. Wash off the cream and remove the vinyl fully with a damp cloth.
5. Remove the etched lettering and reveal it.
6. Now cut the frame's size of a piece of aquarelle paper. Add water loads and color touches.
7. Let the aquarelle dry and put it in the etching frame.
8. Enjoy your hang-up!

"Bed and Breakfast" Guest Room Wood Sign

Supplies

- Vinyl
- Electronic cutting machine
- FolkArt Color Shift acrylic paint (aqua flash)
- Painted panels
- Paintbrush

Instructions

1. Click right to save and use the PNG in any cutting software you have.
2. Don't be afraid if you have no cutter. Just print it out, use carbon paper and paint it manually to transfer it to the wood.
3. For the sake of vinyl, I used the electronic cutting machine.
4. Vinyl is used as a stencil, and therefore, the color does not matter.
5. You will weed out the positive space instead of weeding out the negative space.
6. Paint all the pieces you want.
7. When finished, rub it on top and remove the vinyl back.
8. Rub it with the squeegee.
9. Put the wood mark on it and rub the squeegee gently, then take out the transfer ribbon.

10. The paintbrush could get too close to the edges of the wood's surface.
11. The acrylic paint of FolkArt Color Shift is very fun.
12. Squeeze out some on a palette or just peel off a little of the vinyl backrest.
13. Tap onto the paint and dab on a palette of the stencil brush.
14. You don't want a paintbrush loaded or underneath the vinyl stencil to seep it.
15. Take the whole positive space up and down.
16. The FolkArt Color Shift acrylic paint has a certain texture when applied, and a second cover is needed.
17. Allow the paint to dry then.
18. This is a questionable point. Some people like to wet paint and stencils but, honestly, it just requires wet paint to be scrubbed everywhere! Let it dry.
19. Then in a corner, peel the vinyl. Peel it back over the top, just as it rolls over it.

Fast Easter Bunny Nail Art

Supplies

- Nail clean
- Quick-dry top coat—I incline toward Out the Door snappy dry top coat
- Cricut machine
- Free Easter icons SVG cut record
- Gold cement foil

Instructions

1. Paint your nails any way you'd like. I made an ombre look.
2. Upload the Easter icons SVG to Cricut Design Space. Conceal all the icons aside from the rabbit body. Resize the rabbit picture to 0.25 inches wide. Cut the picture using the vinyl setting and gold glue foil.
3. Apply the rabbit cut out to your dry, painted nails.
4. Apply 2–3 layers of top coat to your nail, allowing it to dry between applications.

Printable Easter Egg Garland

You can do this project either with a cutting machine or without. You can likewise set the project up to include a pretty draw line on the off chance that you have a Cricut Explore or a Cricut Air. This is an extraordinary tool to have the option to make a ton of these cute little paper Easter eggs before long!

Supplies

- String
- Hole punch
- White card stock
- Cutting machine or scissor

Instructions

1. Go to Design Space.
2. Upload the PNG record. Pick "Fundamental Upload" and afterward select "Complex Image." You shouldn't have to alter anything.
3. Upload the draw SVG record. Pick "Vector Upload."
4. Once the 2 records are uploaded to your structure library, you can choose them and add them to your Design Space configuration screen.

5. Make sure the drawing layer is the topmost layer and pick "Compose." Join the 2 layers together. You should have the option to build the size of the pictures to pretty much 7 inches vertically for the Print-Then-Cut page size cutoff points.

6. Follow the on-screen directions to print, draw, and cut the art design.

7. Use the gap punch to make an opening at the highest point of each egg. String together any way you'd like. Tie a little bunch at the highest point of each egg so they would lay level when you hang the laurel.

Plastic Spoon Chicks for Easter

Supplies

- 5 plastic spoons
- 5 earthenware pots
- Fine coarseness sandpaper
- Pencil with a new eraser
- Floral froth
- Cardstock
- White strip
- White tissue paper
- Hot stick weapon
- White create stick

Craftsman paint:

- Buttercream, like DecoArt's Buttercream
- Pink, like Pink Chiffon
- Grape taffy
- Pool blue, marginally lighter in shading pale blue
- Spearmint, comparative DecoArt's Leprechaun
- Orange
- Black
- White

Instructions

1. Delicately sand the sparkle of the spoons, dust them off and paint them.
2. Use a square of botanical froth to hold them while they dry.
3. Include white polka dabs up the handles.
4. Paint earthenware pots white and paint the edges with the hued paint. Include coordinating polka specks.
5. Cut flower froth into little squares and paste them inside the pots. Include the bills and the eyes.
6. Cut bits of card stock for the informal IDs. Compose names on and include the "hands" utilizing your finger plunged in the paint.
7. Addition the spoon chicks into the botanical froth. Tie lace into bows and paste to the neck.
8. Load up with tissue paper and paste on the informal IDs.

DIY "Thank You" Card with Gift Card Holder

Supplies

- Cricut machine and Cricut Design Space
- "'Thank you' card with gift voucher holder" Cricut Design Space project canvas
- White cardstock
- Multiple shaded Cricut pens
- Glue
- Gift card of your decision

Instructions

1. This card accompanies a coordinating envelope that you can discover in the project canvas. I've just made the card to exhibit this project.
2. Go to the Cricut Design Space project canvas and adhere to on-screen guidelines to draw and cut the card.
3. Fold along the score lines and paste the gift voucher pocket set up.
4. Write a little note and give your blessing.

Easy DIY Flower Art Napkin Ring

Supplies

- Cricut Explore machine
- Cricut Design Space
- "Garden Birthday Day Party" cut and draw plans
- 12 by 12 inches Standard Grip Cricut tangle
- Cardstock
- Cricut pens
- Glue

Instructions

1. Follow on-screen the directions to draw and cut napkin ring segments.
2. Layer every napkin ring part and paste set up.
3. Wrap the ring and paste close together.

DIY Fancy Heart Card

Supplies

- Cricut Explore machine
- Cricut Design Space
- "Doodle heart and card set" cut structures
- 12 by 12 inches Standard Grip Cricut tangle
- White cardstock - Bright pink vellum
- Gold and silver adhesive foil
- Black Cricut pen
- Glue or double-sided tape

Instructions

1. Follow on-screen guidelines to print, draw, and cut card parts.
2. Layer different front of card segments and paste set up. Take care not to apply the sticker on the edges of the vellum, or you will see the paste. Apply foil accents within the outline.
3. Assemble envelope: Overlay along all score lines. Crease inside pink vellum along the score line. Stick vellum to within envelope utilizing double-sided tape. Along all score lines and sticking side folds set up. Write a note. Include confetti hearts inside the card and seal.
4. **Tip:** Use double-sided tape with the foil and vellum to abstain from seeing paste lines through the vellum.

CHAPTER 34:

Cricut Projects to Practice

Paper Projects

DIY Lunch Notes

DIY printable lunch notes are very useful in every way possible. For one, they are cute stick-on notes you can add to your children's lunch packs and use them as symbols of your unwavering love and support as a parent, even as your child ventures into the real world of school every day. On the other hand, creating these can also be a great way to engage your children's minds because you can get them aboard the design process and have them help you as you craft these wonders, which they would most likely fall in love with once you are done.

This is a very fun and handy back-to-school craft you can work on all year long.

Supplies

- Design space account

- Your Cricut machine
- Any other thing you figure you can make use of

Instructions

1. On the pad where you can start out a new project, cut your design as you follow the on-screen instructions and observe the pen color changes.
2. When you are satisfied with the design you have created, embellish your work by adding effects that make it more breathtaking. Pay attention to your color schemes, and make sure that you use fonts your child can interact with easily. Remember, it is all about them, so the more you stick to bold and more legible fonts, the better it will be for everyone involved.

You can create this project as a single piece with print-then-cut images, or you can create this project as multiple pieces of interconnected layers of designs, which you can group and send over to the machine for cutting.

Framed Paper Succulents

Don't get carried away by the name; you are not about to put a piece of lettuce into your favorite Cricut cutter. So, you can let go of your breath and find out how to create this.

First things first, this project is all about making use of a piece of strong paper to cover up and design frames for flowers. With this knowledge, you can design just about any kind of frame to hold anything. The options are endless, and the designs you can come up with are too much to be limited. Also, this is pretty much easy to be made.

Supplies

- Cricut machine.
- Standard grip cutting mat
- 12 by 12 inches cardstock or a piece of chipboard to fit into the frame you are looking to design
- Scissors for cutting the petals of the flowers you are looking to frame

Instructions

1. First things first, assemble all the things you would need for your project and begin by painting the frame you would use.

2. Make use of some sandpaper to make sure that the frame is as fine as it can get.

3. Cut the cardboard paper, chipboard, or whatever kind of thick paper you are making use of to fit into the inside of your frame. This is where you will glue your succulents. Use the glue to hold the paper in place.

4. Work on the design you want to print out using the device that is connected to the internet. When you are done, allow the machine to cut it and assemble all the pieces when they are cut.

5. Glue the succulents you have created to the inside of the frame, which you covered with cardboard or chipboard. Start with the large succulents first, and gently move on to the smaller ones.

6. Feel free to decide where you want your new beautiful piece to be hanging when you are done. Don't you want the whole world to see what you have been up to?

Vinyl Projects

Customized Vinyl Mugs

These projects allow you to make use of some reasonable amount of vinyl to customize mugs and other kitchen utensils in a bid to make them look better. There are a lot of customization options here, but the idea is for you to allow your imagination and creativity to roam free so that you can create as much magic as you possibly can.

Supplies

- The Cricut Explore machine.
- The design space app and access to it.

Instructions

1. To create these easy vinyl designs on your mugs, simply select the designs you want to create off the design space. If you cannot find what you seek in that space, you can upload an image from your storage devices or get something off the internet.

2. When the image is uploaded, apply all the effects needed from the design space canvas to create super effects just as you love them.
3. In the end, cut these designs and apply them to your mugs.

When using Cricut vinyl on mugs, it is best to handwash them in soapy water before you start making use of the mugs again. This way, you take off everything that should not be in your body system, making sure that you do not put yourself at risk. Get creative with your designs, but make sure that you keep them well organized. Here are some mugs that have been customized using this project.

Customized Vinyl Bowls

These are almost the same as what has been stated in the project above. The only difference is the object that is being customized, and maybe the designs that the artist is creating on their bowl.

Supplies

- Bowls that you are looking to customize
- Designs you want to print on them uploaded into the Design Space

Instructions

1. Follow through the processes outlined above to create your customized bowl.

Cricut Personalized Soap Bottles

Sometimes, you may have so many soap bottles containing different soaps for different occasions that you may get confused as to which is which. To make sure that you do not misplace your soaps or use them for all the wrong reasons, why don't you start by labeling and customizing the bottles?

Supplies

- Vinyl

Instructions

1. Follow through the processes outlined above to create your soap bottles.

As usual, there is no one-size-fits-all approach to this. All you need is to think out of the box.

Others you can give a trial include "5 minutes Citrus coasters," "Oogie boogie treat bags," "DIY mummy and me utensils," etc.

Fabric Projects

Fabric Bookmarks

This project is perfect for children and beginners because it is easy to be created, and doesn't really take up a lot of time. First off, bookmarks are material strips used to mark a place in a book, meaning that the reader still has some sort of business with that page. Sometimes, these do not come with the book, as the owner or the one who is reading can choose to add them themself.

Supplies

- Cricut cutting machine
- Cricut mat
- Cardboard
- 7.5 by 2.5 inches fabric (you can choose to use 1–2 different colors, depends on what you are looking to achieve)

Instructions

1. Cut the fabrics to size. Copy the bookmarks on the design space and fit in as many as you can/want on your cutting mat.
2. Cut the cardboard you are making use of. If you wouldn't be making use of cardboard, interfacing will also be a good option for you to exploit. Depending on how stiff you want the bookmark to feel, you can use stronger interfacing or cardboard.

3. Attach the fabric pieces you have, with the long sides facing themselves. With your sewing machine or hand stitcher, sew the 2 long sides and the bottom together.
4. You have a bookmark casing now. With a little material like a pencil or a really long pin, fold the bookmark right side out.
5. Insert the interfacing you have created into the bookmark that you just folded the right way out now.
6. Fold the top of the bookmark that is still open down, and sew it closed.
7. Iron the bookmark so that it becomes flat and can slide easily through the pages of your book.

2-Minute Felt Masks

Felt masks are sheer, most times colorful masks that are worn to cover just the eyes and a bit above the nose. People can wear these for fun, or an occasion like Halloween, or some kind of party. The great thing about this project is that it is easy to embark upon that even as a newbie, you should have moved the project from fabric to a complete mask in under 30 minutes or a bit above if you are really not good at the Cricut at all.

Supplies

- Cricut cutting machine
- Standard Grip mat
- 0.5 yards of elastic material
- Felt
- Stapler
- Elmer's glue

Instructions

1. Get a picture of the felt mask you would love to create from the Design Space. If you can't seem to find it in that space, you may download it from another place and upload it to your Design Space.
2. Resize your mask to be between 6 by 6.5 inches.

3. Put the felt on your mat and your machine's rotary blade in the B clamp.
4. Select the fabric you want to cut in the Design Space cut menu (felt, in this case).
5. Cut your masks.
6. With the stapler you have, attach the elastics to the masks you have cut out. Use glue to cover the backsides of the staple pins.

Cricut Design Space for Beginners

What Is the Cricut Design Space?

The Cricut design space is the web-based program considered to be the backbone of the Cricut machine. You get to access the thousands of predefined projects (templates) that you can customize to create your personalized designs or start creating yours from scratch on this application. This platform holds about 75,000 images, more than 800 predesigned templates, and about 400 fonts, giving you a vast array of options to choose from when it comes to creating your projects or customizing any of the pre-created projects you will come across on the platform. In a nutshell, the Cricut design space is simply where the magic of designing happens, and access to this platform is the reason why you need to sign up with an internet-connected device in the first place. You can do other things in this space, including uploading your JPEG and SVG images, customizing your fonts to suit your needs, and generally unleash the creative genius in you.

Which Cricut Machines Are Compatible with Design Space?

All the motorized cutting machines they have on the market are compatible. It includes the Cricut Explore, Cricut Explore Air, Cricut Explore Air 2, and the Cricut Maker. With the current version of Design Space, you can use all of these tools to build countless projects for each style.

How Does the Design Space Work?

It is not just enough to know that the CDS is an important tool; you must know how it works. Navigating your way through the CDS can be a bit overwhelming, especially if you are new to the use of this space and the Cricut. This is because of the many functionalities that are found in it. If you are not trained to make use of these functionalities and to know what each of them stands for, you may not be able to make use of the platform and you will see that you will be at a loss for what to do every time you are about to create your designs or launch a project. We will take a deep dive into the CDS and help you better understand what it is all about and how you can find your way around it. When you log into your design space, you will be taken to the application's home screen.

On the home screen, you will see a lot of thumbnail pictures. These are templates that you can customize to create your projects, and as a beginner, you may want to start by trying out this step. It may be a bit difficult to start creating your designs from scratch, so the best move sometimes may be to start out by customizing a template to suit your needs. You can, however, start a new project if you feel that you have what it takes to do so immediately.

This is what the Design Space Home Screen and the working Canvas look like, respectively.

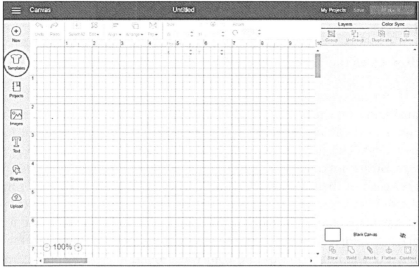

CHAPTER 35:

Easy Projects

Clear Personalized Labels

Supplies

- Cricut clear sticker paper
- High-gloss printer paper for the Inkjet printer
- Inkjet printer (check the ink cartridges)
- Spatula tool

Instructions

1. Create a new project in Design Space.
2. Choose the heart shape from the left-hand side in the "Shapes" menu.
3. Select an image from the "Images" menu on the left-hand side menu.
4. Choose a picture of a flower or search for "M55E."
5. Unlock the flower image, position it in the top-left corner of the heart. Make sure it fits without any overhang.

6. Select the heart and the flower, then click on "Weld" from the bottom-right-hand menu. This ensures that the label is printed together as a unit and not in layers.

7. Select the heart and flowers once again. Then click on "Flatten" to ensure that only the outline shape of the heart is cut out.

8. Choose "Text" from the left-hand menu. Choose a font, and type the text for your label. You can choose a color for your text.

9. Unlock and move the text into position in the middle of the label.

10. Adjust the size to fit comfortably.

11. Select the heart shape and the font. Then click on "Flatten" to ensure the label is cut as a whole and not layered.

12. In order not to waste sticker paper, you should print as many labels per sheet as you can.

13. Choose the square shape from the "Shapes" menu.

14. Position it on the screen, unlock the shape, and set the measurements to a width of 6 inches and a height of 9 inches.

15. Move the first label into place at the top-left-hand corner of the screen.

16. Select the label and click on "Duplicate."

17. Move the second label next to the first one. Give the labels a bit of room between each other and the edges.

18. Fit as many as you can on the sheet, then save your work.

19. Fill in each of the labels with the text you want.

20. If you have space left over when your labels are positioned, you can create smaller ones.

21. You can actually create all different sizes of labels, patterns, and designs.

22. Make sure that all the labels are for print and are flattened.

23. Delete the background rectangle.

24. Select all the labels, and click "Attach" from the bottom-right-hand menu.

25. Click "Make It," and check that the design and wording are correct before clicking "Continue."

26. Choose the high-gloss paper option, and set it to the best quality.

27. Load the sticker paper into the Inkjet printer, and press "Send" to print.

28. Choose "Sticker Paper" for the Cricut materials.

29. Load the sticker paper into the Cricut, and press "Go" when it is ready to cut.
30. The Cricut will cut out the stickers, so you can peel them off the backing sheet as and when you need them.

Custom Coasters

Supplies

- Free pattern templates
- Monogram design (in Design Space)
- Cardstock or printing paper
- Butcher paper
- Lint-free towel
- Round coaster blanks
- LightGrip mat
- EasyPress (6 by 7 inches recommended)
- EasyPress mat
- Infusible Ink pens
- Heat resistant tape
- Cricut BrightPad (optional for easier tracing)

Instructions

1. In Cricut Design Space, open the monogram design. You can click "Customize," and choose the designs that you want to cut out. Otherwise, just go ahead and cut out all the letters.
2. Click on "Make It."
3. On the page displayed, click on "Mirror Image" to make the image mirrored. This must be done whenever you are using infusible ink. For your material, choose "Cardstock." Then, place your cardstock on the mat, and load it into the machine. Press the "Cut" button on the Cricut machine.

4. After the Cricut machine is done cutting, unload it and remove the done monograms from the mat.
5. Trace the designs onto the cut-out. If you have a Cricut BrightPad, you can use it to carry out this step much more easily, as it will make the trace lines easier to identify. Tracing should be done using Cricut Infusible Ink Pens. Use the lint-free towel to wipe the coaster. Ensure that no residue is left behind to prevent any marks from being left on the blank.
6. Make the design centered on the coaster, face down.
7. Get a piece of butcher paper, which is about 1 inch larger on each side of the coaster, and place it on top of the design.
8. Tape this butcher paper onto the coaster, using heat-resistant tape to hold the design fast.
9. Set the temperature of your EasyPress to 00 degrees and set the timer to 0 seconds.
10. Place another butcher paper piece on your EasyPress mat, set the coaster on top of it, face up.
11. Place another piece of butcher paper on top of these. Place the preheated EasyPress on top of the coaster, and start the timer.
12. Lightly hold the EasyPress in place (without moving, or leave it in place right on the coaster if on a perfectly flat surface) until the timer goes off.
13. After this is done, gently remove the EasyPress, then turn it off.
14. The coaster will be very hot, so you should leave it to get cool before you touch it. When it is cool, you can peel the design off of it.

Tassels

Supplies

- 4 by 8 inches fabric rectangles
- Fabric mat
- Glue gun

Instructions

1. Open Cricut Design Space, and create a new project.
2. Select the "Image" button in the lower left-hand corner, and search "Tassel."
3. Select the image of a rectangle with lines on each side, and click "Insert."
4. Place the fabric on the cutting mat.
5. Send the design to the Cricut.
6. Remove the fabric from the mat, saving the extra square.
7. Place the fabric face down, and begin rolling tightly, starting at the uncut side. Untangle the fringe as needed.
8. Use some of the scrap fabric and a hot glue gun to secure the tassel at the top.
9. Decorate whatever you want with your new tassels!

Monogrammed Drawstring Bag

Supplies

- 2 matching rectangles of fabric
- Needle and thread
- Ribbon
- Heat-transfer vinyl
- Cricut EasyPress or iron
- Cutting mat
- Weeding tool or pick

Instructions

1. Open Cricut Design Space, and create a new project.
2. Select the "Image" button in the lower left-hand corner, and search "Monogram."
3. Select the monogram of your choice and click "Insert."
4. Place the iron-on material shiny liner side down on the cutting mat.
5. Send the design to the Cricut.
6. Use the weeding tool or pick, to remove excess material.
7. Remove the monogram from the mat.
8. Center the monogram on your fabric, then move it a couple of inches down to not be folded up when the ribbon is drawn.
9. Iron the design onto the fabric.
10. Place the 2 rectangles together, with the outer side of the fabric facing inward.

11. Sew around the edges, leaving a seam allowance. Leave the top open, and stop a couple of inches down from the top.
12. Fold the top of the bag down until you reach your stitches.
13. Sew along the bottom of the folded edge, leaving the sides open.
14. Turn the bag, right side out.
15. Thread the ribbon through the loop around the top of the bag.
16. Use your new drawstring bag to carry what you need!

Paw Print Socks

Supplies

- Socks
- Heat-transfer vinyl
- Cutting mat
- Scrap cardboard
- Weeding tool or pick
- Cricut EasyPress or iron

Instructions

1. Open Cricut Design Space, and create a new project.
2. Select the "Image" button in the lower left-hand corner and search "Paw Prints."
3. Select the paw prints of your choice and click "Insert."
4. Place the iron-on material on the mat.
5. Send the design to the Cricut.
6. Use the weeding tool or pick, to remove excess material.
7. Remove the material from the mat.
8. Fit the scrap cardboard inside of the socks.
9. Place the iron-on material on the bottom of the socks.
10. Use the EasyPress to adhere it to the iron-on material.
11. After cooling, remove the cardboard from the socks.
12. Wear your cute paw print socks!

Customized Coffee Cups

Supplies

- Adhesive vinyl, permanent
- Cups, any type would work; you can buy reusable cups in bulk and get some in Starbucks cups' size.
- Transfer tape
- Weeding tool
- Cricut machine

Instructions

1. Find and download, then upload SVG files for Starbucks-style cups or make your own to fit the Starbucks aesthetic.
2. You can also make your own by using shapes and designing tools in the Design Space. Make sure to measure the cups so that the personalized logo you are making is proportional to the size of the cup you are planning to customize. You can use shapes and letters with editing tools to make your designs. Letters can be rotated to fit the shape of the circle design, and you can use any font you like, write names, or funny and witty statements. Make sure to set the line type for designs to "Cut." Once you are ready with editing and/or designing, you can click on "Make It" to proceed to cut. Specify "Vinyl" as your material of choice when adjusting settings for cutting.
3. It's time for weeding. Take your weeding tool and remove the parts of vinyl that you don't need in your design. Attach the

transfer tape to the vinyl, and size the transfer tape to fit the size of the design you will use on the cup. Apply the vinyl with transfer tape on the cup and smooth the tape out to remove the bubbles. You can use a spatula for that, but your fingers would also do the work. Remove the transfer tape, and your customized cup is good to go!

Glasswork and Glass Etching

Supplies

- Vinyl
- Stencil
- Transfer tape
- Glassware of your choice
- Etching cream
- Spatula
- Weeding tool
- Painting brush

Instructions

1. Upload SVG files with shapes and silhouettes you want to use for your glassware or find some designs you like in the library of images you have in the Design Space. You will need to resize or size the pieces to fit your glassware size and the part of the glassware you want to apply the vinyl to. Once the shapes are done and sized, you will need to set the line type to "Cut" and choose "Vinyl" as your chosen material after clicking on "Make It." Load the machine and fixate the vinyl piece before cutting.

2. Once the design is cut out and ready, you will need to weed excess parts with the weeding tool. Weed out the positive part

of your design—the inside of the design, so you are left with a pattern and a substantial amount of vinyl around the shape. Next, you will apply the transfer tape on the piece of vinyl with the design pattern. Apply the tape with the vinyl on the glassware and smooth it out across the surface. Remove the transfer tape from the glassware.

3. Use the etching gel by applying it over the cutout part of the design, and don't be afraid to use more etching glue as you want it to stick there. You will remove the excess gel later with a spatula. Before removing extra gel, you need to let the etching gel sit for at least 20 minutes. Once the gel has settled, use the spatula to remove most of the gel. You don't need to throw your gel as you can reuse it—return it to the container, and it will be good to use on more projects. After removing extra gel, remove the remaining gel by washing it with soap and warm water. Peel off the vinyl, then give it another go with soap and warm water. Let the glassware dry, and you have a masterpiece ready to be displayed and used.

Marbled Journal and Vinyl Art

Supplies

- Gold foil vinyl
- Marble paint—several colors of your choice
- White paint
- Transfer paint
- Disposable foil pan—to fit the notebook
- Kraft paper notebook
- Weeding tool
- Cricut machine

Instructions

1. For the first step, you will leave the Design Space waiting as you are going to prepare the notebook and complete marbling first. Combining multiple crafting techniques is essential to becoming an advanced crafter, which is how you will make great use of this project. In case the cover of the notebook you are going to use for the project has a logo or images on it, use a layer of white paint to cover it up before marbling the cover with paint. Let the white paint layer dry for a while as you are preparing the foil pan and marble paint. Fill up the foil pan with water, then add the colors—only a drip or 2 of each color would be enough. Pour the paint drips in the center of the foil pan filled with water. Prepare the paper towels and sink the cover of the notebook into the foil pain. Hold it for a couple of seconds until

the cover gets all the colors on, then place the paper towel between the cover and paper to prevent the water drops from reaching the paper inside the notebook.

2. Let the marble paint on the cover dry as you start the Design Space and prepare vinyl for cutting.

3. Start a new project in the Design Space and upload the SVG file for letters and patterns you want to use on your notebook cover. You can also create your design by using shapes, images, and letters available in the Design Space. Change the line type to "Cut" once your design is ready. Set "Vinyl" as your material of choice after you click on "Make It." Send the design to cutting after loading your machine with gold foil vinyl. Use the weeding tool for removing the negative part of the vinyl design—the background. Peel off the bigger parts of the vinyl and scrape the rest with your weeding tool's help. Apply the transfer tape to the vinyl design—make sure to size the transfer tape to fit the vinyl design. Apply the transfer tape with vinyl on the cover of the notebook. Smooth out the tape to remove any bubbles, then remove the tape. You have just made your planner or an amazing gift for someone.

Candle Lantern

Supplies

- Cricut metallic poster board

- Cricut chipboard

- Hot glue

- Candle—you can use a small lamp as an alternative

- Cricut machine

Instructions

1. You need to download and upload the SVG project file for Cricut Design Space or make your latticework in the canvas (for the latticework) and frames for the lantern that would be made of chipboard. Start a new project and upload your SVG pattern, or start making your own.
2. You only need to make 1 and cut it 8 times as you will need 8 pieces of the frame cut out of the chipboard. The cutting will take some time as you need to make 20 passes for each piece. It may even take 1 hour until you cut them all out and prepare them for latticework.
3. When the frames are all cut out, and there are 8 pieces, you will start making patterns for latticework or find SVG patterns online or in the library of images in the Design Space. Make sure that the width and length of the lattice piece fit the size of frames

so that you don't need to manually recut the latticework before attaching the lattice to frames.

4. You can also make the design tighter and play with shapes and lines to create your patterns. Once you are done with the canvas latticework, set up the material preferences to "Cricut Metallic Poster Board" under "Make It" and load the machine with the specified material. The lattice should be cut with a fine-point blade, while the chipboard should be cut with the knife blade—make sure to always check which blade fits the type of material you are using. Also, make sure to calibrate your blades when using them for the first time.

5. It's time to glue and assemble all parts. So, you should have 4 equal lattice pieces—1 lattice piece for 2 frames. First, add some glue inside the frame and over the edges. Attach the latticework and make sure it fits the frame. Add glue to another frame, then assemble the piece with a lattice to the second frame. Repeat that for the remaining 3 sets of frames and lattice pieces. Glue the 4 pieces together to form a box, and you have a wonderful piece of decorative art for your home or as a gift to someone.

Wall Décor

Supplies

- Vinyl in different colors—you might need a large supply of vinyl, depending on the surface you are decorating
- Weeding tool
- Scraper for pressing
- Cricut machine

Instructions

1. Start a new project in the Design Space and prepare your material. You need to start making your decoration designs by using lines and shapes, or you can browse through endless options in the image library. Alternatively, you can look for free patterns and designs intended for wall art online and upload these designs to the Design Space. Make sure to try out multicolor loading and cutting in case you are using the same designs in different colors. Return to the section with tips for advanced crafters in case you need a reminder on how to do multicolor cuts to cut the time needed for loading and unloading your machine. You can always play with lines to create your shapes and wall art.

2. You can do some antlers wall art for the living room if you like. The design for antlers would look like so, and won't take much to find and upload or make yourself in the canvas.
3. Alternatively, you can work with diamond "sprinkles" as your wall art is made of vinyl.
4. Once you pick your design, upload it or make it by yourself, you can load your machine and click on "Make It" in the Design Space. Specify your material as "Vinyl" then proceed to cut.
5. Decide where you want your wall art to be, on which part of the wall and in which room, as well as the size of the surface you want to cover with wall art. In case you are doing "sprinkles" with diamonds or other shapes, you can scatter the elements across the wall to make an interesting decoration. In the meantime, there is a lot of weeding to do, so get your tool and start weeding the excess vinyl. Once all excess parts of the design are removed, you can start applying your art to the wall.
6. Use a scraper to smooth out the vinyl and get rid of any bubbles. Make sure to plan out where you want the design before applying it to the wall. The vinyl wall art can be later removed by peeling it off the wall so you can change your wall décor whenever you like.

Cricut Puzzle

Supplies

- Cricut chipboard
- Printable sticker paper
- Masking tape
- Cricut machine
- Printer

Instructions

1. First, you need to download the SVG file for puzzle patterns and decide what image you want to use for your puzzle. You can use a family photo, make your designs, download SVG files online, or use images available in the Design Space.
2. You can adjust the size to fit the size of the material you are using—that means that you can make a small puzzle or go for an L-size puzzle design. After you have taken care of the puzzle pattern, you need to upload the image you want to use. Set the image to "Print Then Cut" when adjusting the line type and make sure that the image fits your puzzle pattern size. The image and the pattern for the puzzle will be on the same canvas as you are working on the design. Drag the pattern towards the image, then select the pattern and set it to the front on the editing menu.
3. Once the pattern is set on the front, you will get the idea of how your puzzle will look like after it's been cut out. Once you delete

the parts you don't need and arrange the size of the design, click "Attach" to merge the 2 elements. Make sure to set the line type for the pattern to cut and for the image "Print Then Cut." Prepare the printer as you will be printing the image first on sticker paper.

4. Set up the sticker paper for printing the image. Once the printing is done, use the Cricut chipboard and attach the image by removing the sticker paper and sticking it onto the chipboard. Load the Cricut machine with the image you have created, making the front part of the chipboard. Arrange the "Make It" material settings to the chipboard then send the material to cut. You may need to do 20 passes to cut the puzzle properly. And there you have it! A perfect gift or a perfect way to pass the time and enjoy your customized puzzles.

CHAPTER 36:

More Project Ideas

"Handmade with Love" Tags

Supplies

- Any Cricut machine that you have chosen to purchase
- An active account for Design Space
- A ready-made project from Design Space for project tags. For this project, we will say that you have chosen a tag that says "Handmade with Love," to go with the business example we have used above
- Vinyl and cardstock
- Your choice of a glitter pen color. Here we will say you are going to be using a bright green.

Instructions

1. The first thing that you will need to do is to make sure that you have followed the prompts to draw each layer and then cut each layer as the project requires.
2. Glue your 2 layers of paper together before aligning the hole for your tag at the top of the tag.
3. Add the vinyl you have chosen, and burnish it. This is important because you need to make sure that the vinyl is adhering thoroughly and correctly.
4. Choose what you want to add to the hole in the tag. You can use string, twine, or something more festive if you feel.

Cloud Coasters

Supplies

- Whichever Cricut machine you have chosen to purchase
- An active account for Design Space
- A pair of scissors
- Fusible fleece
- An iron
- A sewing machine
- Cotton fabric and thread to go with it

Instructions

1. Grab your fabric.
2. Cut your fabric and make sure it is 12 inches.
3. Open your Design Space, and hit the button that says "New Project."
4. Click on the button that says, "Shapes," and then insert a shape that looks like a cloud. You are going to do this from the pop-up window.
5. You will need to resize your cloud to 5.5 inches.
6. Click on the button, "Make It."
7. Change your project copies to 4. You will have to do this so that you can have a front and back to each coaster.
8. Click the button, "Apply."
9. Click the button, "Continue."

10. Adjust your settings for the materials to "Medium Fabrics" (like cotton).
11. Load your mat with the attached fabric.
12. Hit "Cut."
13. Repeat 3 steps, but you will be placing the fleece on the cutting mat, not the fabric.
14. Change your cloud shape to 5.375 inches.
15. Select a material and click where it says "View More."
16. Then type in "Fusible Fleece."
17. Cut out 2 of your fleece clouds.
18. Attach one of the fleece clouds to the back of one of the fabric hearts. Use a hot iron.
19. Repeat this step with the second heart.
20. Place your right sides together, and then sew the clouds together. When you do this, make sure that the fleece is attached. Leave a tiny gap in the stitches for turning.
21. You will now need to clip the curves.
22. Turn your cloud so that it is right side out.
23. Press your cloud with the iron.
24. Fold in the edges of your cloud's opening, and then press again.
25. Stitch around your cloud a little bit from the edge. We recommend a quarter of an inch.

You are now done with this project and can give your cute little clouds to someone you care about and brighten their day. The neat thing about this project is that it can go with any shape you wish. You could have so much fun with this by making rainbows, dinosaurs, flags, military camo; the options are endless, and you can gain great ideas for fabrics and materials, to do this project with. It is also a good beginner's project to do because you can get used to different commands on the machine as well.

Fancy Leather Bookmark

Supplies

- Cricut metallic leather
- Cricut holographic iron-on, red for a gold effect
- Purple StrongGrip mat
- Cricut fine-point blade
- Weeding tool
- Pair of scissors for cutting the material to size
- Brayer, or scraping tool
- Cricut knife blade
- Thin gold string or ribbon

Instructions

1. Cut the leather to the size you want it to be.
2. Each leather holder should be approximately 2 feet wide by 6 feet high.
3. Cut the holographic paper to the size you want it to be; this will depend on the font size and wording you choose for the bookmark.
4. Create a new project in Design Space.
5. Select "Shapes" from the left-hand menu.
6. Choose the square, unlock it, and set the width to 2 feet with a height of 6 feet.
7. Choose a triangle from the "Shapes" menu, and set the width to 1.982 and the height to 1.931.

8. Position the triangle in the rectangle at the bottom. Make sure it is positioned evenly, as this is going to create a swallowtail for the bookmark.
9. Select the circle from the shapes menu and unlock the shape. Set the width and height to 0.181.
10. Duplicate the circle shape.
11. Move the one circle to the top right-hand corner of the bookmark and the other to the left. These will be the holes to put a piece of ribbon or fancy string through.
12. Align the holes and distribute them evenly by using the "Align" function from the top menu, with both circles selected.
13. Select the top left hole with the top of the rectangle and click "Slice" in the bottom right menu.
14. Select the circle and "Remove" it, then "Delete" it.
15. Select the top right circle with the top of the rectangle and click "Slice" from the bottom right menu.
16. Select the circle and remove it.
17. Select the bookmark and move it over until you see the other 2 circles.
18. Select the 2 circles and delete them.
19. Select the triangle and the bottom of the rectangle, then click "Slice" from the bottom right-hand menu.
20. Select the first triangle, remove it, and delete it.
21. Select the second triangle, remove it, and delete it.
22. Save your project.
23. You will now have the first part of your leather bookmark ready to print.
24. Place the leather on the cutting mat, use the brayer tool, or scraper it to flatten it and stick it properly to the cutting mat.
25. Position the little rollers on the feeding bar to the left and right so they do not run over the leather.
26. Set the dial on the Cricut to custom.
27. Load the knife blade into the second Cricut chamber.
28. In Design Space, click on "Make It."
29. Set the material to "Cricut Metallic Leather."
30. Load the cutting board and leather into the Cricut, and hit "Go" when the Cricut is ready to cut.
31. When the Cricut is finished printing, unload the cutting board and use the spatula to cut the leather bookmark form out.

32. Use the weeding tool to remove any shapes that should not be on the bookmark.

33. Place the holographic paper on the cutting mat, and put the wheels on the loading bar back into their position.

34. Create a new project in Design Space and choose a nice fancy font. Do not make it any bigger than 1.5 feet wide and 3 feet high.

35. "Save" the project.

36. Click on "Make It," and choose the correct material.

37. Mirror the image.

38. Switch the blade in the second chamber back to the fine-point blade.

39. Load the cutting board, and click "Go" when the Cricut is ready to cut.

40. Gently peel the back off the design, heat the leather, and place the name on the bookmark where you want it positioned.

41. Use the same iron-on method as the method in the "Queen B" T-shirt project below.

42. Your bookmark is now ready to use or give as a personalized gift.

Personalized Envelopes

Supplies

- Envelope 5.5 by 4.25 inches
- Cricut pens in the color of your choice
- Green Standard Grip mat
- Spatula

Instructions

1. Create a "New Project" in Design Space.
2. Choose the square from the "Shapes" menu.
3. Unlock the square, set the width to 5.5 inches and the height to 4.25 inches.
4. Choose "Text" from the right-hand menu.
5. This will be the name and address the envelope will be addressed.
6. Choose a font and size it to fit comfortably in the middle of the envelope.
7. You can choose a different color for the font.
8. Move the text box to the middle of the envelope.
9. Select the entire envelope and click "Attach" from the bottom right-hand menu.
10. When you move the card around the screen, the address text will move with the envelope.
11. Load the envelope onto the cutting board and load it into the Cricut.
12. In Design Space, click "Make It."

13. Choose the material like paper.
14. Check to see if the pen color you need is loaded into the first compartment of the Cricut.
15. When the project is ready, press "Go" and let it print.
16. Flip the card over and stick it onto the mat.
17. Use a piece of tape to stick the envelope flap down.
18. Load it into the Cricut.
19. Change the text on the envelope to a return address, or "Regards From."
20. Change the color of the pen if you want the writing in another color.
21. When you are ready, click on "Make It."
22. Make sure the material is set to the correct setting.
23. When you are ready, press "Go."
24. Once it has finished cutting, you will have a personalized envelope.

"Queen B" T-Shirt

Supplies

- Plain cotton T-shirt in the color of your choice
- Iron-on vinyl also called heat transfer vinyl (HTV, gold)
- Green Standard Grip mat
- Cricut fine-point blade
- Weeding tool
- Pair of scissors for cutting the material to size
- Brayer
- Iron or the Cricut EasyPress Iron
- Cricut heat press mat to iron on

Instructions

1. Start a new project in Design Space.
2. Choose "Templates" from the left-hand side menu.
3. Choose the "Classic T-Shirts" template.
4. From the top menu, choose the type of T-shirt; "Kids' Short Sleeves."
5. From the top menu, choose the size of the T-shirt; "Small."
6. The back and the front of the T-shirt will appear on Design Space in the workspace.

7. From the top menu, select the color of the T-shirt you are using; "Pink."
8. Select "Text" from the left-hand menu and type in "Queen B."
9. Set the font; a great free font for this project is "Bauhaus 9."
10. Position the text on the T-shirt, then set the size and change the color to "Gold."
11. Choose images and find a bee picture. There is a nice free image or some really cute images you can buy.
12. Position the bee above the "B" and set the color to "Gold." You can rotate it into a tilted position.
13. Click on the "Make It" button, and you will be prompted with another screen showing the design on the cutting board. This is because, for iron-on vinyl, you need to mirror the image. You mirror the image to iron it on with the correct side up. Click the "Mirror" button on the left-hand side of the screen. You will see your writing and image look like it is back-to-front. You may want to move the bee over a bit, giving a bit of space between the image and writing.
14. Reset your dial on the Cricut to "Custom."
15. In Design Space, choose the everyday iron-on for your material setting.
16. You can set the pressure to a bit more if you like.
17. You will see a warning letting you know that mirroring must be ON for iron-on vinyl. It reminds you to place the vinyl-facedown as well.
18. Check that you have the fine-point blade loaded in Clamp 2 of the Cricut. Nothing is needed for cartridge one.
19. Cut the vinyl to the space that is indicated by the Cricut Design Space.
20. Place the shiny side of the iron-on vinyl down onto the cutting mat. Use your brayer to smooth out the vinyl onto your mat.
21. Load the cutting into the Cricut, and when the Cricut is ready, click "Go" for it to cut.
22. Unload the cutting mat when it has been cut. Remove the design from the mat, and gently remove the mat side of the vinyl from the carrier sheet (matte side of the vinyl).
23. Use the weeding tool to pick out the areas of the letters like the middles of the B.

24. Place your T-shirt onto the Cricut pressing mat with the middle section where you want the transfer to be.
25. If you are using the Cricut EasyPress, you can go to the Cricut website to find the heat transfer guide and the settings you will need for the press. Follow the instructions with the Cricut EasyPress.
26. For a normal iron, preheat the iron.
27. Place the Cricut heat press mat inside the shirt.
28. Heat the surface of the T-shirt for 5 seconds with the iron.
29. Put the design on the shirt where it is to be ironed on with the carrier sheet up.
30. Place a parchment sheet over the vinyl to protect the iron and the design.
31. Place the iron on the design and hold the iron in place on the design applying a bit of pressure for up to 20 seconds.
32. Turn the shirt inside out, and place the iron on the back of the design for another 20 seconds.
33. When it is done, turn the shirt right side out and gently pull the carrier sheet off.
34. Do not wash the shirt for few hours, after the transfer has been done.

Wedding Invitations

Supplies

- Cricut Maker or Cricut Explore
- Cutting mat
- Cardstock or your choice of decorative paper crepe/paper fabric, home printer (if not using Cricut Maker).

Instructions

1. Log in to the Design Space application and click on the "New Project" button on the screen's top right corner to view a blank canvas.
2. Let's customize an already existing project by clicking on the "Projects" icon on the Design Panel and selecting "Cards" from the "All Categories" drop-down, then type in "Wedding Invite" in the search bar.
3. Click "Text" on the Designs Panel and type in the details of the invite. You can change the font, color, and alignment of the text from the Edit Text Bar on top of the screen, and remember to change the "Fill" to "Print" on the top of the screen.

4. Select all the elements of the design and click on the "Group" icon on the top right of the screen under the Layers Panel. Then, click on "Save" to save your project.
5. Your design can now be printed and cut. Click on the "Make It" button and follow the prompts on the screen to first print your design on your chosen material (white cardstock or paper) and subsequently cut the printed design.

Custom Notebooks

Supplies

- Cricut Maker or Cricut Explore
- Cutting mat
- Washi sheets or your choice of decorative paper/crepe paper/fabric.

Instructions

1. Log in to the Design Space application and click on the "New Project" button on the screen's top right corner to view a blank canvas.
2. Use an already existing project from the "Cricut" library and customize it. Click on the "Projects" icon on the Design Panel and type in "Notebook" in the search bar.
3. Click on "Customize" so you can further edit the project to your preference. For example, the "Unicorn Notebook" project is shown below. You can click on the "Linetype Swatch" to change the color of the design.
4. The design is ready to be cut. Simply click on the "Make It" button and load the washi paper sheet to your Cricut machine and follow the instructions on the screen to cut your project.

Hello Darling Card

Supplies

- Coordinating cardstock
- Cricut scoring tool
- Cricut machine
- Pink and main paper pads
- Glue dots or mini glue dots
- Cricut LightGrip cutting mat

Instructions

1. Open the Design Space and start a new project.
2. Click on the "Images" file to locate the one that you wish to use.
3. Insert that file into the project canvas.
4. Send this file to the Cricut machine, and then use the cut designated for cardstock employing the light cutting mat.
5. Apply your glue dots onto the back of the cards inside.
6. Press the designer cardstock with the glue dots.
7. Repeat this process to create many more cards that will brighten your friends' and families' days.

Calfskin Hair Bow

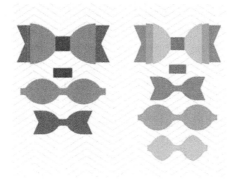

Supplies

- Cricut machine
- Faux calfskin or cowhide
- Transfer tape
- StrongGrasp Cricut tangle
- Bow Cricut configuration space document
- E6000 paste
- French barrette clasps
- Binding clasps

Instructions

1. Line your artificial softened cowhide or calfskin with your exchange tape. This will give something for the texture to clutch instead of leaving fluff everywhere on your tangle and essentially destroying it. This was an immense help, and I will never return to staying the texture ideal on the solid hold tangle again.

2. When you pick the artificial cowhide setting on your Keen Dial, it will slice through the item twice. At the point when your pictures are excessively near one another, occasionally, it will catch and draw the item. To stay away from this, move your pictures to promote separation when you are seeing your tangle. This will spare items over the long haul and spare plenty of headaches. Try not to be hesitant to utilize some scissors if you have one nick in the calfskin.

3. Begin with each one of your pieces laid out. You will need to overlay the longest piece with the goal that the finishes compromise. Secure that with the E6000 stick and a coupling cut. On the off chance that you have made over one bow, right now is an ideal opportunity to gather all the more drawn-out pieces.

4. Next, you will assume the back and position the E6000 stick in the center. Take your bow piece and hold it fast to that, safe with a coupling cut. Enable it to dry only a couple of minutes in the middle of each progression.

5. Next, put some E6000 on the barrette and lay the back piece to it. Take your little centerpiece and apply the paste to that. Overlay it over the bow in the center and around the back of the barrette. Secure that with a coupling cut. I would permit these dry for a couple of hours before you stick them in their hair to make sure they do not get any paste on them.

Valentine's Day Classroom Cards

Materials needed:

- Cricut Maker
- Card designs (Write Stuff Coloring)
- Cricut Design Space
- Dual scoring wheel
- Pens
- Cardstock
- Crayons
- Shimmer paper

Instructions

1. Open the card designs (Write Stuff Coloring) on the Design Space, and then click on "Make It," or "Customize" to make edits.
2. When all the changes have been done, Cricut will request you to select a material. Select "Cardstock" for the cards and "Shimmer Paper" for the envelopes.
3. Cricut will send you a notification when you need to change the pen colors while creating the card, and then it will start carving the card out automatically.
4. You will be prompted later on to change the blade because of the Double Scoring Wheel. It is advisable to use the Double

Scoring Wheel with shimmer paper; they both work best together.

5. When the scoring has been finished, replace the Scoring Wheel with the previous blade.

6. After that, fold the flaps at the score lines in the direction of the paper's white side, and then attach the "Side Tabs" to the exterior of the "Bottom Tab" by gluing them together.

7. You may now write "From:" and "To:" before placing the crayons into the slots.

8. Place the cards inside the envelopes and tag them with a sharp object.

Paper Flowers

Supplies

- Cricut Maker or Cricut Explore
- Cutting mat
- Cardstock
- Adhesive

Instructions

1. Log in to the Design Space application and click on the "New Project" button on the screen's top right corner to view a blank canvas.
2. Click on the "Images" icon on the Design Pane" and type in "Flower" in the search bar. Click on the desired image, then click on the "Insert Images" button at the bottom of the screen.
3. The selected image will be displayed on the canvas and can be edited using applicable tools from the Edit Image Bar. Then copy and paste the flower 5 times and make them a size smaller than the preceding flower to create a variable size for depth and texture for the design, as shown in the picture below.
4. The design is ready to be cut. Simply click on the "Make It" button and load the cardstock to your "Cricut" machine and follow the instructions on the screen to cut your project.
5. Once the design has been cut, simply remove the cut flowers and bend them at the center. Then using the adhesive, stack the flowers with the largest flower at the bottom.

Crepe Paper Bouquet

Supplies

- Cricut Maker or Cricut Explore
- Standard grip mat
- Crepe paper in desired colors
- Floral wire
- Floral tape
- Hot glue
- Fern fronds
- Vase

Instructions

1. Log in to the Design Space application and click on the "New Project" button on the screen's top right corner to view a blank canvas.
2. Let's use an already existing project from the Cricut library and customize it. So, click on the "Projects" icon and type in "Crepe Bouquet" in the search bar.
3. Click on "Customize" so you can further edit the project to your preference or simply click on the "Make It" button and load the crepe paper to your Cricut machine and follow the instructions on the screen to cut your project.

Leaf Banner

Supplies

- Cricut Maker or Cricut Explore
- Standard grip mat
- Watercolor paper and paint
- Felt balls
- Needle and thread
- Hot glue

Instructions

1. Log in to the Design Space application and click on the "New Project" button on the screen's top right corner to view a blank canvas.
2. Let's use an already existing project from the Cricut library and customize it. Click on the "Projects" icon and type in "Leaf Banner" in the search bar.
3. Click on "Customize" so you can further edit the project to your preference, or simply click on the "Make It" button and load the watercolor paper to your Cricut machine and follow the instructions on the screen to cut your project.
4. Use watercolors to paint the leaves and let them dry completely. Then create a garland using the needle and thread through the felt balls and sticking the leaves to the garland with hot glue.

Paper Pinwheels

Supplies

- Cricut Maker or Cricut Explore
- Standard grip mat
- Patterned cardstock in desired colors
- Embellishments
- Paper straws
- Hot glue

Instructions

1. Log in to the Design Space application and click on the "New Project" button on the screen's top right corner to view a blank canvas.
2. Let's use an already existing project from the Cricut library and customize it. Click on the "Projects" icon and type in "Paper Pinwheel" in the search bar.
3. Click on "Customize" to further edit the project to your preference, or simply click on the "Make It" button and load the cardstock to your Cricut machine and follow the instructions on the screen to cut your project.
4. Using hot glue, adhere the pinwheels together to the paper straws and the embellishment.

Paper Lollipops

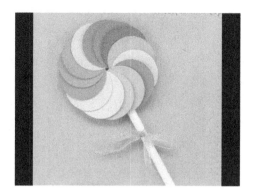

Supplies

- Cricut Maker or Cricut Explore
- Light grip mat
- Patterned cardstock in desired colors
- Glitter
- Wooden dowels
- Hot glue

Instructions

1. Log in to the Design Space application and click on the "New Project" button on the screen's top right corner to view a blank canvas.
2. Let's use an already existing project from the Cricut library and customize it. Click on the "Projects" icon and type in "Paper Lollipop" in the search bar.
3. Click on "Customize" to further edit the project to your preference or simply click on the "Make It" button and load the cardstock to your Cricut machine and follow the instructions on the screen to cut your project.
4. Using hot glue, adhere the down between the lollipop circles. Brush them with craft glue and sprinkle them with glitter.

Paper Luminary

Supplies

- Cricut Maker or Cricut Explore
- Standard Grip mat
- Shimmer paper sampler
- Weeder
- Spray adhesive
- Frosted glass luminary

Instructions

1. Log in to the Design Space application and click on the "New Project" button on the screen's top right corner to view a blank canvas.
2. Let's use an already existing project from the Cricut library and customize it. Click on the "Projects" icon and type in "Paper Luminary" in the search bar.
3. Click on "Customize" to further edit the project to your preference, or simply click on the "Make It" button and load the shimmer paper to your Cricut machine and follow the instructions on the screen to cut your project.
4. Cut and weed the design, spray the shimmer paper's back with spray adhesive, and adhere to the glass luminary.

CHAPTER 37: Project Ideas for Kids

Shark Pencil Case: Return to Fun School!

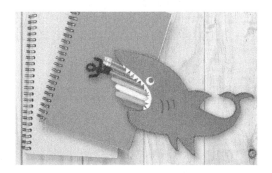

Supplies

- Cricut machine
- Felt
- Ball Chain Keychain
- Googly eyes
- Scissors
- Silver heat transfers and iron

Instructions

1. Upload the picture of the shark to your cutting software.
2. I've been using my Cricut Air 2 Explorer.
3. Simply cut the shark off the machine.
4. Easy, take just 1–2 minutes at any time.
5. Excess vinyl is weeded out.
6. Eye and gill slits included.
7. Place on top of the box with the plastic.
8. Slightly iron over the shark at medium height.
9. The case is with nylon, so if it gets too hot, it will melt.

10. Then let it cool completely.
11. Next, peel the plastic off and roll it back over the top.
12. All right, we're 5 minutes.
13. After that, take a felt piece and cut 2 identical bodies of fish. I modeled these gold-fish crackers slightly larger than cheesy. And I finished with 2 eyes googly (one on both sides).
14. Stick on one fish hot ball chain keychain.
15. Add the other fish body right at the top, covering it with a chain (if the ball chain keychain is not lying around, use some yarn).
16. Every side of the fish has a hot glue eye.
17. Finally, crochet it as a cute shark snack to the zipper!

DIY Rainbow Catcher

Supplies

- Cricut Explore or Cricut Builder (you can use your Cricut Joy, but it'll be very small with your rainbow)
- Standard Grip mat for Blue Light Grip or Green
- Fine-point blade (comes with your machine)
- 2 (12 by 12 inches) black cardstock parts
- Tissue paper in 7 different colors
- Contacts paper
- Washi or other adhesive tapes
- Stick adhesive
- Scissors
- SVG rainbow

Instructions

1. Add the rainbow shape to Cricut Design Space. There are 2 similar pieces, both of which were cut from black cardstock.
2. Add to Cricut Design Space the rainbow parts.
3. Break and rub off the supporting paper with a sheet of contact paper larger than your rainbow bits. Use a bit of washi or other tapes to put sticky-side up and adhere to your work table, which helps prevent it from moving.
4. Then put one of your black rainbow details on the contact paper and press it to stick to it.
5. To make your rainbow suncatcher, cut tiny pieces of tissue paper out of 7 colors and adhere to the contact paper.
6. The rainbow adheres to tissue paper.

7. Cautiously glue the other black rainbow outline on the first outline board after you have used your tissue paper, making it up as neatly as practicable.
8. On top of the first, stick the second rainbow.
9. Then break another strip of contact paper and put it gently on top of the rainbow, the very same size as the first one.
10. Starting in the middle, but the second piece of contact paper on top of the rainbow.
11. Then slit the edge of your rainbow suncatcher all the way through, leaving a tiny 1/8-inch contact paper boundary to help keep it together.
12. Split across the rainbow's edge.
13. Hang up then.
14. With this DIY rainbow suncatcher, bring a little joy to your window! Break the frame with your Cricut Explore or Maker, and then construct the vibrant rainbow using contact paper and paper towels!

Making Paper Stamps

Supplies

- Cricut Explore/Machine for silhouette cutting
- Images (I have used different images which are free with the Cricut Access available in Cricut Maker software)
- Sheets of craft foam
- Blocks of wood
- Tacky adhesive

Instructions

1. Collect supplies.
2. Add select photos to Cricut Design Space. I have selected different images (a unicorn, a light, a core, a dinosaur, etc.), and the images are scaled according to your wood planks. Mine had sizes of around 2 inches each.
3. Set up the foam cutting unit.
4. To cut on your Cricut unit, use a thick grip mat and position foam mats.
5. Break the visuals. With the deep cut cutter, used in the Cricut Explore Computer to cut 6 photos in less than 5 minutes!
6. To stick to wooden boards, use tacky glue and allow it to dry overnight.
7. To draw the picture on the opposite side of the sheets, use the opposite portion of the foam surface (it looks like a stencil) to mark each stamp with the illustration.
8. Instead of painting, you can even cut vinyl, but I simply drew the tiles' picture.

Cute Paper Insects

Supplies

- White vellum
- Felt wool-blend
- Low-temp hot glue handgun
- 2 (11 inches long) bits of wood trim
- Handicraft tape
- 11 by 17 inches stock of cream cards
- Twine of cotton
- Cutting-machine vinyl iron-on
- Smooth fabric for ironing cotton
- Text-weight or card inventory certificates
- Double-sided roller of adhesive
- Fusible web bonding
- Ironing with EasyPress
- Scissors
- Weeding method

Instructions

1. Split both bits of text-weight or card stock paper and bee wings vellum.
2. Apply double-sided adhesive to the top layers of insects and wing edges on the hand.
3. Place the layers and push them into shape.
4. Repeat with the leaf layer phase.
5. Print the poster concept on the stock of 11–17 inches cream cards and stick bugs in place.
6. Complete the template by inserting leaves.
7. Tape cotton twine for a poster hanging.
8. Glue the bits of wood trim to the back and front of the poster art top.

Tip: The downloadable poster template is accessible as a document in the digital folder with all the SVG files removed. Be sure to pick "Full Size" from the print menu before printing. You should visit the nearest office supplies store to print the poster if you do not even have large-format printers.

Princess Crown and Wand Stick

Supplies

- Broad ribbon between 1 inch and 1/4 inch
- Glitter card inventory
- Scissors
- Reduced-temp hot glue handgun
- 12 inches dowel of timber

Instructions

1. Split crown bits from the warehouse of glitter cards.
2. Put 2 dots of hot glue on the back of a broad herb.
3. With the flower in the middle, place and connect both sides of the crown.
4. Scale and glue back to match the head of the crown.
5. Split bits of the wand from the stock of glitter items.
6. The specifics of the glued flower are pieced together so that all sides have a shimmer.
7. Apply the 1-inch-wide ribbon to the 12-inch wooden dowel frame. At a slight angle, wind ribbons up the dowel and glue it into position at the end.
8. Split 2 1/4-inch-thick ribbon pieces, each 10 inches long.
9. Glue to the top of the stick at halftime.
10. The adhesive stick and the specifics of the flower on the back of a broad flower.
11. Apply generous amounts of adhesive to the big flower and match the second flower with it.
12. Press in position and allow to cool.

Making Paper Animals

Supplies

- Needle and thread for sewing
- Text-weight or paper stock card
- Tool for curling
- Twine in cotton
- Iron and base ironing
- The double-sided roller of adhesive
- SVG file
- A 10 inches hoop for embroidery
- Tool for weeding
- Big needle
- A 1-inch bead of wood
- Scissors
- Iron-on vinyl cutting-machine
- Smooth ironing fabric made of cotton

Instructions

1. From text-weight or card stock material, cut all shapes.
2. Switch the informative bear over. In the back foot, put double-sided tape, keeping clear of the feet.
3. Connect the informative bear to the bear's silhouette.
4. Repeat the measures with acorns and mushrooms.
5. Using hot glue to bind bear weapons to mushrooms and leaves.
6. Leaves fold in half near score lines.

7. For forming leaves, use a curling tool.
8. Using the needle to make a small hole on top of the head of the bear. Thread strings into the hole.
9. For all of the mushrooms, acorns, and leaves, add holes and a loop.
10. Pull the outer portion out of the embroidery hoop. Attach the inner hoop with one strip of cotton twine.
11. Apply 2 more bits of cotton twine to the hoop. Collect the 3 pieces and tie them.
12. Slide the wood bead onto the collected twine using a broad needle.
13. Tie 3 bears between each cotton twine based on the hoop.
14. Finish by adding all the mobile leaves, acorns, and mushrooms.

Envelopes for Birthday Parties

Supplies

- Green mat (a fresh blue mat may also be used)
- Rating wheel or stylus (you should use just the stylus if you have an Explore).
- Fine-point blade
- Good strength adhesive
- Cricut Maker/Explorer
- To be answered
- Iron (or EasyPress Mini).
- Cricut reflections
- Document sticker and printer

Instructions

1. The realistic file has to be published. Go to the Design Space canvas region and press the "Upload" button on the left of the canvas panel. Click "Upload Picture" and follow the prototype upload instructions. If the file has been published, click "Recently Updated Photos" and link it to the computer.
2. Looking at the layer board of the sheet, you can see all the layers in the pattern.
3. The envelope is secured by 2 cut sections.
4. Place where you need folds.
5. In order to edit the packet, the layers are first "Ungrouped." Choose the rectangle, adjust the "Line Type" to "Score," then

you have to use either the scoring device or the scoring style on your computer.

6. Split lines must be left as "Line Type" of "Delete."

7. Finally, pick all the layers and press on the bottom of the Layers screen "Attach." Attachment is really necessary. The project would be all over the place if you do not do that by clicking on "Create That."

8. You possibly should press on the tiny lock to activate the proportions of your cube. The card should be 6 by 4 inches.

9. Please remember that you would require huge pieces of paper in several situations to produce envelopes. In my opinion, the most exquisite documents are available in 11 by 11 inches papers, so your packet can not be bigger than that.

10. The scale of your project will not be greater than 11.5 by 11.5 inches if you choose the standard mattress or 12 by 24 inches. If Design Space causes a mistake, it is typically because the design is too big.

11. After the square has been sized, pick and rotate the envelope addition, so the final scores cover the card design. Leave a little space, because the actual card must not be squeezed into the envelope.

12. When the envelope has been sized, cut the card prototype and press on "Make It."

13. You can use the scoring type for the folds while operating with a Cricut Explore unit. The great feature about the stylus is that the stylus and fine-point blades can be mounted at the same time.

14. If you have a Cricut Design Space template select the wheel for scoring lines, and if you do not, click "Edit Software" and choose "Scoring Type."

15. Place the document on the protected mat or pleasant side down. The color of the paper I used on both sides did not matter. Mount "Wheel/Score Type" score and blade with a fine-point blade. Load the Cricut mat and click the "Go" button blinking.

16. Note: If you use the scoring circle, you need to mount it first, then add the blade when the scoring lines for your Cricut are finished. Unload the mat after cutting; I still bent the mat such that the paper can be separated from the mat through gravity. It also stops the content from producing undesirable waves.

Charming Driftwood Sign

Supplies

- Wood plank
- Some paint
- Vinyl
- Piece of rope

Instructions

1. Select an appropriate size of a wooden piece with some suitable length. As you are using it, so it's totally up to you which size you prefer.
2. Draw a shape and image on a piece of paper. Place this image on the wooden plank and draw the shape by using a paper image as a stencil with some prominent marker color.
3. Paint the image or letter with any bright color or with any color of your choice.
4. In the final step, add vinyl covering. It is ready to use, now pass some thread, rope, or any other hanging material.

Party Decor Medallions

Supplies

- 45 same-size records
- Posterboard
- Scale
- Scissors
- Adhesive/Glue
- Vintage milk caps
- Twine
- Scrapbook
- Scallop punch

Instructions

1. In the first step, measurements are made, and cutting is applied to paper. Fold many papers and cut them in once, paper with measurements of 6, 5, and 4 inches in width for small, medium, and large medallions.
2. By holding one end of the paper, fold it, repeat the folds backward and forward. All of the paper strips should be folded in the same way.
3. Now attach all of the strips with the help of glue, but in the way, they become in the form of a seamless strip. Squeeze the strips from the end and pull all of the strips to form them in a shape of a circle.

4. Using glue, take the record and attach it from a lower portion of the paper medallion. Now take 2.5 inches of scallops and fix them with each other.
5. Apply some glue to the center and fix the milk cap and center of the circle. On the backside of the center top of the medallion attach a twine piece; pass a string into it, now it is ready for hanging on the wall or in any other place.

Chalkboard Calendar

Supplies

- Wooden board
- Wooden filler
- Scale
- Paints
- Cutter

Instructions

1. A large cardboard piece, any used cardboard can be reused. Use some wood filler to fill or fix the holes, if any.
2. Paint the board with any of your favorite or desired colors.
3. By using Silhouette SD cut the chalkboard and carefully draw some squares with exact measurements. Mark the area by using chalk ink markers.
4. Now make some holders by using a Mason jar and pipe clamp. You can assign any sign or add any of the tags and any kind of references to it.

Family Birthday Wooden Board

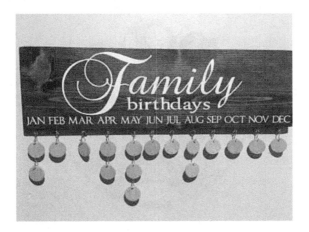

Supplies

- Wooden board
- Chalk paints
- Paint brushes
- Finishing cloths
- Plastic gloves
- Sandpapers
- Old rags
- Lettering vinyl

Instructions

1. Apply a coat of chalk paint to the wooden board, let it dry. Then do another coating of paint for a fine look. Give some time, like 2 hours, to complete its drying period.
2. Now take some wood finishing cloth. Using an old rug, wipe all of the extra paint. Then give again some time to get it dry.
3. Designing family members' names and counting age numbers style of quoting them is a personal choice. Very slightly and carefully use sandpaper.
4. Now apply the vinyl, in lettering. The color and design of the letter are totally up to your choice.

Vinyl Clock

Supplies

- Vinyl record
- Old clock machine
- Glue/gum

Instructions

1. The vinyl clock project is very interesting. It can be implicated in so many ways. First of all, cut the vinyl record in a shape of your choice, square, triangle, flower, circle, and any shape. Set the clock mechanism in the center of a vinyl record.
2. Use glue to fix it right in the center. The vinyl clock is just ready for use. Place it on your desk by attaching some stand to it or hang it on your wall.

Pallet Sign

Supplies

- Scrapbook paper in the colors of your choice
- Mod podge
- Paper trimmer
- Paintbrush

Instructions

1. Using your mod podge, coat the wood boards and the backside of your triangles.
2. Place the triangles one at a time on the board, coating the top with another thin coat of mod podge. Allow your sign to completely dry, and then give it a final coat of mod podge.
3. That is it. The last tip, if you are looking for pallet sign ideas, 48x40 has tons of them on the internet.

Caddy's DIY Utensil

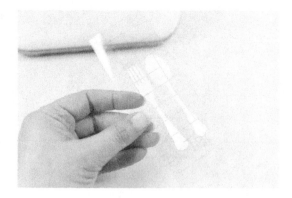

Supplies

- Cricut Explore, Cricut Builder, or Joy Cricut
- Blue mat for Light Grip or green mat for Standard Grip
- Fine-point blade
- White or other vinyl co-ordinating adhesive
- Tool for weeding
- Tape move
- Scraper
- Scissors
- Caddy and Caddy
- Space file concept Cricut

Instructions

1. Make sure you've got a machine chosen in the upper right corner of the Cricut Design Space before you start.
2. Begin by opening the file for Cricut Design Space. You'll see a picture of a spoon and a fork. If you like a particular utensil style better, you can also check for other utensil images.
3. From there, use the size tool on the edit bar at the top to resize your utensils to match your utensil caddy. Mine ended up being 3 inches wide
4. Size tool for height should be set to 3.

5. Then, in the upper right, press "Make It." You'll be taken to the Prepare screen from there.

6. You can see a pop-up screen that asks for your mat range if you cut this on your Cricut Joy. You can cut standard vinyl on a mat, or you can use smart vinyl, which doesn't require a mat. If this is cut on Cricut Explore or Cricut Creator, you can go straight to the screen for Prepare. You can rearrange and rotate the images from here to fit better on the vinyl. All you have to do is tap on one of the photos and use the little rotate icon to rotate the picture. It will rotate it at set times if you hold down the shift key.

7. When you have your photos on the material where you want them, press "Continue" to go to the Make screen.

8. Your Cricut machine will attach to your computer on the Make screen. Then you will pick your content.

9. You will be prompted to insert your blade into your machine once you pick your stuff if it's not already there.

10. Make a screen displaying loading tools and prompt materials.

11. Insert your Cricut material or mat. The Joy will automatically feed the material/mat into the machine, but on Cricut Explore or Creator, you'll need to press the arrow button.

12. Then either press "Go" or the blinking "C" (Explore or Maker) in Cricut Design Space (Cricut Joy). Your Cricut will cut your material easily!

13. It's time to place those freshly cut decals on your caddy now. You're going to weed away the extra vinyl around your fork and spoon first.

14. These decals are big enough that you can peel and stick them on like stickers if you have a steady hand.

15. Cut a piece of transfer slightly larger than your decals tape and peel off the backing paper. Then put it on top of your decals, sticky side down. Use a scraper to clean your decals with the transfer tape.

16. Switch tape with a scraper tool to utensils.

17. Then peel the vinyl backing sheet off the transfer tape, and the labels should adhere to the transfer tape. If you notice the vinyl is not holding, read "Using Transfer Tape" for tips.

18. Then break the 2 pieces apart. Put the decals on the caddy of your utensil, making sure they are straight and balanced. To burnish it, press down on the vinyl.
19. The transfer tape will then peel back. The decals should stick to your caddy, and you're done!
20. You can even monogram almost everything with your Cricut or another cutting machine, from tote bags to T-shirts, home decor, to party props.

DIY Fabric Foliage Bouquet with Corsage

Supplies

- Red pom poms (1-inch size)
- Cricut Create Computer (optional, you can use the file to cut by hand)
- Green light perceived
- Thread in color synchronization (green and red)
- 12 by 12 inches Cricut Cloth Cutting Pad (optional if the PDF is used for hand cutting)
- Kelly Green Thought, The Thought
- The Tacky Adhesive of Aleene
- PDF file cut (get it free below or use your file)
- Scissors
- Pins of defense
- Ribbon
- Sewing machine (optional but strongly recommended)

Instructions

1. Position the deep greenish leaf on the edge of the pale greenish leaf and stitch the middle of the leaf with a straight stitch (do not reach the end of the tip of the leaf). You should hand-stitch or stick the ends together if you don't have a stitching device.

2. Upload the picture in Design Space by using a Cricut Create Computer (you need support uploading in the software). In Graphic Room, scale the picture (Kelly Green—2.78 by 2.08 inches, Light Green—2.94 by 2.38 inches).

3. Organize the foliage and add the ends together to make yours.

4. Attach the strawberries to the surface (if you intend to sew the berries onto the foliage later, you might not need a lot of glue). Using the ribbon to create a bow and stitch the berries. Let it dry with glue.

5. Stitch the foliage with the berries. Everything you need to do is literally tack them into place. To make a circle, cut a small square of pale green fabric and sew the peak and the base to the back of the brooch/boutonniere.

6. In the loop (for a boutonniere or button corsage), you can push a safety pin or move a similar string through loops (for a bracelet corsage or headband).

7. Wearing foliage in your hair. Simply wrap a longer ribbon in the back around the loop, and you have a headband. Simply wrap a longer ribbon in the back around the loop, and you have a hairband.

Cool Tote Bag

Supplies

- Heat or Iron Press
- Crafty Color Shimmer Chimp HTV
- Device for weeding
- Empty pocket for tote
- Essentials of Crafty Color Chimp HTV
- Cricut cutting machine

Instructions

1. To suit the tote bag, import the cut files into Cricut Software and scale them. The tote pouch I'm using is 11 inches broad, so I've made it 5 inches broad for my build.
2. Select the "Create It" icon and then display your photos in the next pane by pressing the "Mirror" button.
3. With the transparent carrier sheet facing down, place the thermal transport vinyl on the cutting board and load the pad into the unit. Click the "Start" button, and it will go to work on the computer. For each color of vinyl you're using, repeat this move.
4. Remove the excess vinyl from all over the cut photos and use a weeding method to assist with the smaller bits if appropriate.

5. Focus the pocket with the monogram, cover with a Teflon sheet (or thin towel), and push for 17 seconds with a hot iron.
6. Allow the material for heat transfer to cool before the carrier sheet is removed.
7. To apply the ribbon layout around the logo, repeat the steps above.
8. Over the clear logo offset, line the glitter monogram, cover it with a Teflon board, and click for 15 seconds.
9. Pull the carrier sheet after cooling and show the layered pattern. This tote bag would then put your body free all summer long.

CHAPTER 38:

Advanced Project Ideas

Fabric Wreath with Flowers

Supplies

- A ring from an old lampshade
- Ribbon to wrap the lampshade
- Cricut Maker
- Cricut felt in various colors
- Rotary blade
- 12 x 12 inches Cricut mat for fabric
- Hot glue gun and sticks of glue
- Felt balls
- Wreath forms

Colors:

- Mauve
- Olive green
- Marigold

- Salmon
- Charcoal
- Peach
- Blue
- Pink
- Dusty blue
- Pale green

Instructions

1. You need to log in using your Cricut Design Space account.
2. In the Cricut Design Space, you will need to click on "New Project" and then select the image that you would like to use for your flowers. You can use the search bar on the right-hand side at the top to locate the image that you are wishing to use.
3. Next, click on the image and click "Insert Image" so that the image is selected.
4. Click on each of the files in the image file and click the button that says "Flatten" at the lower right section of the screen. This will turn the individual pieces into one whole piece. This prevents the cut file from being individual pieces for the image.
5. Now, you should resize the image so that it is the size that you wish it to be. This can be any size within the recommended space for the size of the canvas.
6. If you want duplicates of the image for a sheet of flowers, you should then select all and then edit it and click "Copy." This will allow you to copy the whole row that you have selected. Once you have copied, you can then edit and paste the multiple images to make a sheet. This is the easiest way to copy and paste the image over and over again.
7. Using the project listed in the Cricut manual, you can find the directions for the flowers. Once the flowers are cut out, you can begin to place them together with the instructions listed below.
8. Using each one of the succulents, place the tabs together using glue. Secure your leaves together. Repeat each piece until they are done. Stack them together to create a succulent. Use the hot glue and place the smaller circle in the center of the finished

ones. Each flower should be stacked 3 pieces tall with a small dot in the center.

9. Once you have cut the flowers out, you can begin to glue the pieces together. Start by folding the 8 tabs into the petals and gluing them down. Repeat this step with each piece. Stack them together so that each petal is offset. Once you have stacked your pieces, you can use rolled pieces or a felt ball.

10. Using the glue, place the 6-tab pieces on each one of the petals. Then, proceed to stack them, making sure to use the 10-petal ones first. Offset each petal section so that it is not laying on top of each other in order. Finish it all off with a ball that is rolled into the center.

11. Glue the poppy tabs to each other to secure the petals. Repeat each piece of petal together to create the second poppy. Lay them together in a staggered form. Finish the flower off with a rolled center or ball made of felt.

12. After the flowers and the succulents are assembled, you can begin to arrange them all over the ring covered in ribbon. Using the glue, place the flowers in the order that you want to cover the ring or in a decorative fashion.

Sugar Skulls with Cricut

Supplies

- Printer
- Toothpicks
- Standard cardstock
- 12 by 12 inches Standard Grip mat for Cricut
- Sugar skull print-then-cut image
- Cricut Explore machine
- Cricut Design space software
- Glue

Instructions

1. You need to log in using your Cricut Design Space account.
2. In the Cricut Design Space, you will need to click on "New Project" and then select the image that you would like to use for your sugar skulls. You can use the search bar on the right-hand side at the top to locate the image you wish to use.
3. Next, click on the image and click "Insert Image".
4. Click on each of the files in the image file and click the button that says "Flatten" at the lower right section of the screen. This will turn the individual pieces into one whole piece. This prevents the cut file from being individual pieces for the image.

5. Now, you should resize the image so that it is the size that you wish it to be. This can be any dimension within the recommended space for the size of the canvas.

6. If you want duplicates of the image for the sheet of sugar skulls, then you should select all and then edit the image and click "Copy." This will allow you to copy the whole row that you have selected. Once you have copied, you can then edit and paste the multiple images to make a sheet. This is the easiest way to copy and paste the image over and over again.

7. Follow the instructions on the screen for printing, then cut the sugar skull images.

8. Using glue, piece the front and back of the sugar skull together to create the topper with the toothpick inserted into the pieces center.

Faux Leather Pendant

Supplies

- Necklace chain
- Jewelry pliers
- Cricut gold pen
- Cricut Explore Air 2
- Cricut strong mat grip
- Cricut Faux leather
- Jump ring
- Fabric fusion

Instructions

1. Start by opening the Cricut Design Space. Choose the size that you want the pendant to be. This can be a circle pendant. Using the machine, make another circular-sized pendant.
2. Attach the jump ring here later after the circles have been made.
3. Next, open the text section in the Design shop and type in the exact initials that you would like to use.
4. Select the section that has a writing style option from the menu and adjust the font of the lettering to whatever you wish.
5. Drag your letter to the center part of the circle and resize it to fit the appropriate size.
6. Be sure to make a front and a back. This will ensure both sides of the piece look like leather.
7. Create your circle so that it matches the other one minus the letter.

8. Make this an attached set.
9. Using the Cricut pen, begin to cut the pieces. As it is cutting the leather, it will print the initials.
10. Use your fabric fusion glue to join the 2 pieces of leather together, making the pendant.
11. Using the pliers for jewelry, you can twist on the ring for the necklace.
12. Attach your pendant and jump ring, and then string it onto the chain.
13. The pliers can close the jump ring off.

Feather Earrings with Faux Leather

Supplies

- Fabric fusion
- Paintbrush
- Washi tape
- Metallic paint
- Cricut Explore Air
- Cricut faux leather
- Cricut Standard Grid cutting mat
- A hole puncher
- Jewelry pliers
- Jump ring
- Chain
- Earring findings
- Jewelry pliers

Instructions

1. Use the cut file for the jewelry that you would like to cut for the pattern. Cut 2 pieces for each piece of jewelry.
2. Make sure that you have 2 pieces per item so that you can glue them together. This makes them look like leather on both sides.
3. Mirror the pieces, so they match.
4. Using your washi tape, mark off a section that is the top half of the faux leather piece. Press this tape firmly in place so that you can prevent the leakage of the paint.

5. Paint the end that you would like to be painted. After it is painted, let it completely dry. Repeat for the other pieces that you are painting.
6. Once it is dried out, remove your washi tape.
7. Now, use the fabric to fuse the 2 pieces of each mate. These pieces should be flawlessly fit together. Use the directions on the bottle to adhere these pieces together.
8. Use a strong needle or a micro puncher to make a small but big hole to attach the hardware.
9. Use the pliers to open the jump ring and then loop it into the earrings. Attach the jewelry to the earring pieces or the necklace pieces.

Woodland Fox Bookmark

Supplies

- Cricut weeding tool
- Multiple colors of cardstock
- Adhesive
- Standard Grip cutting mat
- Cricut machine

Instructions

1. Open your Design shop and use the design file that you have created for this bookmark.
2. You may have to purchase the file needed to design this bookmark.
3. Cut 2 pieces for the bookmark. One for each side of the bookmark. This helps it to be sturdier.
4. You will need to glue the 2 identical pieces together.
5. Once you send the image to the Cricut machine, you can begin to place your paper's color on the mat. Then cut it out. Continue to do this until all the pieces and colors have been cut.
6. Weed out any unnecessary pieces that come out with the fox.
7. Glue the fox together and then glue it to the bookmark backing. You should not use too much glue. This will keep the cardstock from being soggy. Use a heavy book and place the bookmark in between the pages to get the glue to set and the bookmark not to wave.

DIY Mermaid Birthday Card

Supplies

- White cardstock
- Cricut Explore Air machine
- Light Grip cutting mat
- 0.4 mm. Cricut pen

Instructions

1. Open your Design shop file and chose the "Image" option. If you have Cricut Access, you should be able to use the mermaid image for free; if not, it will cost you some money.
2. Use your white stock by placing it on the cutting mat and insert it into the machine. Set the dial to "Cardstock." Insert your pen set to black into the pen holder of the cartridge.
3. Send your project to the Design Space and wait patiently for it to process and draw the image.
4. When the card is done, present it to the expected birthday girl.

Snowman Lantern

Supplies

- Cricut Maker or Cricut Explore
- Standard Grip mat
- Vinyl in desired colors
- Transfer tape
- Scraper
- Weeder
- Glass etching cream
- Glass faced lantern

Instructions

1. Log in to the Design Space application and click on the "New Project" button on the screen's top right corner to view a blank canvas.
2. Click on the "Projects" icon and type in "Snowman Lantern" in the search bar.
3. Click on "Customize" to further edit the project to your preference, or simply click on the "Make It" button, and load the vinyl sheet to your Cricut machine, and follow the instructions on the screen to cut your project.
4. Using a weeder tool, remove the negative space pieces of the design.

5. Use the transfer tape to apply the vinyl cuts to the glass face of the lantern.

6. Then use the scraper tool on top of the transfer tape to remove any bubbles, and then just peel off the transfer tape.

7. Lastly, apply the etching cream following the instructions on its package, and rinse off to remove the vinyl.

"Trick or Treat" Bag

Supplies

- Cricut Maker or Cricut Explorer
- Standard Grip mat
- Transfer tape
- Scraper
- Everyday vinyl
- Small craft paper bags

Instructions

1. Log in to the Design Space application and click on the "New Project" button on the screen's top right corner to view a blank canvas.
2. Click on the "Images" icon and type in "Halloween" in the search bar, then click on "Insert Images" at the bottom of the screen. The image selected is shown in the picture below.
3. You can edit either or both the image as needed by clicking on applicable tools on the Edit Bar.
4. Select the entire design and click on the "Group" icon. Then click on "Save" to save the project.

5. Simply click on the "Make It" button and load the vinyl sheet to your Cricut machine and follow the instructions on the screen to cut your project.

6. Carefully remove the excess vinyl from the sheet.

7. To easily paste your design on the craft bag without stretching the pieces, put the transfer tape on top of the cut design. Now, slowly peel the paper backing on the vinyl from one end to the other in a rolling motion to ensure even placement, and use the scraper tool on top of the transfer tape to remove any bubbles, and then just peel off the transfer tape.

Personalized Mugs (Iron-On Vinyl)

Supplies

- Cricut Maker or Cricut Explore
- Standard Grip mat
- Printable Cricut iron-on or heat transfer vinyl
- Cricut EasyPress Mini
- EasyPress mat
- Weeding tool
- Ceramic mug

Instructions

1. Log in to the Design Space application and click on the "New Project" button on the screen's top right corner to view a blank canvas.
2. Click on the "Images" icon on the Design Panel and type in "America" in the search bar. Click on the desired image, then click on the "Insert Images" button at the screen's bottom.
3. Click on the "Templates" icon on the Designs Panel located on the left of the screen, and type in "Mug" in the templates search bar, and select the mug icon.
4. You can change the type and size of the template to decorate mugs with non-standard sizes by clicking on the "Size" icon and select "Custom" to update your mug size.
5. You can further edit your design by clicking on the "Shapes" icon adding: hearts, stars, or other desired shapes to your design.

6. Click on "Save" at the top right corner of the screen and give the desired name to the project, for example, "Mug Decoration" and click "Save."

7. The design is ready to be printed and cut. Simply click on the "Make It" button, and follow the prompts on the screen for using the inkjet printer to print the design on your printable iron-on vinyl, and subsequently cut the design.

8. Note: One side of the printable iron-on dark sheet is white with a matte finish; the other side is printed with blue gridlines. Print on the matte side; the side with the blue gridlines is the iron-on backing which will be removed before applying your design to your material.

9. Carefully remove the excess material from the sheet using the weeder tool, making sure only the design remains on the clear liner.

10. Using the Cricut EasyPress Mini and EasyPress mat, the iron-on layers can be easily transferred to your mug. Preheat your EasyPress Mini and put your design on the desired area and apply pressure for a couple of minutes or more Wait for few minutes before peeling off the design while it is still warm. (Since the design is delicate, use the spatula tool or your fingers to rub the letters down the mug before starting to peel the design).

Personalized Coaster Tiles

Supplies

- Cricut Maker or Cricut Explore
- Standard Grip mat
- Printable Cricut iron-on, or heat transfer vinyl
- Cricut EasyPress Mini
- EasyPress mat
- Weeding tool
- Ceramic coaster tiles

Instructions

1. Log in to the Design Space application, and click on the "New Project" button on the screen's top right corner to view a blank canvas.
2. Let us use our image for this project. Search the web to find a monogram image you would like and store it on your computer.
3. Now, click on the "Upload" icon from the Designer Panel on the screen left.
4. A screen with "Upload Image" and "Upload Pattern" will be displayed.
5. Click on the "Upload Image" button. Click on "Browse," or simply drag and drop your image on the screen.
6. Select the image type "Simple" and save the image as a "Print-Then-Cut Image."

7. Choose the uploaded image by clicking on the "Insert Images" and edit the image as needed.

8. You can personalize the monogram by adding text to the design by clicking on the "Text" icon and typing in "Your Name," or any other phrase.

9. For the image below, the font "American Uncial Corn Regular" in regular and color green were selected.

10. Select the text and the image and click on "Group," then copy-paste your design as many times as needed and save the project.

11. You can resize the design as needed to match your coaster's size, although the recommended size is 4 by 4 inches for most common tile coasters. The design is ready to be printed and cut. Simply click on the "Make It" button and follow the screen prompts for using an inkjet printer to print the design on your printable iron-on vinyl and subsequently cut the design.

12. Carefully remove the excess material from the sheet using the weeder tool, making sure only the design remains on the clear liner.

13. Using the Cricut EasyPress Mini and the EasyPress Mat, the iron-on layers can be easily transferred to your mug.

14. Preheat your EasyPress Mini, put your design on the desired area, and apply pressure for a couple of minutes or more. Wait for few minutes before peeling off the design while it is still warm.

Vinyl Herringbone Bracelet

Supplies

- Cricut Maker or Cricut Explore
- Standard Grip mat
- Vinyl (midnight)
- Weeder
- Scraper
- Transfer tape
- Metal bracelet gold

Instructions

1. Log in to the Design Space application and click on the "New Project" button on the screen's top right corner to view a blank canvas.
2. Click on the "Images" icon on the Design Panel, and type in "#M33278" in the search bar. Select the image and click on the "Insert Images" button at the bottom of the screen.
3. Click on "Customize" to further edit the project to your preference, or simply click on the "Make It" button, load the vinyl sheet to your Cricut machine, and follow the instructions on the screen to cut your project.
4. With a weeder tool, remove the negative space pieces of the design. Use the transfer tape to apply the vinyl cuts to the bracelet. Use the scraper tool on top of the transfer tape to remove any bubbles, and then just peel off the transfer tape.

Window Decoration

Supplies

- Cricut Maker or Cricut Explore
- Cutting mat
- Orange window cling (non-adhesive material that has static cling so it can be easily applied on the glass

Instructions

1. Log in to the Design Space application and click on the "New Project" button on the screen's top right corner to view a blank canvas.
2. Click on the "Projects" icon, click on the "All Categories" to select "Home Decor," then type in "Window" in the search bar.
3. Click on "Customize" to further edit the project to your preference, or simply click on the "Make It" button and load the window cling to your Cricut machine and follow the instructions on the screen to cut your project and transfer it onto the window.

Car Decal

Supplies

- Cricut Maker or Cricut Explore
- Cutting mat
- Vinyl
- Transfer tape
- Scrapper

Instructions

1. Log in to the Design Space application and click on the "New Project" button on the screen's top right corner to view a blank canvas.
2. Let's use our image for this project. Search the web to find the image that you would like and store it on your computer. Now, click on the "Upload" icon from the Design Panel on the left of the screen.
3. A screen with "Upload Image" and "Upload Pattern" will be displayed. Click on the "Upload Image" button. Click on "Browse" or simply drag and drop your image on the screen.
4. Your uploaded image will be displayed on the screen, and you would be able to select if you would like to upload the image as a simple "Single Layer" picture or complex "Multiple-Layers" picture. For the decal image below, we will select "Simple" and click on "Continue."

5. Save the image as a "Print-Then-Cut" image by clicking on the picture on the left then click "Save" at the screen's bottom right.

6. Select the uploaded image and click on "Insert Images," then edit as needed.

7. Click on "Customize" to further edit the project to your preference, or simply click on the "Make It" button and load the window cling to your Cricut machine and follow the instructions on the screen to cut the design.

8. Carefully remove the excess material from the sheet. To easily paste your decal on the car window without stretching the pieces, put the transfer tape on top of the cut design. After you have cleaned the car window, slowly peel the paper backing on the vinyl from one end to the other in a rolling motion to ensure even placement. Now, use the scraper tool on top of the transfer tape to remove any bubbles, and then just peel off the transfer tape. And you are all set!

Holiday Mirror Decoration

Supplies

- Cricut Maker or Cricut Explore
- Cutting mat
- Vinyl
- Transfer tape
- Scrapper

Instructions

1. Log in to the Design Space application and click on the "New Project" button on the screen's top right corner to view a blank canvas.
2. Click on the "Images" icon and type in "Reindeer" in the search bar. Select a picture that you like and click on "Insert Image."
3. Now type in "Wreath" in the search bar and scroll down to find the image used in this project. Click on it, and a small icon will be added to the "Insert Image" bar at the bottom of the screen. Click on "Insert Images" at the bottom of the screen.
4. Edit the design and click on the "Fill" icon from the Edit Bar at the top of the screen to select "Print" and then change the color

of the deer to red. Click on the lock icon at the bottom left of the deer image to adjust the image inside the wreath.

5. Select the entire design and click on the "Group" icon under the Layers Panel. Then click on "Save" to save the project.

6. The design is ready to be cut. Simply click on the "Make It" button and load the vinyl sheet to your Cricut machine and follow the screen's instructions to cut the design.

7. Carefully remove the excess vinyl from the sheet and put the transfer tape on top of the cut design. After you have cleaned the mirror, slowly peel the paper backing on the vinyl from one end to the other in a rolling motion to ensure even placement. Now, use the scraper tool on top of the transfer tape to remove any bubbles, and then just peel off the transfer tape.

Wine Glass Decoration

Supplies

- Cricut Maker or Cricut Explore
- Cutting mat
- Vinyl (gold)
- Transfer tape
- Scrapper
- Wine glasses

Instructions

1. Log in to the Design Space application and click on the "New Project" button on the screen's top right corner to view a blank canvas.
2. Let's use text for this project. Click on "Text" from the Designs Panel on the left of the screen and type in "Wine O'clock" or any other phrase you may like.
3. The font "Anna's Fancy Lettering—Hannah" in purple was selected for this project. But you can let your creativity take over this step and choose any color or font that you like. Select and copy-paste your image for the number of times you want to print your design.

4. Click on "Save" to save the project then click on the "Make It" button and load the vinyl sheet to your Cricut machine and follow the instructions on the screen to cut the design.

5. Carefully remove the excess vinyl from the sheet. To easily paste your design on the wine glass without stretching the pieces, put the transfer tape on top of the cut design. After you have cleaned the surface, slowly peel the paper backing on the vinyl from one end to the other in a rolling motion to ensure even placement. Now, use the scraper tool on top of the transfer tape to remove any bubbles, and then just peel off the transfer tape.

Treasure Chest Jewelry Box

Supplies

- Plain wooden box with lid
- White vinyl
- Vinyl transfer tape
- Cutting mat
- Weeding tool or pick a small blade

Instructions

1. Select the "Image" button in the lower left-hand corner and search for "Keyhole."
2. Click your favorite keyhole design and click "Insert."
3. Select the "Text" button in the lower left-hand corner.
4. Choose your favorite font and type "Treasure."
5. Place your vinyl on the cutting mat.
6. Send design to Cricut.
7. Make use of a weeding tool or pick to remove the excess vinyl from the design.
8. Apply separate pieces of transfer tape to the keyhole and the word.
9. Remove the paper backing from the tape on the keyhole.

10. Place the keyhole where the lid and box meet so that half is on the lid and half is on the box.
11. Rub the tape to transfer the vinyl to the wood, making sure there are no bubbles. Carefully peel the tape away.
12. Use a sharp blade to cut the keyhole design in half so that the box can open.
13. Transfer the word to the front of the box using the same method.
14. Optional: Add details with paint or markers to make the box look more like a treasure chest. Add wood grain, barnacles, seashells, or pearls.
15. Store your jewelry in your new treasure chest!

Motivational Water Bottle

Supplies

- Sturdy water bottle of your choice
- Glitter vinyl
- Vinyl transfer tape
- Light grip cutting mat
- Weeding tool or pick

Instructions

1. Measure the space on your water bottle where you want the text and create a box that size.
2. Select the "Text" button in the lower left-hand corner.
3. Choose your favorite font and type the motivational quote you like best. Something like "I sweat glitter," "Sweat is magic," or "I don't sweat, I sparkle."
4. Place the vinyl on the cutting mat.
5. Send the design to Cricut.
6. Use a weeding tool or pick to remove the excess vinyl from the text. Apply transfer tape to the quote.
7. Remove the paper backing from the tape.
8. Place the quote where you want it on the water bottle.
9. Rub the tape to transfer the vinyl to the bottle, making sure there are no bubbles. Carefully peel the tape away.
10. Bring your new water bottle to the gym for motivation and hydration!

Customized Make Up Bag

Supplies

- Pink fabric makeup bag
- Purple heat transfer vinyl
- Cricut EasyPress or iron
- Cutting mat
- Weeding tool or pick
- Keychain or charm of your choice

Instructions

1. Measure the space on your makeup bag where you want the design and create a box that size.
2. Select the "Image" button in the lower left-hand corner and search "Monogram."
3. Choose your favorite monogram and click "Insert."
4. Place vinyl on the cutting mat.
5. Send the design to your Cricut.
6. Use a weeding tool or pick to remove the excess vinyl from the design.
7. Place the design on the bag with the plastic side up.
8. Carefully iron on the design.
9. After cooling, peel away the plastic by rolling it.
10. Hang your charm or keychain off the zipper.
11. Stash your makeup in your customized bag!

Dad Joke Vinyl T-Shirt

Supplies

- Your favorite white shirt
- Cricut Creator (or any other automated cutting machines using SVG files) or Explore Air 2 cutting machine
- Iron-on (vinyl heat transfer) in different shades (Expressions of Cricut Vinyl)
- Instruments for weeding (Amazon Cricut)
- EasyPress 2 and its mat

Instructions

1. To keep doing the "Dad Jokes"? I guess you're asking about RAD jokes! Ha! Open Cricut Design Space (or another device software), and append an SVG image.
2. Drop the imported picture onto a new canvas, size it to fit the shirt (we recommend making it around 10 inches long for the shirt of a mature male), and in the upper right corner, click the green "Print It Now" icon.

3. The remaining vinyl is scraped off using the weeding equipment to remove the iron-on vinyl with the grinding machine.

4. Next, in the Online Quick reference source, use EasyPress 2 to apply the template to the top, observing the time and temperature configuration needed. Short, quick, and completely enjoyable! That will give Dad a great present for Father's Day, Christmas, Birthdays, and more!

5. This approach even performed on a hat very well! Use your Sport Flex Iron-On adhesive or Infusible Ink and EasyPress Miniature on this polyester trucking cover for a super fun gift idea.

Quiver and Arrow

Supplies

- 4 (20 inches) wooden round dowels
- Spray paint, in the colors you would like the Cupid arrows to be
- Twine, lace, jute, or braided rope—whatever dowels you like to wrap with
- Cylinder jar for your quiver—I bought mine from Walmart
- Packaging sheet or print paper to adorn the bottle
- Scrapbook paper in the colors that you want the arrows and wings to be—I used gloss cardstock. You should use a matching scrap of paper

Instructions

1. Brush the dowels with color.
2. To achieve the perfect look, hot glue the ribbon on the dowel— I twisted mine and hot fused both ends.
3. Cut out the arrow and feathers. Apply hot glue to the arrows and feathers.
4. Cut the paper to the width and length of the cylinder (scrapbook or wrapping Fasten the document to the cylinder.
5. To hold the cupid arrows in place, insert the corresponding paper shred inside if you'd like to add a matching brace.
6. Now you can put the cupid arrows anywhere you can, it will look amazing on a door or wall, and your buddies will ask you to make them more! These are beloved by both my kiddos and they both have a collection in their bed.

St. Patrick's Day Shirt

Supplies

- Cricut Maker or a machine to cut
- Cricut Design Space account
- Cut design with shamrock and doodles
- Green infusible ink pen 0.04
- Infusible Cricut Tin Jacket
- EasyPress 2
- Card warehouse
- Butcher text
- Paper on a laser printer

Instructions

1. Upload and size the file to fit your shirt.
2. Send out to cut (draw) the project. Don't forget to have an image mirror. Place the paper with a laser printer on a Standard Grip cutting mat. Keep sure to follow the infusible ink pen prompts.
3. Delete the laser printer paper from the cutting mat once the image has been drawn.
4. Place a cardstock sheet inside the shirt where you want your design to be.
5. Place on the shirt, image side down, the laser printer paper with design. Cover with butcher paper.

6. Following Cricut's recommended heat setting, press the image onto the shirt with the EasyPress.
7. Remove from the shirt the butcher paper, laser printer paper, and card stock and be St. Paddy's Day pinch-proof.
8. If you're acquainted with the cutting Cricut device family, you're likely familiar with all of the various projects done by you with these instruments, too. The electronic cutting machine or Cricut Joy appears to fit in the right with many types of material that the cutting tool can cut.

Coasters Using Infusible Ink for Christmas

Supplies

- Cricut Maker or Explore
- Infusible ink rounds from ceramic coasters
- Buffalo plaid (Infusible ink transmission sheets)
- EasyPress
- EasyPress mat
- Butcher's article
- White cardstock

Instructions

1. The prototype is accessible in Design Space with the terms "Everything is good" and "All is Light."
2. On the tile coasters, the infusible ink appears so shiny and glossy. I think they'd be great in your house as holiday decor or attach them to a gift package of mugs and hot chocolate.
3. Open the file for "Christmas Coaster Concept."
4. Print out the patterns from the move sheets of Infusible Paint. Don't hesitate to get the concept replicated.
5. Weed the layouts.

6. Click, in the "Heat Guide," to follow the instructions. With a sheet of cardstock underneath the coasters and a strip of parchment paper and over the edge of the infusible paint, push for 220 seconds at 390 degrees F.
7. Once the coaster has settled, gently cut the transfer cover.

PART 8:

FREQUENTLY ASKED QUESTIONS

CHAPTER 39:

About the Machines

Here are the answers to some of the most frequently asked questions by the Cricut user community:

Do I Need a Computer to Use My Cricut Machine?

No! If you have the Cricut Explore Air or the Cricut Maker, you can use the built-in Bluetooth to connect to your mobile device and download the Design Space app on it.

Does My Cricut Machine Have to Be Connected to the Internet?

Your Cricut machine does not work alone; but instead, it has to be connected to the Design Space. The Design Space uses an internet connection, except you're using the offline version on your iOS device.

What's the Difference Between the Cricut Explore One and the Cricut Explore Air 2?

The Cricut Explore One has a single tool carriage, so if you do more than one action (cut and write or cut and score), it will need to do it in 2 steps, and you'll need to switch out the tools between them. The Cricut Explore Air 2 has 2 tool carriages to do both functions in one step with no need to switch tools. Explore Air 2 also has built-in Bluetooth connectivity.

What Is the Thickness of a Material That the Cricut Maker Can Cut?

3/32 inches of 1 inch or 2.4 mm. when using the rotary blade or the knife blade.

How Do I Get a Good Transfer Using the Cricut EasyPress?

Use the EasyPress on a firm and even surface. Check the iron-on material and the base material for the recommended settings and use those. Be sure to apply heat to both the front and back of the project for the recommended amount of time.

How Much Pressure Does the Cricut EasyPress Need?

Check the recommendations for the material you're using. Some will call for "firm" pressure, meaning you should use 2 hands and about 15–20 lbs. of body weight. Others need "gentle" pressure, meaning you should use 1 hand with about 5–10 lbs. of body weight. Use your EasyPress on a waist-high table for the easiest way to apply pressure.

Do I Move the Cricut EasyPress Around Like an Iron?

Keep the EasyPress in one spot for the recommended amount of time. Moving it might smear or warp the design.

Why Should I Use the Cricut EasyPress?

It heats more evenly and more quickly than iron and is easy to use. It will give you more professional-looking iron-on projects and takes 60 seconds or less.

How Do I Protect Surfaces While Using the Cricut EasyPress?

Cricut recommends using the Cricut EasyPress mat, which comes in 3 different sizes. However, you can also use a cotton bath towel with an even texture folded to about 3 inches thick. Do not use an ironing board, as the surface isn't even enough, and it's too unsteady to apply appropriate pressure. Silicone baking mats and aluminum foil don't provide enough insulation and can get dangerously hot.

What Is the Fast Mode?

This is a feature on the Cricut Explore Air 2 and the Cricut Maker. It allows you to cut and write twice as fast when the machine is set to vinyl, iron-on, or cardstock.

Do I Need a Printer to Use My Cricut?

In a nutshell, no. Using your Cricut with the materials that we have laid out in this book does not require a printer's ink, although some materials on the Cricut market are clearly meant to be printed on before use.

When you don't use these items, you can find that you will get the most out of your system without that feature.

When you want to print designs, then cut them down, this is known as the Print-Then-Cut process, and on the internet, there is a wealth of information on that. You can make tattoos, iron-on decals, and so much more!

CHAPTER 40:

About the Materials, Tools, and Accessories

I'm Just Getting Started. Do I Need to Buy All of Cricut's Accessories Right Away?

No, you won't need all the tools at once, and depending on what crafts you want to do with your Cricut computer, some of them you won't ever need at all. In fact, as you get more use out of your computer, you can use crafting things you probably already have on hand to get started. Buying equipment and accessories here and there, spending a small fortune on accessories and equipment, is by no means necessary, just to do your first Cricut design project.

What Is a Cricut Tote Bag?

If you plan to travel with your Cricut machine and supplies or need somewhere to store them when you're not using them, you can purchase a Cricut tote bag.

The Cricut machine tote bag is for all the cutting machines. It can fit anyone you own. The Cricut rolling craft tote bag is for supplies only, and the cutting machine can't fit in it. The bags come in purple, navy, and raspberry.

There is also the tweed Cricut tote bag, which is an older version of the new tote bags.

Will My New Cricut Explore Machine Come with a Carry Bag?

Sadly, it won't. This doesn't mean that you cannot buy a carry bag or machine tote back from Cricut separately.

Will a Cricut Maker Fit into the Tweed Machine Tote?

Yes, it will. If you need somewhere to place your Cricut Maker for convenience, you can easily purchase a machine tote from Cricut.

Do I Have to Buy a Wireless Bluetooth Adapter When I Buy an Explore Machine?

If you bought the Explore Air and Explore Air 2, you don't have to buy a Wireless Bluetooth Adapter. But this is not the same for the Explore One, and so you can buy the Cricut Wireless Bluetooth Adapter if that's what you wish.

The Cricut Maker Can Know the Blade I Loaded Without a Smart Dial. How?

The machine moves the carriage to the right before cutting your project. This is called homing. Here, the device will scan the blade and know which one you installed.

What Exactly Is a SnapMat?

A SnapMat is an iOS-exclusive feature that lets you get a virtual preview of yourself. This gives you the ability to align your designs in Design Space so that they fit perfectly with what you put on your mat. This functionality allows you to place images and text over your mat's snapshot so that you can see exactly how your layout should be in the Design Space.

What Are the Benefits of Using SnapMat?

The SnapMat gives you the certainty that your images will be located in the right place when you send your design to cut through your Cricut. It will show you where your pictures are to be drawn, how cuts are made, and how the text lines up. With a SnapMat, you can tell your Cricut to cut a specific piece of a pattern that you've stuck on your mat, write in specific stationery areas, gift tags, envelopes, or cards, and you can get the most out of your scraps and spare materials left from past projects.

Can I Include Multiple SnapMat Mats at One Time?

The SnapMat can snap one mat at a time. If you want to snap multiple mats, you can do so individually and work that way through your designs. This ensures that each mat is shot correctly and that each one is done accurately.

Is There Somewhere Else Where to Order Weeding Tools?

Harbor Freight and other similar hardware stores sell sets of hooks that are identical to Cricut's weeding method. Such weeding hook sets usually have a very low price point and do the job much like the patented weeding hooks from Cricut. Consider looking at Harbor Freight or another hardware store for a suitable substitute on a budget and in bulk if you think this is a tool you use a lot and need to replace sometimes!

Why Do I Weed Away My More Complex Designs?

There is one method known as Reverse Weeding for more complex designs.

It is a technique mostly performed on vinyl when a design is incorporated in the design with lots of very thin or curly sections. Stick the transfer tape to the front of the pattern as you pass through the vinyl.

Use your scraper to completely burn down the vinyl template transfer tape. It will help it stick to it, and nothing unexpected can come up when you get to this hack's weeding point.

After you have done so, remove everything from the contact film, then use your weeding tool to remove from the transfer tape the excess vinyl. This has been found to remove a great deal of tearing and stretching that can occur with these ventures.

When all the excess has been removed from your product, burn it onto your product piece as usual and then remove the transfer tape just as you would otherwise.

When They're Packed, My Mats Keep Curling. Where Should I Store Those?

Among many craftsmen in the group, it has been found that the best way to store the Cricut craft mats is to use wall space and command hooks. It stops them from falling behind their chairs, getting stuck on their table in piles, or being hurt in the shuffle.

They're always kept straight and secure if you have them hanging up on the wall, and they're always right where you need them to be.

Why Won't My Transfer Tape Work?

More often than not, it's not working when you try to use standard transfer tape with glitter vinyl. It requires the Cricut Strong Grip transfer tape. It's too strong to use with regular vinyl, though, so keep using the regular transfer tape for that.

When It Comes to Tape Transfer, Do I Have Any Alternatives?

One hack that several crafters, writers, and YouTubers swear by is purchasing contact paper from either Target or the Dollar Tree and using it as a transfer tape! Contact paper is available almost anywhere, and for a very fair price, you can get a lot of it. The adhesive on contact paper is designed to be removed with little or no residue after months or even years of use. This consistency makes it a perfect replacement for transfer tape, which we depend on to keep all our project parts between the carrier sheet and our project materials exactly in place!

My Mat Isn't as Sticky as It Was Before. What Can I Do?

You will note that as time goes by, there are areas where your mat will slowly lose its grip on your projects. Try using masking tape or painter's tape to hold your projects in place before giving up and tossing your mat out while it still has some of the traction left over. When they are being cut, this will keep the materials in place, but the adhesive is not strong enough to ruin your project or mat, and it will not leave any residue.

Using a fresh mat with a firm grip on your crafting can be an invaluable advantage, and it helps your projects move so smoothly. Getting the grip on the mat is like getting a pair of extra hands when you're working.

However, realists in the crafting community know that it isn't always possible to replace your mats as soon as they start losing their grip.

Why Do I Apply My Designs with No Bubbles or Wrinkles to a Rounded Surface?

You will find it much easier to lay the decal flat if you cut irregular slits in the transfer tape if you pass a decal to anything that is rounded, like a cup or mug. However, this makes it easier to reuse the bit of tape, this way, you can find that they can lie much more readily on the floor.

How Do You See the Cut Lines on the Material in the Glitter Iron?

Because of the existence of glittery iron-on deflecting light in any direction, it can be very difficult to locate your cut lines, and as a result, weeding will take a little extra contact. However, if you use a small amount of baby powder and brush it over the back of your picture, you'll see those cut lines far clearer.

With this, you just need a very small amount of powder, and you will find that the powder in no way interferes with the material or its adhesion!

Is There a Structured Way of Storing My Scraps of Material?

One of the many beautiful things about organized people is that they love to tell others how to organize themselves! The Cricut culture online has been blown up with this hack recently. Keep a binder with page protectors, and use them as pockets for all of your paper-size or smaller content scraps. You can arrange your scraps in whatever way you want for only a couple of bucks, hold them all together, and never worry if they have had to wrinkle or ruin to be included in your future ventures!

What Type of Mat Should I Use?

Each mat has a specific use. Here's each one and some suggestions of what material to use with them:

- **Blue:** Light Grip Mat—Thinner paper, vellum, construction paper, sticky notes, light vinyl, and wrapping paper.
- **Green:** Standard Grip Mat—Cardstock, thicker paper, washi paper, vinyl, and bonded fabric.
- **Purple:** Strong Grip Mat—Thick cardstock, magnet sheets, chipboard, poster board, fabric with stiffener, aluminum foil, foam, leather, and suede.
- **Pink:** Fabric Grip Mat—Fabric, bonded fabric, and crepe paper.

How Do I Wash My Mats?

Place the mat in the sink, supported by a firm flat surface. Running lukewarm water over it uses a hard-bristled brush to gently scrub it in circles until the mat is clean. Pat dry with a paper towel and let it air dry for the stickiness to return.

Is There a Difference Between Digital and Physical Cartridges?

A cartridge, in the Cricut sense, generally refers to image sets. So, a cartridge is made up of images that have the same theme. Cartridges can be either digital or physical, although a lot of the physical cartridges have been retired. You can purchase the digital cartridges on cricut.com.

What Is Infusible Ink?

Infusible ink is a new system from Cricut that infuses ink directly into compatible Cricut blanks. There are infusible ink transfer sheets and infusible ink pens and markers. They are applied using heat, such as with the Cricut EasyPress.

How Much does a Cricut Cardstock Weigh?

80 lbs.

What Are the Care Instructions for Cricut Iron-On Material?

Wash and dry the item inside out in a delicate style. If you notice areas of the iron-on material coming off after being washed, iron it again, following the full application of instructions.

What's a Quick Reference List of Materials I Can Cut?

- **For the Explore machines:** All paper, all cardstock, vinyl, bonded fabrics, corrugated paper, sticker paper, and parchment paper.
- **For the Maker machine:** all of the above, plus fabric, textiles, and thin wood.

Do I Have to Use Cricut Brand Materials?

No! You can use any brand of materials that you want. Thickness and quality are the only things that matter.

What Pens Can I Use in My Cricut Machine?

The Cricut brand pens will, of course, fit into your machine. However, some others will fit in the pen holder as well. Some users have found ways to adapt other pens, but the pens and markers in the following list don't require any adjustments:

- Wal-Mart Leisure Arts markers
- Target Dual Tip markers
- Pilot Precise V5 pens
- Thin Crayola markers
- Dollar Tree Jot markers
- Bic Round Stic pen

What Is the Cricut Adaptive Tool System?

This is a new feature in the Cricut Maker. It adjusts the direction and pressure of the blades throughout the cutting process. It allows for much more precise cuts and much higher cutting pressure.

What Is the Scoring Wheel?

A scoring wheel is a tool for the Cricut Maker, as it uses the Adaptive Tool System. It creates fold lines in thicker materials. The Scoring Stylus also makes fold lines.

How Small Can the Rotary Blade Cut?

Cricut recommends keeping designs above ¾ inch. Any smaller than that, the blade might gouge into your mat as it turns, damaging the mat and dulling the blade.

Where Do I Buy Cricut Blades?

You can buy blades where Cricut brand products are sold, including craft stores, superstores, Cricut's website, and other online stores.

How Do I Sharpen the Blades on My Cricut?

A very common Cricut trick in use is to cover your Cricut mat with a clean, fresh piece of foil and run it through with your blade to sharpen.

Running the blades through the thin metal will help revitalize their edges and give them some extra staying power before it's time to buy replacements.

Another way to do this is to make a foil ball, remove the blades from the housing and insert them several times into the foil ball before you find a shine on the edge. This will give you a better understanding of how sharp your blades are getting before you finish with them, and it seems like a more expedient way to sharpen many blades in one sitting, but the feedback seems to be just as good as letting your computer do the work for you on one blade at a time.

Why Does My Blade Cut My Support Sheet?

It could be due to inappropriate seating on the blade in the package, so move the package back, bring the blade into it again, load it up again, and try again. It could also be because the content dial is not adjusted correctly. You can plunge the needle right through the whole material and the back if you cut anything very slim but have the dial set to cardstock.

My Material Is Tearing! Why?

The most common reason is that your mat isn't sticky enough. It could have lost its stickiness, or you aren't using the right mat for the material. It could also be that the blade needs to be replaced or sharpened, or you're using the wrong type of blade. Materials can also tear if the machine is in the wrong setting.

What Is the Custom Material Setting For?

If you're cutting something besides paper, vinyl, iron-on, cardstock, fabric, or poster board on the Cricut Explore or Cricut Maker, you can choose "Custom." This will open the material menu in Cricut Design Space. Select "Browse All Materials" and select the correct one. If you don't see your material listed, you can choose something close or create your own. If you create a custom material, you'll adjust the cut pressure, set if it uses multi-cut, and select the blade type. For help, you can look at the settings for something close to the material you're using. If you have enough of the material, do several tests with different settings to see what works best.

CHAPTER 41:

About Cricut Design Space

How Do I Install Design Space?

Design Space will give you a prompt to download and install the plugin. Click "Download" and wait for it to finish. Once it does, click the file to install the plugin. You might get a box asking for permission; if so, allow it. Follow the prompts through the installer. You're now ready to use Design Space!

Do I Need to Pay to Use Design Space?

No, you don't. Design Space comes completely free. You only need a subscription if you plan on using Cricut Access. But, if you need the basics, then you can open a Design Space account for free.

Do I Use the Same Design Space for Both the Explore Series and Cricut Maker?

Your Design Space will not change even if you are changing from one Cricut machine to another. Also, no matter which one you're using, you always have to use Design Space. But, Cricut Maker has more Design Space benefits than the Explore series.

If I Upgrade from an Explore to a Cricut Maker, Will I Lose My Projects and Cartridges?

No, you won't. All your information is not linked to the Cricut machine. Instead, it is connected to your Cricut ID in the Cricut Cloud. As long as you're using the same ID, you will have access to all your information and projects when you get a new Cricut machine.

Where Can I Find Images to Use for My Project?

One of the advantages with Cricut is that you can upload files from any source so long as you have the legal rights to use this image, as the space for Cricut Design and the ability to house so many different file types is fantastic. If you do sell your designs, it is incredibly important to use copyright-free images or purchase the images you include in your designs.

Where Can I Use Cricut Design Space?

You can use Cricut Design Space through your web browser on PC or Mac after downloading the plugin. You can also download the app on your tablet or smartphone on iOS or Android.

Can Cricut Design Space Work on More Than One Mobile Device or Computer?

Yes, it can! Cricut Design Space, as mentioned earlier, is cloud-based. No matter where you are or the kind of device that you are using, you can always use this application as long as it is compatible.

If you're logged in at home, you can also log in on your phone if you're on the go.

Is It Necessary to Turn All My Images into SVGs?

No, if you have a JPG or PNG, you don't need to convert the images to SVG format. However, if you want SVG files in your project, many free online tools can help you with this method. Try to bear in mind that you may have less flexibility to modify your image's components if you convert your file form to an SVG.

Can I Upload Images Through the Android App?

Hey! Cricut recognizes how important mobile connectivity is for its users, so this feature has been made available on all platforms, including Android, where you can access the Cricut Design Space.

What Types of Photos Can I Upload to IOS or Android Apps Via Cricut's Design Space?

Any pictures saved to your Apple or Android computer in the Photos or Gallery app can be uploaded! You can also upload SVG files.

If you are trying to upload a PDF or TIFF file, you should remember that Cricut Design Space does not support these.

Can I Save Ready-To-Make Projects to My Device?

When you want to save your computer to a Ready-to-Make website, so you can use it offline, you can save it to your PC. That is achieved by selecting "Customize," pressing "Save As," then select "Save to that iPad/iPhone." It is important to remember that images and details of the project will not be stored offline. If you need these, it may be helpful to take screenshots of certain things or print them out so that you can return to them when operating in offline mode.

I Bought Images with Cricut Access, Are They Available Offline?

Yes, you can download the photos you purchased with your Cricut Access membership while your membership is active. That means photos in that category can be used for up to 30 days without an internet connection or before the subscription needs to be renewed, whichever comes first. At that point, you'll be prompted to reconnect your computer to the internet so that you can renew your subscription and license to continue using those offline photos.

How Many Times Can I Use an Image Purchased in the Design Space?

Any design asset or feature you purchase from the design space will be yours to use as much as you like when you have an active Cricut Design Space account. Feel free to cut as many designs as you want from your purchased images.

Can I Download Fonts to Use Offline?

Yeah! Fonts are amongst the assets you can download for later, offline use to your computer! Here's how to add your font to your iPhone:

- Tap the "Text" button.

- Tap the "Select" button in the upper left-hand corner of the front display.

- Tap your chosen font to pick it.

- Tap the "Add" button in the upper right-hand corner of the screen.

- Now that you've followed these steps, these fonts can be used offline on your iOS device!

Where Can I Get Images to Use with My Cricut?

The wonderful feature about the Cricut Design Space, and its ability to host so many different types of files, is that you can upload images from any source, as long as you have the legal right to use it. Pulling photos from Google Image Search is done by craftsmen, but if you're selling the design in some way, you're going to want to make sure that the photos you're using are either open-licensed or bought for use and distribution.

How Many Images Can I Download?

Cricut Design Space does not put a limit to the number of images that you can download in a single day. You can only select 50 images to download at one time, but there is no limit to how many times that process can be repeated in one sitting. With this feature, when you're offline, you'll have access to everything you need.

Where Can I Look at My Downloads?

Go to the "Images" screen to display your downloaded files. If you're there, tap the "Filter" button, pick the "On This iPad/iPhone" option, and all displayed images will be all locally stored images. If you are currently in offline mode, then the "Images" screen will be your default view.

Can I Delete Items I've Downloaded?

Sure, just go to "Files" and pick "Photos saved to this iPad/iPhone" if you're online, and remove with the pop-up "Delete" button. It should be noted that if a non-downloaded image is wrongly selected the "Delete" button would simply be a "Download" button.

How Do I Delete Images I Uploaded Through the Mobile App?

It is another fantastic feature that every available version of this app can run, whether you have a Mac, PC, iOS, or Android computer! Open the Design Space app to complete the task on your mobile device.

To find it, pick "Download" in the options list below; you will need to swipe. Select "Open Uploaded Images" after you have taped on that. When you are in the photos you have posted, select the one you want to delete. Click the "Info" tab, with a green circle and a lower-case "I." You can easily remove your picture from there!

What Sort of Things Can't I Do in Offline Mode?

Features that are only available online are Print-Then-Cut Configuration, Personalized Products, New System Setup, Views of Categories and Cartridge, and Image Upload services. If you want to do any of these things, just connect your computer to the internet, and you can do it without a problem.

Is Offline Mode Available on the Desktop?

Yes, the offline mode feature is available exclusively for iOS devices at this time. At this time, there are no signs as to whether Cricut plans to add other channels to this feature or not.

Can I Update My Projects in the Cloud with Offline Changes?

Yeah, just save your projects to the "Projects" screen with the same name as the project's previous version. This will absolutely overwrite the project you were currently saving to The Cloud with the adjustments you made while offline.

How Do I Save Offline Changes to My Projects?

Suppose you are going to work on a project in offline mode. In that case, tap "Save," and the file you saved to your device will be updated automatically without having to reselect the option "Save to This iPad/iPhone" if there is no internet connection.

Can I Download an Entire Cartridge to Use in Offline Mode?

It is not possible to download a whole cartridge of content in one step, but you can download as many of the individual assets as you want from any cartridge or category.

What Is Available for Offline Download?

You can download any element or asset that you own or have purchased rights through Cricut Design Space for offline use. This includes images you uploaded from other devices, images, or assets that you obtained through active membership in Cricut Access. It is up to you to pick what assets you want to make available for offline use.

How Do I Save Projects That Allow Me to Use Them Offline?

This step can only be accomplished with an active internet connection, so be sure to download before going offline. Open a project that you want to save for use offline and select the option "Save As." Select the option "Save to This iPad/iPhone," which will allow you to use the project without any connection later.

Is There a Limit to How Long My Offline Images Are Available to Me?

For 7 consecutive days, free images obtained via the Cricut Design Space (including simple shapes) can be used without refreshing the internet connection. After that point, permissions will expire but can be easily renewed by connecting to the Internet and relaunching the Cricut Design Space application.

I Accidentally Welded 2 Images. How Do I Un-Weld Them?

Sadly, there is currently no dedicated unwelded option in Design Space. However, if you weld a picture, if you haven't saved the changes to your project, you can still click "Undo." It is recommended that you save your photos at each point locally, so you have clean photos to work with for each project.

How Do I Look at All the Projects I've Saved to My Device?

Tap the "Menu" button to see this that looks like 3 stacked bars. It will be at the top of the page for "Projects." Tap the button that says, "My Projects on this iPad/iPhone," while there. If you're still offline, that will be your default "Projects" screen view.

What Happens If I Sign Out of My App?

Any asset you control somehow is connected to your Cricut ID attached to The Cloud. What this means is that if you sign out of the app after installing something, you will once again need to log into the app with an internet connection to access certain things, tasks, photos, etc.

How Do I Convert to Metric Units?

To switch to centimeters from inches on a laptop or desktop, open the "Account" menu; you'll see 3 stacked lines in the upper left corner, then select "Settings." You'll see the options to select inches or centimeters.

What Does the "Select Visible" Option Do?

The "Select Visible" option at the bottom of the "Images" screen will select all of the images currently on the screen you are viewing. This feature can help you to quickly group images with as little hassle as possible for fast download.

Do I Need to Buy All My Cricut Fonts?

Cricut Design Space can use fonts installed on your computer when you browse for your fonts. The fonts can also be purchased or used for downloading via the Cricut Design Space with little to no problems. Across the Web, too, there is a range of resources for this.

Nevertheless, if you use a font, make sure you have a license to use it for the reasons you want to employ it! Fonts have copyrights, just like images, and can be limited to what you can do with them.

Why Don't My Pictures Appear Right on My Mat?

Once you press "Print It," it is likely that your print version doesn't look like anything in Design Space. When this happens, go back to Design Space, highlight all your photos, click "Team," then click "Attach," and all your project cutting needs will be kept right wherever they are.

How Do I Use Design Space on My Chromebook?

Unfortunately, Cricut's Design Space is not currently designed for Chromebook OS compatibility. It is because the need for the application to download the plugin is a significant obstacle to the operating system, but that doesn't mean that there will be no compatibility shortly.

How Does My Machine Connect to Design Space?

The Explore Air 2 has built-in Bluetooth, so it can connect to any device that has that capability. The Explore One has to be connected directly to your computer, or you can purchase a Cricut Wireless Bluetooth Adapter.

What Is Cricut Access?

This is Cricut's subscription service to their library of images and fonts in Cricut Design Space. It gives access to more than 30,000 images, 370 fonts, and premium project ideas, as well as 10% off all purchases on the Cricut website.

There are different types of plans available, ranging from $4.99–9.99 per month.

Why Am I Getting Error Messages About the Design Space Plugin?

If you're getting error messages or having difficulty using Design Space, you may need to reinstall the plugin. Expand your computer's system tray on the lower right-hand side of the screen and locate the Cricut icon. Right-click on it and click "Exit." Open your web browser and navigate to design.cricut.com and sign in with your Cricut ID. Once prompted, download and install the plugin again.

Where Do I Go to Buy Materials?

When it comes to buying your Cricut products, there's almost an infinite number of places you can get them. As the Cricut is such a powerful tool with the ability to cut so many fabrics, you won't be able to go into any art or fabric stores without tripping over new products that you can use for your latest and greatest craftsmanship.

When you keep learning more about how and what you can do with Cricut, you'll find out which materials and brands best match your needs. From there, by shopping online, you can always find what you need to get the best prices and quantities of the items you want, which will help you stretch your dollar the best you can.

Are the "Despeckle" and "Smooth" Tools Available in Design Space Through Windows, Linux, and Android?

Those features are unique to the iOS platform at the time of writing. That means that this functionality is only available to Apple users, and there is currently no hint as to whether or not that will change in the future.

Conclusion

There is no imaginable limit to all the incredible things you can achieve with the powerful tools that you will use to create your next craft. These tools are versatile, and, combined with your creative ideas, there is no limit to what you can achieve.

Cricut Design Space gives the crafter the power to create unique crafts, only limited by their imagination. If you run out of ideas, Design Space ready-to-make projects are loaded with ideas, as is the Cricut website.

Learning any new software program takes time, patience, and practice. Remember to have fun and don't give up if, at first, you don't get a design right. The more you work on the Design Space canvas, the more familiar you will become with it.

Some people prefer to use the Cricut machine to create their decorations, while others can even make some money out of their projects. Just think of customized T-shirts or mugs, as these items are trendy today.

Slowly, Cricut is expanding its user base, and more people are becoming fascinated by these machines. Whether we are talking about decorations enthusiasts or just people who are very good at crafting, this brand has become a niche market leader. Since the machines are being sold on different sales channels, not only on the Cricut Shop, this brand is expected to become a lot more popular. Cricut has a few models in use nowadays. The most important ones are the Explore Family (Explore, Explore One, Explore Air, and Explore Air 2) and the ultimate one, the Cricut Maker.

If you are not accustomed to any Cricut machine, and if you are interested in finding out how these machines work, then it's better to start with a lower version like the ones from the Explore Family. However, Explore Air 2 has become an exciting machine, as it offers plenty of features for just a small amount of money. If you use the Cricut Access subscription, you will have access to most of the designs, images, and other files shared with this service. Trust me, the Cricut Access subscription is worth it, but you need to go through all possible resources if you want to learn how these machines function genuinely. This book is the perfect guide for using these machines and the Design Space application. Therefore, you will need to make sure to apply all the tips, tricks, and information provided in the pages you have just read to get better use out of these machines.

Good luck.

HERE ARE THE BONUSES!

FOR READERS OF THIS BOOK ONLY

Scan this QR code with your smartphone or go to https://campsite.bio/jennifermichaels for accessing a collection of video tutorials, official manuals, best communities to meet other makers, thousands of project ideas, and millions of free SVG files and images.

Made in the USA
Las Vegas, NV
01 November 2023

80013289R00236